Nyāyaratnadīpāvali of Ānandānubhava

Nyāyaratnadīpāvali of Ānandānubhava

Translated and Annotated by

KANSHI RAM

Volume I

INDIAN COUNCIL OF PHILOSOPHICAL RESEARCH

and

MOTILAL BANARSIDASS PUBLISHERS
PRIVATE LIMITED • DELHI

First Edition : Delhi, 2015

In arrangement with
Indian Council of Philosophical Research
Darshan Bhawan, 36 Tughalakabad Institutional Area
New Delhi- 110 062

ISBN : 978-81-208-4001-0

MOTILAL BANARSIDASS
41 U.A. Bungalow Road, Jawahar Nagar, Delhi 110 007
8 Mahalaxmi Chamber, 22 Bhulabhai Desai Road, Mumbai 400 026
203 Royapettah High Road, Mylapore, Chennai 600 004
236, 9th Main III Block, Jayanagar, Bengaluru 560 011
8 Camac Street, Kolkata 700 017
Ashok Rajpath, Patna 800 004
Chowk, Varanasi 221 001

Printed in India

by RP Jain at NAB Printing Unit,
A-44, Naraina Industrial Area, Phase I, New Delhi–110028
and published by JP Jain for Motilal Banarsidass Publishers (P) Ltd,
41 U.A. Bungalow Road, Jawahar Nagar, Delhi-110007

Dedicated to
Swami Divyanandaji Sarasvati, M.M. Kailas Ashram, Rishikesh, who kindly helped me in comprehending the difficult passages of the Nyāyaratnadīpāvali.

Foreword

The present volume *Nyāyaratnadīpāvali* of Ānandānubhava with a translation and annotation by Professor Kanshi Ram is the product of the translation project launched by Indian Council of Philosophical Research (ICPR), New Delhi. The *Nyāyaratnadīpāvali* is an authoritative text that has inspired several post-Śaṅkara Advaitins who have contributed to the debate on the Advaita tradition with its roots in the Upaniṣads and its continuity through the writings of Gauḍapāda and Śaṅkara.

On the evidence of style and diction, it is clear that Ānandānubhava knew his Navyanyāya, through the works of Gaṅgeśa Upādhyāya. Ānandānubhava formulated the logical framework of Advaita, and added to it his very insightful śāstric analysis. His writings influenced great scholars like Citsukha, the author of Tattvapradīpikā and Vimuktātman, the author of Iṣṭasiddhi.

Professor Kanshi Ram's excellent modern translation of Ānandānubhava makes available to the contemporary reader both in the east and the west an important work on Advaita, and is likely to prove to be a valuable contribution to philosophical scholarship and debate. On behalf of the ICPR I thank Professor Kanshi Ram for his painstaking and laudatory effort

PROF. MRINAL MIRI
Chairman, ICPR

Topical Contents

Acknowledgements

It was Baba Mastaramji, my guru, who initiated me into the Advaita system of philosophy and encouraged me to study Śaṅkara while I was busy doing my post-doctoral work on Vijñānabhikṣu's system of philosophy. I take this opportunity to pay my homage to him.

I would like to thank Professor Godabarisha Mishra, former Member Secretary, Indian Council of Philosophical Research, who entrusted me with the onerous task of translating the Nyāyaratnadīpāvali of Ānandānubhava. Professor V. N. Jha, former Director, Advanced Centre of Study in Sanskrit, Pune also encouraged me to take up such a śāstric work to translate. It was at his and Professor Godabarisha Mishra's instance that I accepted this proposal. After translating a few pages, I found that a mere translation was not enough in understanding the text as the work is written in a pithy and logical style. So, I made a proposal that it would be better if the translation be accompanied by elaborate annotations on the basis of the Vedāntaviveka, a very lucid and elaborate commentary by Ānandajñāna (Ānandagiri) on the Nyāyaratnadīpāvali. Professor Godabarisha Mishra readily accepted the suggestion. The result is the present work containing the annotated translation of the first chapter of the Nyāyaratnadīpāvali.

Whenever I came across difficult passages in the Nyāyaratnadīpāvali, I approached Swami Divyanandaji Sarasvati of Kailas Ashram, Rishikesh. He was kind enough to discuss these passages so that the philosophical issues propounded in them may be properly comprehended and explained.

I express my gratitude to Professor Mrinal Miri, Chairman, ICPR for his support and encouragement in bringing out the work on the Nyāyaratnadīpāvali of Ānandānubhava. This speaks volumes for his love and concern for the traditional Indian Philosophy.

During the period I was doing this work I had weekly sessions of academic disçussion on the topics, expounded by Ānandānubhava in the Nyāyaratnadīpāvali, with Professor Mithilesh Chaturvedi and Dr. Omnath Bimali. These sessions greatly helped me in comprehending the textual intricacies both grammatical and philosophical and also in elucidating the text fairly clearly. I gratefully acknowledge their contribution in this regard. Whenever I came across a problem of philosophical significance I made it a point to share it with Professor Mishra who himself has contributed a lot to the Advaita Philosophy.

Dr. Manendra P Singh, the incumbent Member Secretary, ICPR, was always ready to help me whenever I sought his advice with regard to the procedural matters concerning the publication of the manuscript of the Nyāyaratnadīpāvali. Dr. Mercy Helen, Diretor (P&R), ICPR, also assisted me during the process of the publication of the present manuscript. I am thankful to both of them for their support.

Besides preparing the index, Dr. Ratish Chandra Jha, Assistant Professor, Sanskrit Department, Hans Raj College, very carefully went through the whole manuscript and spotted both typographical and other errors. For this he deserves my thanks and blessings.

Mr. J. P. Jain, Managing Director, Motilal Banarsidass Pvt. Ltd. took special care to nicely execute the job of printing the present manuscript. Dr. Wachaspati Pandey, editor, Motilal Banarsidass, also helped me in doing away with different kinds of shortcomings of the present manuscript. I express my thanks to both of them.

It is a pleasant duty to recall the care and concern with which my wife, Kesar, attended to my needs during the period I was engaged in doing the present work.

Introduction

The Nyāyaratnadīpāvali, authored by Ānandānubhava, is a significant work on the Advaita Philosophy written in a śāstric style. It was critically edited by V. Jagadisvara Sastrigal and Kalyanasundara Sastrigal for the Government Oriental Manuscripts Library Series No. 166, Madras. It was published in 1961 along with the comprehensive and perspicuous gloss entitled 'Vedāntaviveka' by Ānandajñāna (Ānandagiri). As is clear from the colophon of this work, Ānandānubhava was a pupil of Nārāyaṇajyotis. His date appears to depend on the date of Vimuktātman on whom Ānandānubhava commented, and Citsukhācārya who quoted and criticised Ānandānubhava in his well-known work Citsukhī. He is said to have written the Padārthatattvanirṇaya and the Iṣṭasiddhivivaraṇa. The former seeks to refute the categories of the Vaiśeṣika system of philosophy. It was commented upon by the illustrious Ānanadagiri. The latter work is a gloss on the Iṣṭasiddhi by Vimuktātman who is believed to have flourished between the last quarter of the tenth and the first quarter of the eleventh century. These chronological limits regarding Vimuktātman are based on the fact that he has quoted from the Naiṣkarmya-siddhi of Sureśvarācārya.[1] The date of Citsukhācārya is believed to be about 1220 A.D.[2] Moreover, in the Nyāyaratna-dīpāvali there are references to Kumārila Bhaṭṭa, Prabhākara, Viśvarūpa, Maṇḍana, Vācaspati, Sucaritamiśra, Ānandabodha, Udayana, etc. Ānandabodha who wrote the Nyāyamakaranda was a well-known exponent of the philosophy of Advaita. He is believed to have flourished in 1200 A.D.[3] From what has been said in the foregoing, it is clear that Ānandānubhava

1. *Encyclopedia of Indian Philosophies*, Vol. XI, p. 73, MLBD, Delhi, 2006.

2. *Ibid.*, p. 603.

3. *Nyāyaratnadīpāvaliḥ*, Madras Government Orietal Series, 166, 1961, p. xi.

could not be earlier than Vimuktātman and later than the well-known Advaita Philosopher Citsukhācārya, that is, his period can reasonably be placed between 1000 A.D. and 1220 A.D.

The Nyāyaratnadīpāvali consists of four chapters. The scheme adopted in this work does not differ much from that which is followed in the Brahmasūtras. It has been established in the first chapter that Brahman is both the efficient and the material cause of the universe. Besides, the philosophical issues of significance have also been discussed in the first chapter, for example, the validity of Vedic testimony, the non-human origin of the Vedas, the eternity of varṇas, the intrinsic and extrinsic nature of validity, intrinsic nature of the validity of Vedic testimony, the criticism of the Mīmāṁsā view that the purport of the scriptural enunciations is action and that the scriptures do not expound anything that is not connected with action, to wit, they do not dwell upon an existent entity, potency as a separate category, the deliberation on the scriptural statement '*neha nānāsti kiñcana*', the identical nature of Existence, Consciousness and Bliss, Bliss as the nature of soul, positive nature of Bliss, self-luminosity of the soul, the nature of māyā, Brahman in association with māyā as the material and efficient cause of the creation, the impartite (*akhaṇḍa*) nature of the meaning of the identity propositions (the mahāvākyas), etc. The second chapter discusses elaborately the theories of errors, which is very essential to comprehend the indeterminability (mithyātva) of the phenomena. The positive nature of ajñāna is also established in this chapter. In the third chapter, it is established that the immediate knowledge (*aparokṣajñāna*) can also arise from the verbal testimony. In this chapter the theory of the combination of knowledge and action (*jñānakarma-samuccaya*) as a means to Liberation has also been thoroughly discussed and refuted. A very significant philosophical issue, that is, the locus of avidyā has also been discussed in this chapter. The fourth chapter discusses the nature of release and liberation during living state.

The importance of the present work is evident from the fact that none other than Citsukhācārya followed its style and method of presentation of philosophical issues, albeit with more precision and lucidity, and quoted and criticised its views on the intrinsic nature of validity, the import of Vedic injunctions, the process of verbal cognition, etc. The significance of the Nyāyaratnadīpāvali becomes all the more clear from the fact the illustrious Ānandajñāna (Ānandagiri) wrote an elaborate and lucid commentary entitled Vedāntaviveka on it. The work is difficult as it is written in a terse, śāstric and logical style. The analysis of philosophical problems is done with the help of syllogistic propositions. Their treatment and the discussion based on the fallacies of reason render the work rather abstruse.

The present volume contains the annotated translation of the first chapter of the Nyāyaratnadīpāvali in which several important philosophical issues have been discussed as given above. Since the nature of the work is terse and also teems with logical niceties, the annotations based on the commentary of Ānandajñāna have helped in bringing out the import of the philosophical issues more lucidly.

Although the Madras Government publication is critically edited, it contains many errors. It is the typographical and punctuational errors that sometimes make the comprehension of the text rather difficult. At some places in the text, even the topical headings are not consonant with the text so demarcated. The demarcation itself is defective at several places. I have tried my level best to give the correct text in the Devanāgarī and also punctuation marks wherever they help in making the sense of the text easy of comprehension. On page 115 of NRD, I have emended the demarcated text. The topical heading '*Prābhākaraśaṅkāsamādhānam*' should have included the text beginnig with '*na*' occurring in the first line on page 115 of NRD, and not '*na*' in the fourth line as is given in the present edition.

I have given the text in Devanāgarī along with its topical headings as I have found them in the Madras Government publication except some headings given in the 'Topical Contents'. The obvious errors have been corrected. This renders the text somewhat easy to understand.

The Sanskrit text is followed by the translation in English which is further followed by annotations based on the Vedānta-viveka by Ānandajñāna. I have tried to explain the syllogistic propositions with the help of illustrations from the basic Nyāya texts, such as Tarkasaṅgraha, Nyāyasiddhāntamuktāvalī, etc. so that the fallacies may be understood easily. This facilitates in appreciating the Advaita position vis-a-vis the Buddhist, Nyāya, Mīmāṁsā, etc.

It is a relatively free translation so that it may enable the reader to understand what Ānandānubhava has got to say on the philosophical issues he has taken up for deliberation. For the same reason, I did make the proposal to the ICPR to include the annotations based on the Vedāntaviveka, the elaborate commentary on the present work written by Ānandagiri so that the issues discussed in the text may be rendered easy of comprehension.

I place this work before the learned readers. I hope that I would be benefited from the feedback both in respect of errors and conceptual inadequacy or ambiguity as these shortcomings might remain in such a work even though it has been carefully gone through and proof-read by me and Dr. Ratish Chandra Jha. I will definitely emend the present work in the light of the suggestions received whenever I am called upon to do so.

Abbreviations

Bh. G. : Bhagavadgītā

Bṛh. Up. : Bṛhadāraṇyaka Upaniṣad

BS : Brahmasūtras

BSS : Brahmasūtraśāṅkarabhāṣya

Chā. Up. : Chāndogya Upaniṣad

ÇS : Citsukhī

MS : Mīmāṁsā sūtras

NRD : Nyāyaratnadīpāvali

Tai. Up. : Taittirīya Upaniṣad

VV : Veḍāntaviveka

NP : Nayanaprasādinī

॥ श्रीरस्तु ॥

॥ ओं महागणपतये नमः ॥

आनन्दानुभवपूज्यपादविरचिता

॥ न्यायरत्नदीपावलिः ॥

प्रथमोऽध्यायः

हरिं हार्दं प्रणम्याथ वेदान्तार्थप्रसिद्धये ।
सन्न्यायरत्नदीपानामावलिः क्रियते मया ॥

यद्यपि वेदान्तार्थः स्फुटं भाष्यादिषु प्रतिपादितः तत्रभवद्भिः भाष्यकारादिभिः तथाप्यभिनवदुस्तर्कतिमिरतिरोहित इवासौ अतस्तत्प्रकाशनाय प्रयत्यते ।

Translation : Paying obeisance to Hari who dwells in the heart, I now compose the garland of the lamps of jewels in the form of unblemished principles in order to establish the import of the Upaniṣads (Vedānta).

Although the import of the Upaniṣads has been clearly expounded by the honoured authors of commentaries on the Brahmasūtras, Upaniṣads, etc., still an effort is being made here to bring to light the import of Vedānta as it appears to be clouded by the darkness of new fallacious arguments.

Annotation : Ānandānubhava, the author of *Nyāyaratna-dīpāvali*, invokes Hari and pays obeisance to Him so that the work which he has undertaken to bring to light the import of Vedānta may be completed without any interruptions and may grow and continue to be of advantage to those desirous of attaining liberation (*mokṣa*) by deliberating on the Ultimate Reality delineated in the Upaniṣads. The invocation is also purported to preserve the tradition of the cultured in this respect. The words *hari* and *hārda* occurring in the invocatory verse respectively represent the terms *tat* and *tvam* and signify God and the individual self. Both the terms end in the same case-ending. This indicates that the identity of the two is the subject-matter of the present work.

In consonance with Śaṅkara's interpretation of the word *atha* in *athāto brahmajijñāsā*, BS 1. 1. 1, the word *atha* occurring in the invocatory verse here points towards the qualifications of a person who is eligible to study Vedānta and deliberate on the nature of Brahman. That the seeker ceases to be afflicted with the effects of ignorance by realising the oneness of Brahman and the individual self is the purpose of the present treatise. The anubandhas demonstrated here belong to the discipline of Vedānta. So, this treatise is a prạkaraṇa of Vedānta (*śāstrīyānubandhacatuṣṭayavaiśiṣṭyād asya prakaraṇatvam*, VV. p. 2). Moreover, the present work expounds, in a unique style, all the tenets discussed in the Śārīrakaśāstra and also performs a specific function of removing the confusion created by the fallacious arguments against the views of Advaita Vedānta. Therefore, the present work has rightly been designated as a prakaraṇa by Ānandajñāna.[1]

बौद्धकृतवेदाप्रामाण्यपूर्वपक्षः

ननु वेदस्यापि न विवक्षितार्थता, अप्रमाणत्वात्; किमु वेदवादिनोऽप्यनिष्टार्थानां वेदान्तानाम्? तथा हि — यानि परस्परविरुद्धानि वाक्यानि न तानि प्रमाणानि यथा उन्मत्तवाक्यानि; तथा हि — 'ब्राह्मणो न हन्तव्य' इत्यादि क्वचिद-हिंसोच्यते। 'ब्रह्मणे ब्राह्मण'मित्यादि ब्राह्मणादिपशुविधानम् तथा नैष्ठिकं ब्रह्मचर्यमुच्यते, 'न काञ्चन परिहरेत् तद्व्रतम्' इति गुर्वङ्गनादिगमनं च। तथा ब्राह्मणस्य सुरापानविधिनिषेधौ।

एवं ब्रह्मणि 'एकमेवाद्वितीय'मित्यादौ विरोधो द्रष्टव्यः। अत एवोक्तम् — त्रयो वेदस्य कर्तारो मुनिभाण्डनिशाचराः' इति।[2]

न च प्रकरणादिभेदाद् व्यवस्थया अविरुद्धार्थता, तद्भेदस्य प्रक्रियासिद्धत्वात्। तस्माद् विरुद्धार्थत्वाद्वेदा न प्रमाणम्।

---

1. *śāstraprakaraṇayor ekārthatve'pyavāntarakāryabhedopapatteḥ śāstrakāryāntare sthitatvam apyāstheyam. yathāhuḥ —*
śāstraikadeśasambaddhaṁ śāstrakāryāntare sthitam, āhuḥ prakaraṇaṁ nāmeti.... VV. p. 2. Also cf. *The Naiṣkarmyasiddhi of Sureśvara*, ed. R. Balasubramanian, Madras, 1988, p. 6.
2. VV, pp. 4-5

Buddhist view that the Vedas are not valid

Trans. : Even the Veda, being inauthentic, does not have anything purposeful to expound, much less the Vedānta texts which are antagonistic even to the views of the followers of the Vedas. To explain, the statements which are mutually contradictory are not authentic like the statements of a drunk. To illustrate, at one place non-violence is prescribed by stating 'The brāhmaṇa should not be killed', etc. (At another place) there is a prescription for the brāhmaṇa, etc. to be made a sacrificial animal for the welfare of the brāhmaṇas, etc. In the same way, life-long celibacy is enjoined (at one place) and (at another) a vow is prescribed not to say 'no' to any woman, implying thereby not to say 'no' even to the wife of the preceptor. In the same manner, the prescription to drink wine and its prohibition (are also available in the Vedas).

In a similar manner, in respect of the nature of Brahman contradiction can be seen in such statements as 'The Reality is only one and non-dual', etc. It is this reason that it has been said 'The three are the creators of the Vedas : the ascetics, dupes and the demons.'

(The pūrvapakṣin says that) it cannot be accepted that the resolution of contradiction in the meanings conveyed by Vedic sentences can be achieved by virtue of the difference that exists in the contexts. According to him, this difference is a result of the methodology of exposition (*prakriyā*) (and thus this cannot offset the actual difference that exists in the acts enjoined). Therefore, being contradictory in nature, the Vedas do not constitute a verbal testimony (says the pūrvapakṣin).

Ann. : The Buddhist opponent puts forward an argument to prove the inauthenticity of the Vedas. He says that the Vedas are not authentic since they have contradictory statements like those of a drunken man. Hence, the view that the Vedas have something meaningful to communicate does not hold good. To explain, at one place the killing of a brāhmaṇa is prohibited but, in a human sacrifice (*puruṣamedha*), it has been prescribed that he should be made a sacrificial animal to propitiate Brahmā for the welfare of the brāhmaṇas (*brahmaṇe brāhmaṇam ālabhate kṣatrāya rājanyam,* see VV p. 4). Thus, there is a contradiction between the injunction of killing and its prohibition. Similarly, a vow of life-long celibacy is ordained for a brahmacārin who takes a vow to stay at the guru's āśrama for the whole life emaciating his body (*atyantam ātmānam ācāryakule'vasādayannityātyantikaṁ brahmacaryaṁ vidhīyate*, VV, p. 4). Contrariwise, a vow has been prescribed in the context of the Vāmadevya upāsanā not to dishonour the wish of a woman desirous of having physical relation. The author of the Nyāyaratnadīpāvali, on behalf of the pūrvapakṣin, cites from Chāndogya Upaniṣad 2. 13. 2 in order to point out the contradiction in Vedic statements. In the context of Vāmadevya upāsanā, the votary has been prescribed that he should not say 'no' to any woman who approaches him with a desire for physical relationship, which is opposed to the vow of absolute celibacy. According to the opponent, a woman may be the wife of the preceptor, which is implied by the expression *kāñcana*. That is why probably the author refers to the wife of the preceptor. However, others have interpreted the Upaniṣadic text '*na kāñcana pariharet tadvratam*' in the following sense : The person who is devoted to Vāmadevya Sāman has to observe a vow 'not to say 'no'' to any of his wives desirous of having physical relationship.[1] In a similar manner, there is a general Vedic prescription for a brāhmaṇa not to take wine (*surā*). On the other hand, wine has been prescribed for a brāhmaṇa in the *sautrāmaṇi* sacrifice.

The pūrvapakṣin says that a satisfactory resolution of the contradiction existing in the Vedic statements cannot be achieved by invoking the difference in contexts, etc. The reason is that the difference in the contexts is an outcome of the methodology of exposition (*prakriyā*) adopted by the exponents of Vedic views. So, the difference in the contexts is based on prakriyā (methodology of exposition), and not on evidence. Thus, it cannot duly resolve the contradiction which exists in the actual acts prescribed by the Vedic injunctions (cf. VV, p. 5). So, according to the pūrvapakṣin, the Vedas, enjoining contradictory acts, cannot constitute a valid means of knowledge.

किञ्च यदाप्तवाक्येतरवाक्यं तदप्रमाणम् यथोन्मत्तवाक्यम् आप्तवाक्येतरवाक्यं च वेदः। विपक्षे चाप्तप्रणीतता वेदस्यापद्येत। दूषणान्तरविरहः पुनः स्पष्ट इति

1. Cf. *The Word Speaks to the Faustian Man*, Soma Raj Gupta, MLBD, 2001, pp. 159-60

न विव्रियते। तस्मात् सिद्धम् वेदस्याप्रामाण्यम्। किमु वेदवादिनोऽप्यनिष्टार्थानां वेदान्तानामिति।

Trans. : Morever, the sentence spoken by a person other than a trustworthy one is not a testimony like a sentence spoken by a drunken man and the Veda consists of sentences which are other than those spoken by a trustworthy person. In case the Veda is accepted as a contrary instance (*vipakṣa,* i.e. an evidence like a sentence of a trustworthy person), then the contingency of its having been authored by a trustworthy person would be incurred. The absence of other fallacies, (*viruddhatva,* etc.) being obvious, is not being explained. Therefore, it is proved that the Vedas are not an authority, much less the Upaniṣads which are unfavourable even to the Vedavādins (upholders of Vedic rituals).

Ann. : If somehow the asiddhi fallacy of the probans in the preceding syllogism was established, then the pūrvapakṣin would advance the following syllogism to prove the inauthenticity of the Vedas : The Vedas do not constitute a verbal testimony since they contain sentences which are other than those made by trustworthy persons like a sentence spoken by a drunken man. It cannot be accepted that the Vedas, as a contrary instance, contain the statements of a trustworthy person. In that case, the contingency of the Veda having been authored by a trustworthy person would be incurred, which goes against the theory of non-human origin of the Vedas (*apauruṣeyavāda*)[1] held by the Mīmāṁsakas and the Advaitins. The opponent avers that the syllogism, put forward by him to prove the inauthenticity of the Veda, does not suffer

1. Both the Mīmāṁsakas and the Advaitins subscribe to the concept of *apauruṣeyatva* that the śrutis are of non-human origin. Nonetheless, there is some difference between the Mīmāṁsakas and the Advaitins in this regard. The former recognise the absolute eternalness of the Vedas whereas for the Advaitins there is nothing eternal and absolutely real, except Brahman. Consequently, the Advaitins construe *apauruṣeyatva* of the śrutis as not pronounced by any person, according to his independent will. It is therefore held by them that though at the beginning of creation the śruti passages are transmitted by Īśvara, he does not exercise his will in doing so but only reproduces the passages as they were in the previous creations. Cf. Citsukhī, pp. 267-80. On the other hand the Naiyāyikas hold that the Vedas are *pauruṣeya* since they are originated by Īśvara.

from any other fallacy such as *viruddhatva* (*sādhyābhāvavyāptiḥ*, probans' concomitance with the absence of the probandum) as is clear from the fact that the probans obviously does not reside in the vipakṣa (i.e. in a sentence spoken by an authentic person). In this way, the syllogistic proposition proves beyond any doubt that the Vedas are not a valid means of knowledge and, hence, carry no sanctity as an authority. When the Vedas are not established as a reliable authority, the authenticity of the Upaniṣads would be considered much less as they are not favourable even to the Vedavādins who subscribe to the view of Vedic rituals. Consequently, both the Vedas and the Vedānta do not constitute a verbal testimony.

वेदप्रामाण्यव्यवस्थापनम्

उच्यते । न तावद् अत्र विरुद्धार्थता सामान्यविशेषविषययोः क्वचिद्भिन्नार्थत्वात् प्रकरणादिभेदादधिकारिभेदाच्च व्यवस्थोपपत्तेः । इत्थं व्यवस्था चागमवादिभिः सर्वैरभ्युपेया । अन्यथा क्षणिकविशुद्धबोधविधिः सर्वशून्यताविधिश्च विरुद्धचेत । तस्माद्वेदस्यासिद्धा विरुद्धार्थता । परस्परेति च धर्मिनिर्देशेऽसाधारणता । सामान्यनिर्देशे च त्वदीयागमेन ते व्यभिचारः तस्यास्मदागमेन विरुद्धार्थत्वात् । द्वितीयप्रयोगेऽपि वाक्यत्वं भागासिद्धम् । गीतिरूपेषु सामसु वाक्यत्वानभ्युपगमात् । विवादपदं वाक्यं धर्मीति चेत् । न । तवागमभागे बाधात् सिद्धसाधनत्वाच्च ॥

Establishment of the view that the Vedas are an authority

Trans. : To this our reply is : There is, in fact, no contradiction here (in the Vedas) since, in some cases, the spheres of the general and the specific have different prescriptions and that can be duly resolved by taking recourse to difference in contexts, etc. and in qualifications (eligibility conditions). This kind of arrangement should be accepted by all the adherents of the Āgamas. Otherwise a prescriptive statement in consonance with the view of momentary pure consciousness would be contradictory to that which is consonant with the view of all-emptiness. Thus, the view that there is contradiction in the statements of the Vedas remains unestablished. If the term *paraspara* stands for the Veda, then the fallacy of reason known as *asādhāraṇa anaikāntika* would be applicable. If the term *paraspara* is taken to be a general reference, then it will incur the fallacy (known as *sādhāraṇa anaikāntika*) in your case as your Āgama is (at least) contradictory to our Āgama (thus the probans would exist where the probandum does not exist). In the second syllogistic proposition, the probans in the form of the property of being a sentence suffers from the defect known as *bhāgāsiddha* since it is not accepted to be present in the metrical hymns of the Veda. If a sentence (in general) is to be made the subject (*dharmin* or *pakṣa*), then the sādhya is stultified in the case of your Āgama (because your Āgama is not inauthentic from your own point of view). Additionally, it would be a case of proving that which has already been proved (from the siddhāntin's point of view).

Ann. : There is no contradiction in the statements of the Veda prescribing killing and prohibiting it as the statement which prohibits killing is of a general nature, whereas the statement enjoining killing relates to a specific context. So, having different contexts, the injunctions relating to killing or prohibiting it can be treated as not being contradictory. The same is the case about life-long celibacy and having physical relationship with a woman. When a student stays in the āśrama for study, he is to observe celibacy. On the other hand one is allowed to have a physical relation with a woman when he is observing a particular vow (cf. *āśramaprakaraṇe naiṣṭhikaṁ brahmacaryam ucyate. vrataviśeṣādhikāre ca aṅganāsaṅgo' bhidhīyate. tathā ca prakaraṇabhedāt brahmacaryavidhiniṣedhayor aviruddhatetyarthaḥ*. VV, p. 6). So far as the apparent contradiction regarding the Upaniṣadic statements is concerned, it may be said that they have been given keeping in view the capability of seekers. This is commonly seen in differing life-situations. This comes to mean that the non-dualistic statements about Brahman are meant for the seekers equipped with higher spiritual capacity, whereas the dualistic statements have in view the seekers of lesser capability. Consequently, it can be said that there is no contradiction in the statements of the Veda in this respect. Similarly, the statements concerning the prescription and prohibition of wine can be explained. This kind of methodology should be admitted in respect of śāstric injunctions.

Otherwise, the contradiction existing in the injunctive statements made in the context of the views of momentary pure consciousness and those of all-emptiness shall defy resolution. Consequently, it may fairly be held that the Vedic statements are actually not contradictory although they seemingly prescribe acts of a contradictory nature.

Now the siddhāntin takes up the job of pointing out fallacies in the arguments put forward by the pūrvapakṣin. What does the word *paraspara* in the syllogistic proposition '*yāni parasparaviruddhārthāni vākyāni na tāni pramāṇāni yathā unmattavākyāni*' stand for? Ānandagiri in his Vedāntaviveka suggests that it could stand either for the Veda or Āgama. If it stands only for the Veda, then the contradiction in the Vedic statements cannot be illustrated by the statement of a drunken man since this kind of contradiction exists only in the Vedic statements and not anywhere else much less in the statement of a drunkard. Hence, the probans (*hetu*) is rendered fallacious (*asādhāraṇa anaikāntika* cf. *sarvasapakṣavipakṣavyāvṛto'sādhāraṇaḥ*, TS) since it does not reside in the *vipakṣa* (inauthenticity does not exist in the Buddhist Āgama which is, therefore, *vipakṣa* in this case) and in the statement of a drunken man, which exemplifies *sapakṣa*, but only in the *pakṣa*, that is in the Vedic statements only. Thus this is a case of the fallacy known as *asādhāraṇa anaikāntika*.

If the word *paraspara* in the hetu (*parasparaviruddhārthatvāt*, also cf. *kiṁ ca hetau parasparaśabdena vedo vyapadiśyate āgamamātraṁ vā*, VV, p. 6) is taken to stand for a general reference, then the Āgama could also be taken as *dharmin* (*pakṣa*). In this situation, another problem would crop up. Although the Āgama has authenticity for the opponent but it lacks authenticity so far as the siddhāntin is concerned. Thus, the probans is again rendered fallacious (*sādhyābhāvavadvṛttiḥ sādhāraṇo'naikāntikaḥ* : the reason (*hetu*) which resides where the probandum (*sādhya*) does not exist). In this situation the occurrence of the probans in the locus where the probandum does not exist can be demonstrated as follows : It is obvious that the statement of an Āgama belonging to the opponent that only void exists is opposed to the statements of the Veda that the self should be known as it truly is and that this was Being alone in the beginning, i.e. before creation. Thus the contradiction of the statement of the Veda exists in the Āgama of the opponent where authenticity (the absence of the absence of validity = *sādhyābhāva*) from the pūrvapakṣin's point of view exists. Consequently, the state of being contradictory exists where the sādhya (invalidity) is absent (cf. *astītyevopalabdhavyaḥ sadeva saumyedamiti vedavākyena tvadāgamavākyaviśeṣaṁ śūnyatāpratipādakaṁ viruddhaṁ prasiddham*, VV, p. 6).

The other syllogism is put forward to prove that the Veda lacks authority since the Veda does not contain sentences of a trustworthy person. Moreover, in such a situation the probans (*hetu*) would not be residing in the whole of Vedic corpus (*pakṣa*) as the metric hymns of the Sāmaveda are not accepted as sentences. Consequently, the hetu is rendered fallacious as it does not reside in a part of the *pakṣa* (*bhāgāsiddha*). Secondly, if a sentence in general is accepted as *pakṣa*, it would also include a sentence of the opponent's Āgama, which is authentic in his view but inauthentic according to the siddhāntin. This will lead to the fallacy known as *bādha* since the absence of invalidity is definite so far as one's own scripture is concerned. It contradicts the siddhāntin's view of invalidity regarding the opponents' treatise. In spite of difference in respect of Śūnyavāda and Vijñānavāda, there is no inauthenticity in the opponent's Āgama. Moreover, the defect of proving that which has already been proved (*siddhasādhana*) is also incurred since the inauthenticity of the opponent's Āgama is already established according to the siddhāntin's view (*asmābhistvadāgamavākyārthānām apramāṇatvopagamāt tatraivāsmākaṁ siddhasādhyatvam*, VV, p. 7).

अथ विमतो वेदो धर्मीति चेन्न। अस्याश्रयासिद्धेः। न हि लोकसिद्धमपि ते बाह्यमक्षणिकं प्रामाणिकं किंचिदस्ति यद्यस्ति तदापि क्षणिकस्येन्द्रियाग्राह्यत्वादसिद्धिरेव। प्रामाण्यसाधनेऽप्येवमस्माकं धर्म्यसिद्धिरिति चेन्न। क्षणिकस्यापि त्वया सिद्ध्यभ्युपगमात्।

Trans. : Supposing the Veda under dispute is the subject (*pakṣa*) of the syllogistic proposition, then this cannot be so, for the locus (the subject) itself does not exist. There is nothing external non-momentary current among the people which is established by proof according to your view. If it is accepted, then also it continues to be non-existent (unestablished) since the momentary cannot be grasped by the senses. (If you say that) the subject is not established even in our inferring the authority (of the Veda), then this is not so since you do postulate the existence of the momentary.

Ann. : The use of the expression *vimato vedaḥ* 'disputed Veda' ensures the exclusion of both the metrical hymns of the Veda which do not fulfil the criterion of being a sentence and the Āgamas of the Buddhists from becoming the subject (*pakṣa*) of the syllogistic proposition. Still, the Veda cannot be accepted as the subject of inference (*dharmin*) as the Buddhists do not subscribe to the view that the Veda is established as an entity by proof. To explain, according to the Śūnyavādins, the Veda cannot be the subject of inference as nothing exists as per their view. So far as the Vijñāna-vādins are concerned, nothing external exists and consciousness (*vijñāna*) cannot be admitted as the subject of the syllogistic proposition as they do not consider its authenticity to be under dispute. So far as the Sautrāntika and Vaibhāṣika schools are concerned, they do accept the stream of incessantly continuing instants. Consequently, *dharmin* or the subject of inference may be accepted as existent. However, the Veda, being momentary as per the view of momentariness, cannot be accepted as comprehensible to the auditory sense and, thus, it is as good as non-existent. Nonetheless, the siddhāntin avers that, according to the Sautrāntika and Vaibhāṣika Buddhist views, the Veda may be construed as the subject of inference. The reason is that, although the Veda is not enduring (in accordance with the view of momentariness), even then it can logically be accepted as established in accordance with the Buddhist view of momentariness. Hence the pūrvapakṣin's view does not hold good that, in a similar manner, the subject of the syllogistic proposition to prove the authority of the Veda from the siddhantin's point of view also would not exist.

लोकसिद्ध एवास्तु धर्मीति चेन्न। बाधापत्तेः। ऋग्वेदोऽयमिति ह्यबाधित-महाजनप्रसिद्धेर्धर्मिसिद्धिरास्थेया। न प्राकृतप्रसिद्धेः। अन्यथा भागे सिद्ध-साधनताप्रसङ्गात्। तथा च सति महाजनप्रसिद्ध्यन्तरबाधो दुर्वारः। प्रामाण्य-प्रसिद्धिबाध्या न बाधिकेति चेन्न। तद्बाधानुपलब्धेः। अनुमया बाधकल्पने चान्योऽन्याश्रयत्वापत्तिः।

Trans. : If only that which is current among people, i.e. established, be accepted as the subject of inference, then this cannot be accepted as such because inauthenticity that is going to be inferred would be contradicted (as those who believe in the authority of the Veda also subscribe to the view that the Veda is absolutely valid and authentic). From the uncontradicted or unsublated perception of the distinguished (cultured) men that 'this is the Ṛgveda', the Veda as the subject of inference should be taken as established and not on the basis of the belief of the ordinary people. Otherwise, the defect of proving that which has already been proved would be incurred in a part of the subject (since the siddhāntin does not consider the statements of the Jain or Buddhist ascetics to be valid or authentic). And in that case also the stultification of the view about the inauthenticity of the Veda accepted by the cultured cannot be avoided.[1] If it is said that the conviction of the authenticity of the Veda is to be contradicted and that it is not to contradict the inauthenticity of the Veda, then this cannot be maitained since the contradiction of the authenticity of the Veda is not (perceptually) available. In case the contradiction of the authenticity of the Veda is assumed on the basis of the inference of the inauthenticity of the Veda, then it would lead to the defect of mutual dependence.

Ann. : Now Ānandānubhava starts taking stock of another viewpoint. He suggests that if it is not possible to accept the validly cognised entity as subject of the inference, then an entity about which the distinguished and cultured men are convinced could be taken as the subject of the syllogistic proposition. The belief of the ordinary people should not be given precedence in this regard as it would lead to another fallacy. In other words, the subject of the inference should not be decided on the basis of popular belief. If this is done, then a defect of partially proving the already proved would be incurred as in that case the statements of the Jaina or Buddhist monks would also become the subject of the inference and they are decidedly inauthentic according to the siddhāntin. In this way this will become a case of proving that which is taken as already settled.

1. *ye hi mahājanā vedaṁ vidanti te tasya prāmāṇyamapi pratipadyante. tena mahājanapratītavedasyāprāmāṇye bādhāpattirityarthaḥ.* VV, p.8.

The conviction of the distinguished about the veracity of the testimony of the Veda definitley contradicts the view about its inauthenticity. Nonetheless, the opponent retorts saying that the view about the authenticity of the Veda cannot contradict the view about its inauthenticity since what is to be contradicted cannot contradict anything else and that in this case it is the authenticity of the Vedic testimony which is going to be contradicted. If, to prove this point of view, the pūrvapakṣin takes recourse to the inference of the inauthenticity of the Veda to contradict the view about the authenticity of the Veda, then it leads to the defect of mutual dependence in the following manner : The inference of the inauthenticity of the Veda stultifies its authenticity and when the stultification of the authenticity of the Veda is thus obtained, the syllogism is invoked to prove the inauthenticity of the Veda. In this way the defect known as mutual dependence results. (*vedāprāmāṇyānumānād vedaprāmāṇyaprasiddhibādhasiddhiḥ tatsiddhau ca tadaprāmāṇyānumānasiddhiriti parasparāśrayatvāt.* VV, p. 8). It is on account of this defect of mutual dependence in respect of the pūrvapakṣin's view that the doctrine of those who are convinced about the veracity of the verbal testimony of the Veda finds itself endorsed.

आप्तवाक्येतरवाक्यत्वं च वेदस्य वेदवादिनां केषांचिदसिद्धम्। अज्ञातार्थाविषयत्वं चास्माकं सर्वत्रोपाधिः। किञ्चाप्रामाण्यं किं प्रमाणादन्यत्वमुत प्रमाणाभावत्वमुत तद्विरोधिता। आद्ये सिद्धसाधनता। ज्ञानं ह्यस्माकं साक्षात्प्रमाणम्। तदन्यत्वं च वेदेषु सिद्धम्। द्वितीये भावत्वग्रहविरोधः। तृतीये त्वनुपलम्भबाधः। दृष्टान्ते च साध्यविकलता। न हि प्रमाणेनैव वेदेषु विरोध उपलभ्यते। अतन्निवर्त्यत्वात्। अथ प्रमासाधनेतरत्वमप्रामाण्यं साध्यम्। न। तस्याग्निर्हिमस्य भेषजमिति भागे सिद्धत्वात्। तर्हीतरभाग एवास्तु धर्मी। हेतुदृष्टान्तौ तु पूर्वोक्तावेव।

Trans. : The probans 'being a sentence other than that of a trustworthy person' does not exist in the Veda according to the view of some of the upholders of the Veda (the Naiyāyikas accept that the Vedas are authored by God, that is, the Vedas are *pauruṣeya*). (Secondly) in our view there is an upādhi consisting in the non-objecthood of an unknown entity applicable everywhere (i.e. which is possible in the present syllogism as well as in the preceding one). Moreover, what does non-validity (*aprāmāṇya*) signify? Does it mean a state of being other than the means of a valid cognition or the absence of the means of a valid cognition or the state of being contrary to the means of a valid cognition? The first alternative suffers from the fallacy of proving that which has already been proved as we construe knowledge as an immediate means of a valid cognition (being self-luminous) and the state of being other than that exists in the Veda (this constitutes *siddhasādhanatā*). The fact that the Veda (without any reference to a counter-positive) eternally exists is falsified if the second alternative is accepted. In the third alternative, the fallacy known as bādha consisting in non-availability becomes applicable and the illustration (then) ceases to have the *sādhya* in it (as the statements of a drunk do not set aside the means of a valid cognition; cf. *pramāṇanivartakatvamapramāṇatvam ityatra doṣāntaramāha — dṛṣṭānte ceti. na khalūnmattavākyāni pramāṇaṁ nivartayanti. tannivartyatvādityarthaḥ*, VV, p. 9). There is nothing in the Vedas which is contrary to the means of a valid cognition. The reason is that the Veda and the means of a valid cognition are not mutually exclusive (*pramāṇabhūtajñānena nivartakena nivartyena vā vedeṣu nivartyeṣu nivartakeṣu vā virodho nādhigataḥ*, ibid., p. 9). Or, it may be that the inauthenticity, which consists in being other than the means of a valid cognition, is the sādhya. That is also not the case (since the state of being other than the means of a valid cognition exists in a Vedic statement that restates that which has already been perceptually verified). As such, this exists in a section of the Veda, that is, in the statement 'the fire is the remedy of cold'. Then, let the other part of the Veda (which does not have restatements) become the dharmin. The probans and the illustration would verily be the same as already stated.

Ann. : The reason consisting in being a sentence other than that of a trustworthy person is fallacious in accordance with the view of a section of the upholders of the Veda since the Naiyāyikas hold that the Vedas are authored by God. Moreover, the reason in this case is vitiated by the presence of an upādhi consisting in the non-objecthood of an unknown entity which is possible in this inference and the one already stated. The non-objecthood of an unknown entity is concomitant with invalidity (*aprāmāṇya*). To explain, where there is invalidity, there is necessarily non-objecthood of an unknown entity since objecthood of an unknown entity is a necessary condition of a valid cognition according to the view of the siddhāntin. Secondly, it is not necessary that the non-objecthood of an unknown entity is concomitant with the probans consisting in 'being a sentence other than that of a trustworthy person' as it is given in our experience that the Veda makes known that which is not known (*nāpi sādhanavyāptiḥ anavagatārthāvagatihetutāyā vede svānubhavasiddhatvāt*, VV, p. 9). This means that the reason is fallacious (*vyāpyatvāsiddha*).

Ānandānubhava now discusses the meaning of *aprāmāṇya* by taking into consideration the three denotations of the particle *nañ*. To the question whether *aprāmāṇya* means 'the state of being other than the means of a valid cognition', he replies that if we accept this, then the defect of proving the already proven becomes applicable since knowledge is an immediate means of valid cognition being self-luminous according to the view of the siddhāntin and the state of being other than that exists in the Veda (cf. *jñānaṁ hyasmākaṁ sākṣāt pramāṇam. tadanyatvaṁ ca vedeṣu siddham*, ibid., p. 9). He explains the untenability of the second alternative as follows : If one says that the Veda is not a means of valid cognition, this obviously implies the non-existence of its being a valid means of cognition (*tadabhāvatvaṁ ced aprāmāṇyaṁ tadā vedo'pramāṇam iti vadatā tasya pramāṇābhāvatvam uktaṁ bhavati*, ibid., p. 9). Thus, there being no counter-positive of the Veda which is accepted as eternal, the second interpretation is set aside as it goes against this fact that the Veda is eternal (*tathā ca pratiyoginirapekṣatayā bhāvatvena bhāsato vedasya tadabhāvatvamabhidadhannanubhavavirodhena nirasyo bhavati*, ibid. p. 9). In the third alternative, the particle *nañ* is accepted to mean 'contrariness (*virodhitva*)'. Since there is no contrariness in the Veda in the manner as it exists in the statements of a drunken man since these statements do not set aside a valid cognition rather they are themselves contradicted by a valid cognition. In this way the sādhya (*pramāṇanivartakatā*) consisting in 'contradicting a valid means of cognition' does not exist in the statement of a drunk. This renders the reason fallacious as the sādhya ceases to exist in the illustration. Moreover, no contrariness of a valid means occurs in the Veda (*na hi pramāṇenaiva vedeṣu virodha upalabhyate,* see NRD, p. 9). Obviously, a valid means of cognition does not annul the very being of the Veda itself on the empirical plane although the knowledge of non-duality does do away with the very being of the Veda (*advaitajñānasya vedanivartakatve'pi tathāsiddheḥ* VV, p. 9). So, from the point of view of contrariness, the Veda cannot be proved to be invalid. After discussing the three alternative meanings of the paricle *nañ*, Ānandānubhava suggests another meaning of the paricle *nañ* and summarily rejects it. He says that if the meaning of the sādhya of inference, that is, *aprāmāṇya* is construed as 'the state of being other than the means of a valid cognition', then also it cannot be accepted in respect of all the Vedas. The reason is that 'the state of being other than the means of a valid cognition' exists in a section of the Vedas. The Vedic sentence 'the fire is the remedy of cold' of Śuklayajurveda Saṁhitā, 23. 10 narrates the fact which is perceptually verified. Hence, the absence of being a valid means of cognition exists in it as a valid cognition consists in a cognition of an unapprehended entity. Hence, there is a deviation which consists in proving what has already been proved (*siddhasādhanatā*) in this section of the Veda. In this situation, he suggests that the other section of the Veda, which is other than a restatement should be accepted as the subject (*pakṣa*) of inference and the reason and the illustration may be retained as already stated.

अथवा वेदवाक्यत्वं हेतुः उक्तभागो दृष्टान्तोऽस्तु । न । इतरभागस्याज्ञातार्थज्ञापकताप्रतीतिबाधाद् , विपक्षे बाधकविरहादाप्तप्रणीतताप्रसङ्गस्य निराकरिष्यमाणत्वात् । अप्रमाणसाधर्म्यमात्रेणाप्रामाण्ये बौद्धागमवाक्यम् अप्रमाणं प्रसिद्धाप्तवाक्येतरवाक्यत्वाद् उक्तवाक्यवदित्यतिप्रसङ्गरूपबाधकतर्कसद्भावाच्च । तस्माद्वेदस्याप्रामाण्यप्रलापः प्रमत्तप्रलम्ब इवोपेक्षणीयः । प्रामाण्यं चादरणीयम् । प्रयोगस्तु - कारीर्यादिवाक्यं प्रमाणम् अबाधितानुवादेतरवाक्यत्वाद् वैद्यशास्त्रवत् । विपक्षे चोक्तविधवाक्यताभङ्गप्रसङ्गो बाधः । दूषणान्तरविरहस्त्वतिरोहित एव । एवं च सति विवादपदं वेदवाक्यं प्रमाणम् उभयसिद्धाप्रमाणेतरत्वे सति वेदवाक्यत्वात् सम्प्रतिपन्नवदितीतरभागस्यापि प्रामाण्यं सिद्धम् । न च विपर्ययेऽप्येवं प्रयोगः सम्भवतीति वाच्यम् । उक्तप्रमासाधनत्वप्रतीतिबाधस्यात्रापि तुल्यत्वात् ।

Trans. : Or, let 'the state of being a Vedic sentence' be the probans (*hetu*) and the said portion, the illustration. This is not so since the knowledge that the other section of the Veda makes an unknown entity known is contradicted. In respect of the contrary instance (i.e. the Veda is the means of a valid cognition), there is no contradictory argument and (in this case) the contingency of the Veda having been authored by a trustworthy person (since the Veda is accepted as the means of a valid cognition like the sentence of a trustworthy person) will be dismissed. If the invalidity of cognition merely on the basis of a common characteristic is intended to be proved, then this would lead to a contradictory inferential argument : the statement of a Buddhist Āgama is inauthentic since it is different from the statement of a well-known trustworthy person like the statement (of a drunkard) already illustrated. (Given such a situation), the incoherent talk of the invalidity of the Veda deserves to be disregarded like a song sung by an intoxicated man. (On the other hand) the authority of the Veda should be respected. (To endorse this point of view) the syllogistic proposition is as follows : The sentence that enjoins *kārīrī iṣṭi* (*kārīryā vṛṣṭikāmo yajeta*, s. v. *kārīrī*, Mīmāṁsākoṣa), etc. is an authority as it is an uncontradicted statement which is also other than a restatement like that in a medicinal treatise (*vaidyaśāstra*). The violation of the status of being a sentence of the said kind is a deterrent to the contrary instance (i.e. such a sentence is not an authority). The absence of any other fallacy is indeed obvious (since the probans is fully equipped to prove the validity of a Vedic sentence). And given this condition, the sentence of the Veda, being the subject of dispute, is an authority since it is a Vedic sentence other than the one recognised by both the disputants as the means of an invalid cognition like a well-recognised sentence. In this way, the authenticity of the other section of the Veda is also established. That this kind of a syllogism could also prove the contrary does not hold good because the sublation of the cognition of the state of being other than the instrument of a valid cognition is equally applicable in this alternative also.

Ann. : It is to be taken into consideration whether the sādhya consists of the entire Veda or of a particular section of it. In case it belongs to the whole Veda, then the sentence 'fire is the remedy of cold' which occurs in the Yajurveda Saṁhitā restates what is verifiable in experience and hence it does not constitute the means of a valid cognition. The author proposes another syllogism to prove inauthenticity, in which the state of being a Vedic sentence, being proximate, is put forward as the probans (*hetu*) and the statement of the Yajurveda Saṁhitā (fire is the remedy of cold) as the illustration. However, this also does not serve any purpose because the knowledge that the other section of the Veda makes an unknown entity known is contradicted as the illustration conjures up an impression of this kind. Although the Vedic statements enjoining sacrifices to attain heaven, etc. obviously make an unknown thing known as the status of heaven, etc. is not empirically verifiable and, thus, the syllogism to prove the inauthenticity of the Veda is not acceptable (*svargakāmādivākyam anavagatāvagati-hetutvenāvagataṁ tenānubhavaviruddhatvān nedam anumānam*, VV, p. 10). Moreover, there is nothing which can contradict the absence of invalidity in the Veda. In case, in proving the validity of the Veda, the contingency of the Veda having been authored by God is incurred, Ānandānubhava points out saying that this is going to be refuted later on. He further says that, if invalidity is intended to be proved merely on the basis of resemblance with a means of invalid cognition, then, by extending the contrary argument, the invalidity of the statement of a Buddhist Āgama can also be proved since it happens to be different from the statement of a well-known and accepted trustworthy person. The statement of a drunken man may be taken as an illustration. The reason is that accepting such a proposal would lead to the defect of overpervasion (*atipra-saṅga*) and it will act as a deterrent to the acceptance of the validity of the statements of Buddhist Āgamas. It is in this situation that Ānandānubhava says that the view about the invalidity of Vedas is totally uncalled for. On the other hand, the view about the validity of the Vedas is acceptable by all means. To endorse his viewpoint, he puts forward the following syllogism : The sentence that enjoins the *kārīrī iṣṭi*, etc. has authenticity as it is uncontradicted and also other than a restatement like the one occurring in a medicinal treatise. There are two kinds of Vedic statements : 1. those that concern the seen fruits and 2. those that relate to the unseen results. The *kārīrī iṣṭi* belongs to the former kind since its performance brings about rain, which is empirically verifiable. The syllogism has been put forward by the siddhāntin keeping in view this kind of result. On the other hand, the result in the form of heaven, etc. is unseen and cannot be verified at the empirical level. In order to exclude the restatement of the Yajurveda Saṁhitā like 'the fire is the remedy of cold', the state of being a sentence has been qualified by the phrase 'other than a restatement'. Also there are other Vedic statements like '*āditγo yūpaḥ*', etc., the content of which is contradicted by another means of proof, i.e. by perception. The identification of the sacrificial post with the sun, to which the animal to be immolated is tied, is contradicted by direct perception. In order to exclude such statements, the term *abādhita* is given to qualify the probans. The illustration is from a medicinal treatise, which also concerns verified results. Thus the inferential sentence is complete in all respects to prove the authority of the Veda. The supposition of the contrary, i.e. invalidity in this context, is taken care of by the contingency of a break in the state of being a sentence which is other than a restatement and the content conveyed by which is not contradicted by perception. The absence of any other fallacy is evident since the reason is equipped with all the necessary characteristics and hence adequate to infer the authority of the Veda.

Given this conditon, the authority of the other section, which concerns the unseen results, is also proved by the ensuing syllogism: The sentence of the Veda under dispute is an authority since, being a Vedic sentence, it is accepted by both the sides as not being a locus of invalidity (*ubhayasiddhāpramāṇatvānadhikaraṇe sati veda-vākyatvāditi hetuḥ,* VV, p. 11) like a well-known authentic sentence given in experience (*sampratipannavat*). Incidentally, Ānandajñāna has explained the purpose of the constituents of the syllogism in the following way. The term Veda is given to exclude the statement of a drunk man, which is not considered to be authentic and the phrase 'under dispute' is provided to exclude restatements like 'the fire is the remedy of cold', etc. The state of being a sentence does not reside in the lyrical hymns of the Sāmaveda. So, to avoid the stultification in respect of sāmans, the term 'sentence' is given in the inferential proposition.

That this kind of an inferential formulation can also be used to prove the contrary does not hold good because the contradiction of the cognition of the means of a valid cognition is equally available in this alternative also. For the illustration 'the fire is the remedy of cold' being a restatement of a verifiable fact does not allow the cognition of the means of a valid cognition to arise as the instance of validity consisting in making known the unknown obtains only in the Vedic sentences enjoining the sacrifices, etc., and not in sentences which state what is verifiable at the empirical level.

अथवा विवादपदानि वेदवाक्यानि प्रमाणम् अबाधितानवगतार्थबोधकत्वाद् वैद्यशास्त्रवत्। प्रामाण्यं च लोकप्रसिद्धमेव साध्यम् नाज्ञातार्थावगमसाधनत्वम् अतो न साध्याविशिष्टता। विपक्षे वैद्यशास्त्रस्याप्यप्रमाण्यप्रसङ्गो बाधः। न च हेत्वसिद्धिः। तस्यानुभवसिद्धेः। एवं दोषान्तराभावोऽपि द्रष्टव्यः। तस्माद-निच्छताप्यच्छमतिना आयुर्वेदवद्वेदस्यापि प्रामाण्यमेष्टव्यमिति सिद्धम्।

सारमुद्धरते योऽस्माद् ग्रन्थात् स्तैन्यपरोऽधमः।
तस्य पापमतेर्भूयात् प्रतिजन्माशुभं बहु॥

Trans. : Or, the Vedic sentences as the subject of dispute are an authority since they make known that which is unknown and uncontradicted as do the medicinal treatises. Validity which is well recognised by people is the probandum (*sādhya*), and not the state of being the means of making known the unknown object. Hence there is no non-difference of the probans with the probandum. The contingency of incurring the invalidity of medicinal treatises is a deterrent to the contrary instance, i.e. the inauthenticity (*aprāmāṇya*) of the Vedas. And the fallacy known as *svarūpāsiddhi*, i.e. the absence of the probans in the subject (*pakṣa*) does not exist as it is given in our experience that the Veda makes known what is unknown. In this way the non-existence of other faults also should be understood. It is, therefore, established that the opponent possessing a lucid intellect should accept, even though unwillingly, the authority of the Vedas like that of the medicinal treatises.

Having an evil mind and intending to steal, may he who knows the essence from this treatise and uses the logical arguments given here (to usurp the authorship of the present work), experience many inauspicious happenings in each incarnation.

Ann. : To prove the sādhya, which has been proved by using two reasons (*hetus*), the siddhāntin, for the sake of brevity, puts forward another syllogistic proposition using a single reason (*hetu*). The Vedic sentences constitute the subject (*pakṣa*). Validity or *prāmāṇya* is to be proved by means of the probans consisting in being the instrument of making known an unknown and uncontradicted entity. The medicinal treatises constitute the illustration. In this context the siddhāntin draws our attention to the fact that if validity (*prāmāṇya*) is taken in the sense of making known that which has not already been known and which remains uncontradicted, then the hetu and the sādhya would be rendered identical. To avoid this eventuality, validity, in the popular sense, has been accepted as the probandum. Moreover, there is no scope of assuming invalidity in respect of the Vedas since it would occasion invalidity with regard to the medicinal treatises which are not so since their veracity has been verified empirically. This instance would debar the supposition of invalidity with respect to the Vedas. The probans is not vitiated by any other fallacy. There are two explanations to this effect : 1. The state of being a source of a valid cognition exists in the Vedas and this has been verified once and again. 2. The state of being definite about the existence of the probans in the Vedas and hence about the authenticity of Vedic statements is enough to ward off the possibility of any other fallacy in respect of the reason (*hetu*) (*hetordharmiṇi vyāpakatayā vṛtteranubhavato niścitatvāt*, VV, p. 12). That is why it behoves the opponent to willingly accept the validity of the Vedas like that of medicinal treatises.

The verse given at this juncture in the text seems to be odd as the editor has pointed out in the footnotes 1 and 3 (*ayaṁ ślokaḥ asya vyākhyānaṁ ca maṅgalaślokānantaraṁ yojyam iti pratibhāti. mūlagranthe dvitīyaślokatayā sambhāvitasya padyasya vyākhyārūpo-'yaṁ granthabhāgo 'pi tatraiva niveśam arhati).* It appears that both the verse and its meaning fit well immediately after the invocatory verse, and not at this place as is obvious from the translation given above (cf. *yastu vaidikadarśanaśīlastadanusāriṇo'smāt prakaraṇāt sāriṣṭhāṃ upapattim uddhṛtya jānīte tasya pāpebhyo darśanāntarebhyo vyāvṛttamateḥ sarveṣu janmasvāsamantataḥ śubham eva prabhūtaṁ bhūyād iti ślokārthaḥ*, VV, p. 12). This is the first sense which appears to be anomalous. In the second sense, as Ānandagiri explains, it refers to plagiarism which, the teacher wants to tell his disciple, is unethical and hence it should be condemned. In this sense it may, however, be accepted as part of the text at this place (cf. *athavā kaścit kila mandabuddhiḥ svayaṁ granthanirmāṇanai-*

punaśūnyassannetatprakaraṇagatā yuktīruddhṛtya likhitvā svakīyaṁ granthakartṛtvaṁ khyāpayāmāsa. na ceyam ucitā prakriyā śiṣṭānām iti śiṣyaśikṣārthaṁ tādṛśaṁ durācāraṁ tiraskarotīti śrutyaiva śloko vyākhyeyaḥ, VV, pp. 12-13).

वैशेषिकादिकृतवेदपौरुषेयत्ववादः

ननु आयुर्वेदवद्वेदस्यापि प्रामाण्ये पौरुषेयत्वं दुष्परिहरम्। प्रयोगस्तु वेदवाक्यं पौरुषेयम् वाक्यत्वात् कालिदासवाक्यवत्। वैदिक्यानुपूर्वी प्रणेतृपूर्विका वर्णानुपूर्वीत्वात् संप्रतिपन्नवत्। वेदवाक्यमाप्तप्रणीतम् प्रमाणत्वे सति वाक्यत्वादायुर्वेदवाक्यवत्। विपक्षे च कादाचित्कता वाक्यस्य न स्यात्।

Nyāya-Vaiśeṣika view of the human origin of the Veda

Trans. : The pūrvapakṣin says, 'When the authority of the Veda has been proved like that of the Āyurveda, it is difficult to escape the view that the Veda is also of human origin.' (In this regard) the syllogism reads as follows : The Vedic sentence is of human origin since it is like that of Kālidāsa. The Vedic order of words or phonemes proceeds from an author since it is an order of words like a well-known regular order of words. The Vedic sentence is produced by a trustworthy person since, being a verbal testimony, it is a sentence like that of a medicinal treatise. On the acceptance of the contrary view, (*vipakṣa*) (that the Veda is of non-human origin) the non-eternalness of a sentence would not be (logically) justified.

Ann. : If the authority of the Veda is established on the basis of medicinal treatises (Āyurveda), then the consequent logical conclusion that the Veda is also of human origin is inescapable. Thus to prove the human authorship of the Veda, the inferential proposition may be put forward as follows : The Vedic sentence is of human origin since it is a sentence like that of Kālidāsa. The reason is that the Vedic order of words should proceed from an author since it is a regular order of words like a well-perceived word-order. So, the natural conclusion is as follows : The Vedic sentence proceeds from a trustworthy person since, being a verbal testimony, it is a sentence like the one available in Āyurveda. If we do not subscribe to this view, then it would be difficult to hold the non-eternal nature of a sentence, which is established from experience.

न च कश्चिदपि शब्दो न कादाचित्कः अनुभवप्रसिद्धिविरोधात्। अथाभिव्यक्तिविषयतया शब्दस्य कार्यतानुभवस्तद्वत्प्रसिद्धिश्चाविरुद्धा । न । शब्दस्य स्थिरत्वे मानाभावाद् अभिव्यक्तिकल्पनायोगात् । स एवायं शब्द इति प्रत्यभिज्ञारूपं मानमस्तीति चेन्न । तस्या ज्वालाप्रत्यभिज्ञावत् सादृश्यनिबन्धनात् । अन्यथा पाषण्डागमा अपि नित्या इत्यपौरुषेयाः स्युः । तस्माच्छब्दः कादाचित्क एव । प्रयोगस्तु वर्णा उत्पत्तिमन्तः विनाशिनो वा सामान्यवत्त्वे सत्यस्मदादिबहिरिन्द्रियग्रहणार्हत्वाद् घटवत् । वर्णा अनित्या उत्कर्षनिकर्षवत्त्वात् सुखवत् । वैदिक्यानुपूर्वी इदम्प्रथमा वर्णानुपूर्वीत्वात् संप्रतिपन्नवत् । विपक्षे च बौद्धागमस्यापि नित्यत्वप्रसङ्गो बाधः । दूषणान्तरविरहस्त्वतिरोहित एव । तथा शब्दार्थसंबन्धोऽप्यनित्य एव । तथा हि गवादिपदं सङ्केतपूर्वकतयैव व्यवहारपदं पदत्वात् । संप्रतिपन्नवदित्येषा दिक् ।

Trans. : That not even a single word is non-eternal does not hold good since it goes against what is established from experience. (If it is held that) the experience that word is a product can be accounted for by holding that it is perceived when it is manifest (though eternal) (and that), thus, it would not go against what is attested from experience. Such a viewpoint should not be entertained as the view that word is eternal is not acceptable for lack of evidence to the effect that word endures. Moreover, it is not proper to invoke the manifestation-view of word (to say that word is eternal). (In case it is suggested that) recognition (*pratyabhijñā*) is a proof for the eternity of word, (then also it is not so since) the recognition that 'this is the same word' depends on the similarity in the instances of the same word (pronounced at different times) like that of the continuous successive flames of a lamp. If this is not admitted, then the scriptures of the heretics would also have to be accepted as eternal and of non-human origin (*apauruṣeya*). It should therefore be accepted that word is non-eternal. The syllogistic proposition (to prove the non-eternity of word) too is as follows : Letter-sounds have a beginning or subject to destruction since, having a universal, they can be apprehended by the external sense organs of the people like us as we cognise a pot. The letter-sounds are not eternal since they have in different measure excellece and deficiency as pleasure has. The regular order of Vedic letter-sounds or words may be said to be the first (in other words to have a beginning) since this is a regular order of letter-sounds like a perceptually recognised order of letter-sounds. (If this is not accepted, then the contingency of incurring the eternity of the Bauddha Āgamas also would become a deterrent to the contrary view (that word is eternal). The absence of other fallacies is obvious (in our view). Thus, the word, its meaning and the relation between them are definitely not eternal. To explain, the words like *go*, etc. have been assigned meaning by convention in order that they may become usages like other well-known ones. This is the direction (to follow to establish that word is not eternal).

Ann. : The pūrvapakṣin says that the view that word endures and is eternal is against experience. If the holder of the view that word is eternal says that the occasional manifestation of word may explain the product-view of word, then it may, however, be accepted as a product when it is pronounced. In this way, the product-view can be explained and accommodated in a satisfactory way. In other words, it is the eternal word that becomes manifest when it is pronounced. Consequently, it appears to be a product of our voice apparatus. The pūrvapakṣin who holds that word is not eternal does not subscribe to the view that recognition 'that this is the same word' is an evidence for the eternity of word. The argument he advances to reject the standpoint that recognition is an evidence is that recognition can be explained on the basis of similarity and, thus, it does not constitute an evidence to prove the eternity of word. To explain, the flame of a lamp continues to appear incessantly and it is on the basis of similarity between the flame of the preceding moment and that of the succeeding moment that we say that this is the same flame althouth they are different. In the same manner, a letter-sound can be said to be the same though they are pronounced at different moments. So, the recognition mentioned above is illusory as it is the similarity (of different flames or different letter-sounds), which is responsible for such an experience. It is not the eternity of word which occasions such an experience. If this view is not accepted, then the scriptures of the heretics would have to be accepted as eternal and of non-human origin, which is not desirable. It is, therefore, proper to hold that word is not eternal, the pūrvapakṣin concludes.

It has already been made clear that from the point of view of experience as well as in accordance with the common belief of people it is appropriate to hold that word is non-eternal. To further explain the position of the pūrvapakṣin and to prove the non-eternity of words, the author puts forward several inferential formulations to prove the non-eternity of word. The first formulation helps infer that letter-sounds have a beginning since they possess universal and at the same time they can be perceived by our external sense organs in the same manner as a pot is cognised. The pot is obviously has a beginning, in other words, it is produced. So, the letter-sounds are also produced since they are apprehended by our external senses. The second syllogism is as follows : The letter-sounds are not eternal since they have in varying degrees excellence and its opposite. Pleasure (*sukha*) has been given as an illustration. Just as pleasure is sometimes experienced in great measure and sometimes minimally; in the same manner letter-sounds are sometime grasped with clarity and sometime not. It is the varying degrees of clarity, etc. that make letter-sounds ephemeral like pleasure. It may also be acceded that the Vedic order of letter-sounds or words is the first to come into being but nevertheless, it is not different from a word-order like any other well-perceived word-order. The opposite view that word is eternal cannot be subscribed to since, in that case, it would render the Buddhist scriptures eternal. This contingency is a deterrent to the view that word is eternal. In conclusion, the word, its meaning and their relation are not eternal. Moreover, a word is used in a sentence after it has been conventionally invested with a particular signification. It means that first the meaning is assigned to a word and then the relation of the meaning of a word with it comes into existence. So, all the three, the word, its meaning and their relation are not ereрnal.

वेदापौरुषेयत्वसिद्धान्तारम्भः

उच्यते — न तावत् कल्पादौ वेदस्योत्पत्तिः सम्भवति। तदा शरीरादेः पदरचनाहेतोरसम्भवात्। अथ तेन विनापि नित्येच्छादिशालिना अचिन्त्य-

महिम्नेश्वरेण वेदो विरच्यते इति मतम्, स तर्हि स्वमहिम्नैव विरचयेत्, किं प्रयत्नादिना? तर्हि हिरण्यगर्भ एवास्तु वेदस्य कर्ता। 'स वै शरीरी प्रथमः' इति तस्य शरीरित्वागमात्। 'इदं सर्वमसृजत,' इति 'ऋचो यजूंषि सामानी'ति च। वेदस्रष्टृत्वश्रुतेश्च। न। अत्राविर्भावाभिधानात्। प्रलये हि तिरोभूतानामीश्वरानुग्रहाद्धिरण्यगर्भबुद्धावाविर्भावो वेदानामत्रोच्यते न त्वसतां सर्गः। तथा च शास्त्रम् — 'यो ब्रह्माणं विदधाति पूर्वं यो वै वेदांश्च प्रहिणोति तस्मै' इति।

The view of non-human origin of the Veda

Trans. : This is being explained : The origin of the Veda is not possible in the beginning of creation since the physical organism, etc. which are responsible for the composition of words did not exist at that time. Again, it may be held that even without the physical organism Veda may be produced by God possessing eternal will, etc. and inconceivable power. Then let him produce Veda by his own greatness, even sans effort, etc. Thus let Hiraṇyagarbha alone be the originator of the Veda since he is known to have the physical organism as is clear from the statement 'He is the first embodied Being'. It is said in the śrutis 'He created this all' and He produced the Ṛgveda, the Yajurveda and the Sāmaveda'. This is not so since it has been said that they were made manifest. The Vedas which disappeared at the time of dissolution became manifest in the intellect of Hiraṇyagarbha by God's grace. It is not that the Vedas which did not exist were brought into existence. To this effect the scripture says, 'It is God who first brought forth Brahman (Hiraṇyagarbha) and then handed over the Vedas to him.'

Ann. : It is impossible that the Vedas were produced at the beginning of creation since there was no embodied being to produce such works at that time. Nonetheless, if it is conceded that God created the Vedas by his eternal will and inconceivable power, then, in such a situation, let Hiraṇyagarbha be accepted as the author of the Vedas since it is said that he was the first embodied Being and it is also said that it is he who created the Ṛgveda, the Yajurveda and the Sāmaveda. The siddhāntin does not subscribe to this view as scriptures say that the Vedas which submerged (into the primary cause) at the time of dissolution were made manifest at the beginning of creation by God. It is not that the non-existent Vedas were created afresh at the beginning of creation but they were made manifest at the beginning of creation. This view is endorsed by the following scriptural evidence : It is God who first brought Brahman (Hiraṇyagarbha) into existence and then entrusted the Vedas to him.

स्यान्मतम् । स एकमिच्छाकायम् अधिष्ठाय ससङ्केतं वेदं विधाय कायान्तरेण च व्यवहृत्य हिरण्यगर्भादीनां शब्दार्थबोधं जनयतीति । न । इत्थंभावे प्रमाणाभावात् । ननु वेदस्य कार्यत्वादेरेव शरीरादिमत्पूर्वकत्वं सिध्यति । तत्कार्यत्वे पौरुषेयत्वे चानुमानमुक्तम् । तद्दुरुक्तम् । 'अनादिनिधना नित्या वागुत्सृष्टा स्वयम्भुवा' । 'ऋषीणां नामधेयानि याश्च वेदेषु दृष्टयः' । 'वेदशब्देभ्य एवादौ निर्ममे स महेश्वरः' इति स्मृतिबाधात् । तथा 'नाचिकेतमुपाख्यानं मृत्युप्रोक्तं सनातनमि' ति श्रुतिबाधाच्च ।

Trans. : This could also be a view (of the pūrvapakṣin) that God, having adopted a body at His will, having composed the Veda after investing it with a denotative function and having manifested it (at the beginning of creation), explained the meanings of words to Hiraṇyagarbha, etc. (the Siddhāntin does not accept this, since there is no evidence to this effect). (The pūrvapakṣin gives a reply saying that) since the Veda is a product, it is proved that the Veda is preceded by an embodied being and an inferential proposition to the effect that the Veda is a product and hence was authored by an embodied being has already been furnished. (The siddhāntin replies saying that) that which has been said (by the pūrvapakṣin) is not proper (since this suffers from the defect of mutual dependence, see VV, p. 16). (The other fault is that) this contradicts the following statements of the smṛtis : 1. The eternal speech that has no beginning and end was transmitted by the Self-born. 2. The names of the seers and revelations in the Vedas and 3. In the beginning the great Lord created from the words of the Vedas (names, actions and modes of life). Similarly this contradicts the statement of śruti : This eternal anecdote as enunciated by Death and received by Naciketā.

Ann. : The pūrvapakṣin puts forward his point of view that the Veda is of human origin since it can fairly be assumed that God in the beginning of creation created a body for himself and adopted it in order to produce the Vedas invested with a denotative function and transmitted them to Hiraṇyagarbha, etc. explaining to them the meanings of the words therein. The siddhāntin rejects the position of the pūrvapakṣin saying that there is no evidence which can be produced to prove that the Vedas were created by an embodied being. Again the opponent comes up with another argument that it has already been supported by the syllogistic proposition that, being a product, the Vedas were preceded by an embodied being. The siddhāntin again does not accept the opponent's view and endorses his own stand by saying that, if the opponent's view-point was accepted, then the statements of smṛtis and śrutis to the effect that the speech and the Vedas are eternal would be contradicted. The statements of smṛtis which are quoted are : 1. *anādinidhanā nityā vāgutsṛṣṭā svayambhuvā.* 2. *ṛṣīṇāṁ nāmadheyāni yāśca vedeṣu dṛṣṭayaḥ.* 3.*vedaśabdebhya evādau nirmame sa maheśvaraḥ.* The first statement is the first half of the verse quoted by Śaṅkara in his commentary on the Brahmasūtra 1. 3. 28. The complete verse quoted by him is as follows : *anādinidhanā nityā vāgutsṛṣṭā svayambhuvā, ādau vedamayī divyā yataḥ sarvāḥ pravṛttayaḥ.* 'The Self-born projected the eternal divine speech in the form of the Vedas which have no beginning and no end and from which all activities proceeded'. It would be better if the next two quotations are taken as one and be compared with the following verse from Manusmṛti, I. 21:

nāmarūpaṁ ca bhūtānāṁ karmaṇāṁ ca pravartanam,
vedaśabdebhya evādau nirmame sa maheśvaraḥ.

'In the beginning, the great Lord created from the words of the Vedas alone, the names and the forms of the creatures and promoted religious activities.' In consonance with the spirit of the verse of Manusmṛti, I. 21, if the next two quotations are combined the meaning would be as follows : In the beginning the great Lord created from the words of the Vedas alone, the names of seers and all the view-points given in the Vedas.

Another statement is from the Kaṭhopaniṣad, I. 3. 16. The complete mantra from it is as follows :

nāciketamupākhyānaṁ mṛtyuproktaṁ sanātanam,
uktvā śrutvā ca medhāvī brahmaloke mahīyate.

'Relating and hearing this eternal anecdote as received by Naciketā and as told by Death, the intelligent man becomes glorified in the region that is Brahman.'

The spirit of the the mantra of the Kaṭhopaniṣad, I. 3. 16 is that speech in the form of conversation between Yama and Naciketā is eternal. In the same manner, the Vedas should be accepted as eternal. In case the opponent's view-point is accepted, then this statement of the śruti would be contradicted. To avoid the contradiction of the statement of śruti, it is essential that the Vedas are accepted as eternal and hence of non-human origin.

वर्णानित्यत्वानुमानखण्डनम्

किञ्च यत्तावदनित्यत्वसाधनं सामान्यवत्त्वे सत्यस्मदादिबाह्येन्द्रियग्रहणार्हत्वं, तत्रास्मदादीति विशेषणमस्मत्पक्षे व्यर्थम्। त्वत्पक्षे च हेतोर्भागासिद्धिः। उपान्त्यादिशब्देष्वभावात्। न चास्मदादिबाह्येन्द्रियग्रहणार्हः शब्दो धर्मीति वाच्यम्। अस्यापि विशेषणस्य वैयर्थ्यात्। किञ्चैकश्शब्द एकस्यैवेन्द्रियस्य ग्रहणार्ह इति ते स्थितिः। श्रोत्रान्तरे तस्यासमवायात्। अतस्तेऽस्मदादिबाह्येन्द्रिय-ग्राह्यत्वासिद्धेर्विशिष्टधर्मिहेत्वोरसिद्धिः। जात्युपाधावुक्तधर्मिहेतोर्निर्देशान्नोक्तदोष इति चेत्, किमपरजात्यास्मदादिग्राह्यसजातीयत्वमुच्यते, किं वा परजात्या? आद्ये उपान्त्यादिधर्मिभागस्यासिद्धिः। दृष्टान्ते च साधनविकलता, घटे शब्दत्वा-भावात्। अथास्मद्ग्राह्यापरजातीयत्वमात्रं विवक्षितं तदा नित्यरूपेण व्यभिचारः। द्वितीये त्वात्मादिनानैकान्तिकता। अस्मदादिपदं जातीयपदं च विहाय धर्म्यादि-निर्देश इति चेन्न। त्वद्ग्राह्येष्वपि शब्देषु सर्वत्रास्माकं मानाभावाद् भागासिद्धेः। विशेषणं च व्यर्थमित्युक्तम्। यदप्यनुमानान्तरमुत्कर्षनिकर्षवत्त्वादिति तत्राप्यागम-बाधः। धर्मिभागासिद्धिश्च उपान्त्यादीनामस्माकमसिद्धत्वात्। तद्व्यावृत्त्यर्थं विशेषणं पूर्ववद्व्यर्थम्। उत्कर्षादिमत्त्वं च वर्णेषु निजं किं वा औपाधिकमाहोस्वित् साधारणं हेतूक्रियते। आद्ये असिद्धिः। वर्णा निजोत्कर्षादिमन्तः सामान्यवत्त्वे सति श्रावणत्वाद् ध्वनिवदिति चेन्न, उपान्त्यादिधर्मिभागासिद्धेः। तत्रैव तव हेत्वसिद्धेश्च। द्वितीयतृतीययोस्तु कूपकुम्भाकाशादिनानैकान्तम्। यदप्युक्तं वैदिक्यानुपूर्वी इदंप्रथमा वर्णानुपूर्वीत्वात् संप्रतिपन्नवत्। तथा गवादिपदं सङ्केतपूर्वकतयैव व्यवहारपदं पदत्वात् संप्रतिपन्नवदिति। तत्रोभयत्रापि पूर्ववदागमविरोधादि दूषणम्। द्वितीये तूपान्त्यादिभागे व्यवहारानुपलब्धिबाधोऽतिरिच्यते।

Refutation of the view that varṇas are not eternal

Trans. : Moreover, the reason (*sādhana* or *hetu*) to prove the non-eternity of letter-sounds is that which, having a universal, has the capability of being perceived by the external sense organs of the persons like us. In this, the qualifying phrase 'of the persons like us' is of no use according to our view. In your case the reason does not exist in a part of the minor term (*pakṣa* or *dharmin*) since it does not exist in the letter-sounds proximate to the last one (as they are accepted only as inferable by you, i.e. the logicians, cf. VV, p.17). Also it should not be held that the word which is capable of being perceived by the external sense organ of people like us should be accepted as the dharmin (*pakṣa*). The qualifying term *asmad*, etc. of the dharmin also does not serve any purpose. Moreover, according to your view, it is a single word which is capable of being perceived only by one auditory sense organ since it does not inhere in the other (person's) auditory sense organ (*tatraikasya śrotuḥ śrotre yaśśabdo'vatarati nāsau śrotrantarasya śrotre samavaiti,* ibid., p. 17). So, both the qualified dharmin and (the qualified) hetu do not hold good in your view because the capability of being perceived by the people like us exists neither in the dharmin (*pakṣa*) nor in the reason (*hetu*). The pūrvapakṣin says that, if the universal is presented as a distinguishing property inhering in them, then the above-mentioned dharmin and hetu would be free from the defects mentioned above. (The siddhāntin asks :) Is the state of being similar to the lower universal (*aparasāmānya*), capable of being perceived by the persons like us, intended to be con-veyed? Or, is it the state of being similar to the higher universal (*parasāmānya*) that is intended to be conveyed? In case the first alternative is accepted, then the status of the dharmin with respect to the penultimate letter-sound, etc. remains unestablished and the hetu ceases to exist in the illustration as the status of being a word (śabdatva) does not exist in a pot. And if only the status of being similar to the lower universal capable of being cognised by us is intended to be conveyed, then there would be deviation with respect to the eternal *rūpa* (cf. *asti hi salilaparamāṇvādigatarūpādāvasmadbāhyendriyagrāhyaguṇatvāparajātyādhāratvaṁ nānityatā,* ibid., p. 18). In the second alternative, there exists a fallacy of reason known as *anaikāntika* with reference to the soul, etc. If it is said that the mention of the dharmin is without the expressions 'of people like us' and '*jātīya*', then also a part of the dharmin remains unestablished as there is no evidence for us in respect of the words which are capable of being perceived by you. (So, the fallacy known as *bhāgāsiddhi* results). And it has already been mentioned that the qualifying term (*sāmānyavattve sati*, see VV, p. 18) does not serve any purpose. So far as the other syllogism having the reason 'the state of having excellence and its opposite' is concerned, the scriptures (*āgamas*) would become liable to be contradicted. A part of the *dharmin* remains unestablished since we do not recognise the penultimate letter-sounds, etc. to be existent (as they cease to be perceived by the external senses). That is why the qualification 'perceivable by the external senses with respect to the proximate letter-sounds' does not serve any purpose as mentioned before. (However, the siddhāntin now puts forward three queries with respect to nature of the reason :) Do the properties excellence, etc. existing in the reason constitute the letter-sounds themselves? Or, do they exist adjunctivally (*aupādhika*) in them or are they just properties in general? The first alternative (that excellence, etc. are the constituents of letter-sounds) is not established by any evidence. The following syllogistic proposition is not capable of proving this instance : The letter-sounds have their own excellence, etc. since they have a universal and at the same time they have the property of being audible like a sound. (This inferential formulation does not support the contention of the opponent) because the penultimate letter-sound and the preceding ones do not form the minor term (as they cease to exist when the last letter-sound is being heard (*dharmibhāgāsiddhi*)). (For the same reason), the *hetu* consisting in 'the property of being audible' does not exist in them. (Because of these fallacies, the first alternative remains unestablished). So far as the second and third alternatives are concerned, the apparent existence of excellence, etc. in ākāśa, etc. because of the adjuncts, a well, a pot, etc. gives rise to the fallacy of reason known as *sādhāraṇa anaikāntika* (as the reason consisting in excellence, etc. resides in ākāśa where the sādhya (non-eternity) does not exist. Also the statement : The Vedic order of words is the first one (i.e. has a beginning) since it is the sequential order of letter-sounds like a known order of words; likewise the statement : The words such as *go*, etc. become usable after they have been conventionally invested with a denotative function like a known pada; in both these cases, the faults such as the contradiction of scriptures (*āgamas*), *dharmibhāgāsiddhi*, etc. become applicable. In the case of the second syllogistic proposition, additionally, the sublation (*bādha*) consisting in the non-availability of empirical usage becomes applicable in respect of the penultimate letter-sounds (as they cease to exist when the last letter-sound is heard).

Ann. : The pūrvapakṣin proves the non-eternity of letter-sounds by using the following syllogistic proposition : The letter-sounds are not eternal since, having a universal, they can be perceived by the external sense organ of people like us like a pot and other such things. In this syllogism the qualification consisting in 'people like us' does not serve any purpose since the yogin capable of sensing something that is beyond the grasp of senses is not admitted by the Mīmāṁsakas. So there is no one who needs to be excluded by the qualifying phrase 'people like us'. The qualification 'capable of being apprehended by the external sense organ' is also purposeless since there is no letter-sound which, according to the Naiyāyikas, cannot be heard. Thus neither of these qualifications performs the function of differentiating anything since there is nothing which needs to be differentiated by virtue of these qualifications. Thus the fault known as *viśeṣaṇāsiddhi* results. Even if the qualification is admitted as it is, then also the defect known as *bhāgāsiddhi* still remains applicable as per your view since a part of the dharmin consisting of the letter-sounds proximate to the last one is not heard when the last sound is pronounced and hence is construed as non-existent. In this way, the reason is non-existent in a part of the dharmin.

The pūrvapakṣin puts forward another syllogism to prove the non-eternity of the letter-sounds on the basis of their possessing excellence, etc. like pleasure. In this context, the siddhāntin raises three queries regarding the nature of the properties such as excellence, deficiency, etc. : 1. Are excellence, deficiency, imperfection, etc. the natural properties of varṇas? 2. Or, are these properties due to the adjuncts (*aupādhika*)? 3. Or, are they properties in general? Regarding the first question, the siddhāntin (Mīmāṁsaka) says that these properties do not reside in the dharmin (*varṇas*) since, as per their view, these are the properties of sound (dhvani), which manifests the varṇas. Although these properties belong to the sounds, they appear to be existing in the (*varṇas*). Hence, the reason suffers from the fallacy known as *svarūpāsiddhi*. Regarding the second and third alternatives, the same reason is rendered *sādhāraṇa anaikāntika* because it resides where the sādhya (non-eternity) does not exist as in the case of ākāśa, etc. where the adjunctival properties like excellence, etc. appear to reside in association with a well, a pot, etc.

The Naiyāyikas hold that the Veda is of human origin and hence non-eternal since it contains a regular order of words as any other work does. To further stress his standpoint, the pūrvapakṣin says that the relation of meaning with a word is also a product as the word '*go*' is made usable in a sentence when it is conventionally invested with the function of denoting 'a cow'. The siddhāntin retorts saying that if both the above views are accepted, then the scriptures, quoted above, are contradicted as both the Veda and the relation between a word and its meaning have been accepted as eternal. Additionally, so far as the second syllogism is concerned, usability is not available with respect to the letter-sounds proximate to the final one from the convention point of view since they cease to exist when the last letter-sound is actually pronounced and heard. To explain, when the last letter-sound is uttered, the penultimate letter-sound and the preceding ones cease to exist. How can then the reason reside in the letter-sounds which have ceased to exist? In this way a part of the minor term (*dharmin* or *pakṣa*) cannot become a locus of the reason.

If we make the word, having the capability of being audible to our external sense organ, the minor term in order to escape the defect of *bhāgāsiddhi*, then also the qualification does not serve any purpose in the same manner as it does not serve any purpose when it qualifies the reason. Obviously, there is nothing which needs to be differentiated with reference to the word (*dharmin*) which has the capability of being heard by the auditory sense organ of one and all. Moreover, if we take the Nyāya view, then a word can be perceived only by the auditory sense organ in which it inheres and not by the one in which it does not (*tasya śrotrāntare samavāyābhāvāt bhavatpakṣe*, VV, p. 20). Thus, the qualified dharmin and the reason cannot be held to be existent. For the establishment of *dharmin* and *hetu* they may be accepted as the loci of a universal. To explain, the word having similarity on account of the less extensive universal (*aparajāti*) which is perceivable by our external sense organ can be admitted as the subject (*pakṣa*) and that which has similarity because of the less extensive universal comprehensible to our sense organ becomes the reason. The other alternative is that the word having similarity due to the most extensive universal can become the *pakṣa* and that which possesses similarity on account of the most extensive universal comprehensible to the external sense organs of the people like us becomes the reason. In regard to the similarity due to the less extensive universal, the reason becomes fallacious since the less extensive universal (*rūpatva*) resides in the form (*rūpa*) of atoms of water, etc. where non-eternity does not exist. Thus the reason is rendered *sādhāraṇa anaikāntika*. In respect of the similarity on account of the most extensive universal, the same fallacy of reason is applicable since a part of the reason, that is, the most extensive universal comprehensible to our sense organs does exist in souls, etc. where non-eternity (*sādhya*) does not reside. To avoid this contingency, if the dharmin is retained without the qualifying expressions 'people like us' and 'less and most extensive universals', then also the fallacy remains applicable since the words which are comprehended by you cannot be said to be perceived by us as explained above. Thus a part of the minor term does remain unestablished (*pramitasya bhavanmate dharmitvaniyamāditi bhāvaḥ*, ibid., p. 18). It has already been pointed out that the qualifying expressions '*asmadādi*' and 'comprehensible to the external sense organs' are redundant since the Mīmāṁsakas do not accept such a yogin who can apprehend the insensible and there is no word which is not comprehensible to the sense organ (*yogino 'naṅgīkārādasmadviśeṣaṇasyātīndriyaśabdābhāvādbāhyendriyagrāhyaviśeṣaṇasya ca vyarthatetyuktam*, ibid., p. 18). In the same manner the expression '*sāmānyavattve sati*'' qualifying the reason does not serve any purpose.

With regard to the very first alternative of the opponent, the siddhāntin says that the letter-sounds proximate to the last one do not exist when the last letter-sound is articulated as according to the Nyāya view the proximate letter-sounds, being destructible in the third moment, have already ceased to exist after the last sound has been articulated. Hence a part of the word (*dharmin*) remains non-existent. Moreover, the reason does not exist in the illustration as the pot does not have wordness in it (NRD, p. 18).

The other syllogism in which the phrase 'possessing excellence and its opposite' constitutes the reason goes against the Āgama itself. The fault consisting in the non-establishment of a part of the dharmin becomes applicable since the siddhāntin does not recognise the existence of letter-sounds proximate to the last one for the reason just mentioned. The qualifying expression 'comprehensible to the external sense organ' is redundant in respect of the non-existent letter-sounds.

Now the question about the excellence and its opposite being possessed by the letter-sounds is taken up by the siddhāntin. He asks whether the excellence, etc. of the letter-sounds are intrinsic to them or are they due to some adjunctival function. In case the first alternative is accepted, then the reason consisting in 'possessing excellence, etc.' cannot reside in the proximate letter sounds since they do not exist. This is demonstrated in the following syllogism : The letter-sounds have their own excellence, etc. since they have a universal and at the same time they have the property of being audible like a sound. But this is not so because the minor term in the form of penultimate letter-sounds is non-existent. With reference to these penultimate letter-sounds, the hetu conceived by you suffers from the fallacy known as *bhāgāsiddhi* since the proximate letter-sounds do not exist when the last letter-sound is articulated. It is clear that the syllogistic proposition does not prove that the letter-sounds possess excellence, etc. Even if it is conceded that varṇas exist, then also the reason consisting in 'being audible' does not reside in them as according to the Mīmāṁsakas they do not possess the property of being audible. This is actually the property of sound which is attributed to the varṇas.

The line of argument taken by the pūrvapakṣin that the order of varṇas in the Vedas has a beginning like a well-perceived word-order in any available work is also not acceptable since it goes against the Āgamas as expained earlier. So far as the assignment of the function of denotation to a word by a human being is concerned, that is also not so as the relation between the word and its meaning is eternal according to the Mīmāṁsakas. Moreover, the absence of the varṇas (letter-sounds) proximate to the last one is perceived by means of anupalabdhi and hence they cannot become the basis for the inference of the relation between a word and its meanining (cf. *ato'nupalabdhyā bādhānna sambandhānityatvaṁ śakyaṁ anumātum ityarthaḥ*, VV, p. 20).

ननु विवादपदमिति धर्मिनिर्देशे, न धर्मिभागासिद्ध्यादिदोषः। उपान्त्यादीनां तवासिद्धत्वात् प्रकृतविवादागोचरत्वादधर्मिभागत्वात्। नापि व्यर्थविशेषणता, तन्निर्देशस्य निर्विशेषणत्वात्। एवं तर्हि नान्त्यशब्दस्यापि धर्मिता, तस्यापि भवत्पक्षेऽस्माकमसिद्धत्वात्। न चायं धर्मिनिर्देशो निर्विशेषणम्। प्रकरणसिद्ध-शब्दापेक्षया अस्य सविशेषणत्वाद्। अन्यथा धर्म्यनिर्णयप्रसङ्गाद्। अतो व्यर्थवि-शेषणतापि सिद्धा। विवादपदं वाक्यं धर्मी अतः सिद्धसाधनतानिवृत्त्यर्थं विशेषण-मिति चेन्न। उभयवादिसिद्धवाक्यस्य त्वन्मतेऽभावात्। अस्तु तर्हि वेदजन्यम् ज्ञानमुत्पत्त्यादिमच्छब्दजन्यं शाब्दज्ञानत्वात् संप्रतिपन्नज्ञानवदिति प्रयोगः। मैवम्। न हि त्वयाऽस्मत्सिद्धवेदजन्यं ज्ञानमिष्यते किंत्वन्त्यशब्दजन्यम्। तच्चास्माकमसिद्धम्। अतः स्फुटाऽऽश्रयासिद्धिः। अथ प्रयोगः — वर्णत्वमुत्पत्ति-मदाश्रयं वर्णाश्रयजातित्वात् सत्त्ववदिति।

Trans. : If we construe *vivādapadam* 'the subject of dispute' as the dharmin, then the faults *bhāgāsiddhi*, etc. do not apply because the letter-sounds proximate to the last one do not exist as per your view and, hence, they do not form a part of the dharmin and the subject matter of the current dispute. Also there is no purposelessness of the qualification as the dharmin has been mentioned without any qualification. [Although the defects *bhāgāsiddhi*, etc. have been dispensed with (see ibid., p. 20)] the final letter-sound too does not remain as the dharmin since it does not exist for us (when your view is taken into account). And also the mention of the dharmin here cannot be without any qualification as it has to have 'word' as the qualification in deference to the context. Otherwise the fault of non-ascertainment of the dharmin would become applicable (because of the possibility of a great many doubtful provables, see ibid., p. 20). (Once the dharmin is determined in consonance with the context,) then the purposelessness of the qualification: *vivādapadam* is also accepted. (The word in general is obtained by virtue of the context. If it is not qualified, then the fault of *siddhasādhyatā* would become applicable. To avoid this, the qualification of the dharmin is required; see ibid., pp. 20-21).

(In this background, the pūrvapakṣin proposes that) 'the sentence' should be accepted as the dharmin, i.e. as the subject of dispute. The qualification, therefore, may now be needed to dispense with the fault of proving that which has already been proved. (Even then) the siddhāntin does not accept this saying that the sentence which is acceptable to both the disputants does not exist according to the view of the pūrvapakṣin (see VV, p. 21). [Thus the dharmin still remains unestablished.] (Then with a view to doing away with all the defects, the pūrvapakṣin puts forward another syllogistic proposition) : The knowledge generated by the Veda is that which is generated by the words having a beginning, etc. since this is a verbal knowledge as any other known verbal knowledge. The siddhāntin summarily rejects this saying that the pūrvapakṣin does not accept the knowledge generated by the Veda which is established according to the siddhāntin but subscribes to the view that knowledge is generated by the last letter-sound and that is not accepted by us (the siddhāntin). Consequently, the fault known as *āśrayāsiddhi* evidently becomes applicable (in accordance with the siddhāntin's view). (The pūrvapakṣin makes yet another proposal :) The state of being a varṇa resides in that which has an origin since it is a universal located in the varṇas like the existence-universal.

Ann. : The pūrvapakṣin makes an attempt to prove his point of view that the varṇas are not eternal. The dharmin according to him is 'the subject of dispute'. The dispute relates to the word in general in deference to the context. So, it would include even the letter-sounds which are proximate to the last one (cf. *vivādasya śabdamātraviṣayatvādupāntyādiṣvapi pravṛtteḥ bhāgāsiddhitād-avasthyaṁ ityāśaṅkyāha upāntyādīnāmiti*, ibid., p. 20). However, the proximate letter-sounds do not exist when the last letter-sound is articulated and heard and consequently the dharmin does remains partially unestablished (*dharmibhāgāsiddhi*). The pūrvapakṣin clarifies saying that, when the proximate letter-sounds do not exist, they will be kept out of the purview of the dispute and, thus, the fault of partial non-establishment of the dharmin ceases to be applicable (*upāntyādīnāṁ tavāsiddhatvāt prakṛtavivādāgocara-*

tvādadharmibhāgāt, NRD, p. 20). In case 'the word in general' is made the minor term, then every word or letter-sound would be covered by this term. In case the mention of the minor term is accepted to be without any qualifying term, as the pūrvapakṣin says, then the issue of raising the fault of purposelessness of the qualification is rendered redundant. But the dharmin has to be taken as qualified in deference to the context which relates to 'word'. Otherwise it would be difficult to determine the dharmin because of the possibility of a great many inferables (*yadi tu śabdasya viśeṣatayā prākaraṇikaḥ sambandho nāsthīyate tadā vivādagocarasya bhūyasaḥ sambhavena sandigdhaviśeṣyatvād apārthakaṁ pratijñāvacanam āpatediti*, VV, p. 20). When the dharmin is settled by virtue of the context, the requirement of the use of the qualification '*vivādapadam*' is rendered redundant (*astu tarhi dharminirdeśasya saviśeṣaṇatvamityāśaṅkya vivādapadaviśeṣaṇasya vyarthatām āha*, ibid., p. 20). However, the pūrvapakṣin says that the qualified dharmin as '*vivādapadaṁ vākyam* : the sentence as the subject of dispute' is still required to ward off the defect of proving that which has already been proved. This is the reason why the qualified dharmin 'the sentence as the subject of dispute' is required.

When the pūrvapakṣin comes up with the above-mentioned minor term consisting of the 'the sentence under dispute', the siddhāntin says that 'the sentence under dispute' cannot be accepted as the proper dharmin as a sentence accepted by one cannot be construed as accepted by the other as 'a word can be perceived only by one sense organ' according to the view of the pūrvapakṣin (*tvanmate vākyamekaṁ nobhayasiddhamasti. ekasya śabdasyaikendriyagrahaṇārhatvaniyamopagamāt. ato vivādapadasyobhayasiddhavākyasyābhāvāddharmyasiddhiriti*, ibid., p. 21). When the minor term is acceptable to neither side, there is no scope for further deliberation. It is at this juncture that the pūrvapakṣin, with a desire to avoid all kinds of faults, comes up with another syllogism to prove his standpoint : The knowledge produced by the Veda is that which is generated by the words which have an origin, etc. since it is generated by the words as any other known verbal cognition. The siddhāntin does not accept this syllogism since the pūrvapakṣin accepts only that cognition which is generated by the last letter-sound, and not by the Veda. The cognition generated by the last letter-sound is not acceptable to the siddhāntin. Hence evidently, there is no viable pakṣa and this results in the fault known as *āśrayāsiddhi.* Now the pūrvapakṣin puts forward yet another syllogistic proposition in order to prove the non-eternal nature of varṇas : The state of being a varṇa (*varṇatva*) exists in that which has an origin since it is a universal inhering in varṇas like existence-universal. This appears to be a good attempt by the pūrvapakṣin. The illustration of existence-universal existing in a pot looks quite convincing. Obviously, the existence-universal exists in a pot, which is not eternal. Similarly the varṇatva universal resides in a varṇa, which should be non-eternal like a pot. The siddhāntin does not agree with the pūrvapakṣin as the same reason, he points out, can be used to prove the eternity of varṇas with the help of the existence-universal residing in the soul which is eternal (cf.*varṇatvaṁ nityāśrayaṁ varṇāśrayatvāt sattvavat*, VV, p. 21). Obviously, a syllogistic proposition having a fallacious reason cannot prove the probandum (i.e. the non-eternity of varṇas) conclusively because the term *jāti* which constitutes the reason resides in both the eternal and non-eternal entities.

वर्णानां नित्यत्वसिद्धान्तारम्भः

न; नित्याश्रयत्वसाधनेऽप्यस्य धर्म्यादिस्तुल्यत्वात्। विपक्षे च बाधासम्भवो वक्ष्यते। उत्पत्त्यादिमत्त्वं च साध्यं ते दुर्घटम्। उत्पत्तिमत्त्वं हि त्वत्पक्षे प्रागसतः सत्तायोगित्वम्। तच्चाप्रसिद्धम्। प्राक्त्वोत्पत्त्योरन्योऽन्याश्रयत्वात्। न च लोकप्रसिद्धं साध्यम्। त्वया प्रमाणत एव वस्तुसिद्धेराश्रयणात्। विनाशित्वमपि किं विनाशयोगित्वं किं वा तद्योग्यत्वम्, आहोस्वित् स्वप्रच्युत्युपलक्षितसत्तायोगित्वम्। आद्ये, विनाशायोगिना कुम्भादिना व्यभिचारः। द्वितीये, सिद्धसाधनता; स्वरूपं हि ते योग्यत्वम्। तृतीये, दृष्टान्ते साध्यविरहः, स्वशब्दार्थस्य दृष्टान्तेऽनन्वयात्। सैव सत्ता तत्राप्यन्वितेति चेद्, हन्त आत्मन्यपि सैवाऽन्वितेति गतं विनाशित्वलक्षणेनेत्यप्रसिद्धता। तर्हीदमेवास्तु साध्यम्, न तु (पूर्व) साध्यस्य लक्षणं तेनात्मापि सपक्ष इति चेन्न अप्रसिद्धविशेषणत्वात्। न हि वर्णच्युतिरस्माकं प्रसिद्धा। अतस्तल्लक्षितसत्ताप्यप्रसिद्धैव। अनित्यत्वमपि, विनाशित्वं चेद् व्याख्यातम्। सर्वकालानवच्छेदश्चेत् सिद्धसाधनता। इष्यते हि वर्णेषु कालानवच्छेदः। कालसम्बन्धाभावात्। एवं तर्हि कालविशेषेणैवावच्छेदोऽनित्यत्वं साध्यत इति चेन्न। भवदभिमतकालसंयोगादिना तदवच्छेदस्यास्माकमप्रसिद्धत्वात्। अथ कालविशेषे शब्दोत्पत्तिस्तदवच्छिन्नत्वम्। न। तस्य शब्दोत्पत्तिनिरासेन निरस्तत्वात्। तस्मादुत्पत्तिमत्त्वादि साध्यं ते दुर्घटम्। एवं वेदपौरुषेयत्वानुमानेष्वपि यथायोगं दोषो द्रष्टव्यः। तत्रापि ह्युक्तागमबाधधर्मिभागासिद्ध्यादि

तुल्यम्। पौरुषेयत्वं च पुरुषाधीनोत्पत्तिमत्त्वं तदप्युत्पत्तिमत्त्वाप्रसिद्ध्यैव तवाप्रसिद्धम्। बाधकं च तर्कमवोचाम। कल्पादौ वेदस्य शरीरादिकारणासम्भवात् कार्यत्वाद्यसम्भव इति। विपक्षे बाधकतर्काभावाच्च शङ्किताप्रयोजकता।

The theory that the varṇas are eternal

Trans. : No, the same dharmin (*pakṣa*), etc. can equally be employed to infer also the locus of an eternal entity and that the contradiction of the contrary instance is not possible will be explained (in the sequel). Also it is difficult for you to explain the viability of the *sādhya* consisting in the state of having an origin, etc. In your view 'the state of having an origin' consists in the relation of existence universal with that which has no prior existence and this cannot be taken as established because the state of being prior and production are mutually dependent. And that which is current among people cannot become the *sādhya* because, in your view, an entity is admitted to be established only when it is known through a valid means of cognition. (The siddhāntin asks :) What is the state of being destructible? Does it mean having relation with destruction or the state of being capable of having relation with destruction or having a relation with existence-universal which is implied by its (varṇa's) disappearance. On the acceptance of the first alternative, a fallacy known as *anaikāntika* with respect to the present pot becomes applicable (as at the present moment the pot does not have any relation with destruction, though the reason exists in it. In other words, the sādhya does not exist in the illustration, that is, a pot, whereas the reason does; see infra p. 41). If the second alternative is accepted, then there is a defect of proving that which has already been proved since, according to you, the state of being capable is construed as the very being (see VV, pp. 22-23). In case the third alternative is accepted, the sādhya ceases to exist in the illustration as what is meant by the pronoun *sva* (varṇa) does not have any relation with the illustration (the pot, because it does not have *varṇatva* in it). Then, let the same existence universal (implied by the disappearance of varṇas and other entities) have relation also with the pot. In that case the same existence-universal would have relation with the soul also and then the definition of destructibility would just vanish. This amounts to the untenability of the state of being destructible. (In other words non-eternity (with regard to the varṇas) remains unestablished.) Then let 'the state of being related with existence-universal implied by the disappearance of varṇas' be the *sādhya* and not its definition. By this the soul would not become the illustration (*sapakṣa*) as the qualification (*svapracyutilakṣita*) is not an established fact according to us because we do not subscribe to the standpoint that the varṇas are subject to destruction. So, the existence-universal implied by the disappearance of the varṇas is not accepted by us as established. If you construe destructibility as non-eternity, then this has already been explained. If destructibility or non-eternity means the absence of relation of all time, then the fault of proving that which has already been proved becomes applicable as it is held (by the Bhāṭṭas) that the varṇas are not delimited by time because there is no relation of time with them (cf. VV, p. 23). Keeping this in view if it is going to be proved that the non-eternity of varṇas consists in their being delimited by a specific period of time, then this is not the case as the delimitation of varṇas by time through conjunction, etc. accepted by you is not established as per our view. Again, if you construe the delimitation by time in the sense of the production of varṇas at a particular time, [then also this is] not [acceptable] as this has already been demolished with the rejection of the view of the production of varṇas. Consequently, it is difficult for you to establish the *sādhya* consisting in 'having an origin, etc.' In this way, these fallacies of reason could also be extended to the syllogistic propositions used in inferring the human origin of the Vedas. In that case also the contradiction of the Āgamas, partial non-establishment of the dharmin (*bhāgāsiddhi*), etc. already mentioned would become equally applicable. The state of having a human origin consists in being produced under the control of a human being. That too remains unestablished in your case on account of the non-establishment of (the major term) having an origin, etc. The contradictory argument (of the view about the non-eternity of varṇas and the Vedas) has already been explained by us : At the beginnig of the creation, there was no embodied being. Hence, there was no possibility of production, etc. There is no contradictory argument against the contrary instance (that the varṇas are eternal). In the absence of a contradictory argument against the contrary instance, the reason applied to prove the non-eternity of the varṇas is rendered incapable (*aprayojaka*) of proving the sādhya. (In other words the pūrvapakṣin's syllogistic propositions are not accompanied by any favourable argument (*anukūla tarka*) to prove the non-eternity of varṇas. Hence, the siddhāntin's view that the varṇas are eternal finds itself endorsed).

Ann. : The minor term, etc. which are used by the pūrvapakṣin in the syllogism to infer non-eternity of the varṇas may also be used to infer the eternity of varṇas (*varṇatvaṁ nityāśrayaṁ varṇāśrayatvāt sattvavat*, VV, p. 21). Moreover, there is no contradictory argument against the syllogism used to prove the eternity of varṇas. The siddhāntin now discusses various aspects of the probandum (*sādhya*) of the pūrvapakṣin's syllogistic formulation to make his case stronger : Does 'having an origin' mean 'existence having a relation with that which has prior non-existence?' The siddhāntin says that this is not an established fact as the state of being prior and production are mutually dependent. Thus having rejected the view that the varṇas have an origin, he now proceeds to show the impossibility of the destructible nature of the varṇas. He raises three queries about 'the state of being destructible'. 1. Does 'being destructible' mean 'having a relation with destruction'? Or 2. Does it mean 'being capable of being destroyed' (for this interpretation, see ibid., pp. 22-23)? Or 3. Does it mean 'having a relation with existence universal implied by the disappearance or destruction of the varṇas'? If the first alternative is subscribed to, then the fallacy known as *sādhāraṇa anaikāntika* becomes applicable as the pot existing at the present momemt has no relation with destruction but it has the reason (*hetu*) in the form of 'having a universal, etc.' in it. Thus the reason resides where the sādhya does not exist. Obviously this is a case of *sādhāraṇa anaikāntika* (cf. *na tāvad* *vartamāne kumbhādau vināśayogitvaṁ vartamānatvavirodhāt sādhanaṁ tu sāmānyavattve satītyādi tatrāstītyanaikāntikatvam*, VV, p. 22). With regard to the second query about the state of being destructible, the view of the siddhāntin gets endorsed as, in accordance with this interpretation, the varṇas would remain intact even during the state of destruction since the term *yogyatva* is construed as 'its own being (*svarūpa*)' in the light of the interpretation given by Ānandajñāna (*varṇā vināśaṁ prati varṇā iti hi tadā sādhyārthaḥ. tathā ca siddhasādhyatā varṇānāṁ vināśāvasthāyām api varṇatvenāvasthitāvasmatpakṣasyākṣatatvāditi*, ibid., pp. 22-23). In respect of the third query in which destructibility has been interpreted as having relation with existence-universal implied by the destruction of a letter-sound (varṇa), the fault consisting in the absence of the major term (*sādhya*) in the illustration becomes applicable as the existence implied by the disappearance of a varṇa does not reside in the pot. The reason is that the state of being a varṇa, the pronoun '*sva*' refers to, does not exist in a pot. If the existence-universal is taken as implied by the destruction of both the varṇas and non-varṇas, then the existence-universal would be existing in a pot but at the same time it would also happen to reside in the soul which is eternal. In this way the concept of destructibility sought to be proved here goes haywire (see ibid., p. 23). However, the siddhāntin says that he does not subscribe to the view of the non-eternity of varṇas. Hence, the sādhya implied by the destruction of varṇas remains unestablished (see NRD, p. 23).

The view that the varṇas are eternal is strengthened when the concept of destructibility in terms of 'relation of time with an entity' is rejected (see VV, pp. 23-24). Similarly, the view of the human origin of the Vedas should be seen because it would not be consistent with what has been said in the Agamas about the Vedas: The Vedas are not a product because there was no embodied being at the beginning of the cycle (*kalpādau vedasya śarīrādikāraṇāsambhavāt kāryatvādyasambhava iti*, NRD, p. 25). Moreover, there is no such argument as would contradict the view that the Vedas are eternal and *apauruṣeya*. The defects bādha, bhāgāsiddhi, etc. which are applicable in the syllogisms used to prove the non-eternity of the Vedas should be extended to the syllogisms used to infer that the Vedas are of human-origin (*vedānityānumāneṣūktaṁ doṣajātaṁ pauruṣeyatvānumāneṣvatidiśati*, VV, p. 24). That the Vedas are eternal and of non-human origin renders the pūrvapakṣin's syllogisms incapable of proving his case (cf. *vedasyākāryatvāpauruṣeyatvayoḥ bādhakābhāvāccāprayojakatvam uktānumānānām*, VV, p. 25).

वेदेतरागमानामपौरुषेयत्वनिराकरणम्

यत्तूक्तमितरागमानामप्यपौरुषेयत्वप्रसङ्ग इति तद् गोमयपायसीकरणसमं व्याप्तेरभावात्। ननु ते वेद एव व्याप्तिस्सिद्धा। ननु तवापि पयसि गोविकारत्वं सिद्धम्। अनुग्राह्यमानाभावादप्ययमप्रसङ्गः। विपर्यये हि मानासम्भवो दर्शितः। एतेन युगपत्सर्ववर्णोपलम्भो व्याख्यातः। कथं चेत्थंभावस्य प्राप्तिः, युगपदिन्द्रियसम्बद्धत्वादिति चेद्; न, तस्यासिद्धेः। न हि स्वरूपेणैव वर्णा इन्द्रियसम्बद्धाः, किन्तु ध्वन्युपहिता एव। ध्वनिश्च क्रमभावीत्यस्मात्स्थितिः। यत्तु मानं श्रोत्रं समानेन्द्रियग्राह्यसमानदेशसमानधर्मापन्नानां ग्रहणाय प्रतिनियतसंस्कारसंस्कार्यं न भवति, इन्द्रियत्वात् चक्षुर्वत्। शब्दा वा प्रतिनियतसंस्कारसंस्कार्या न भवन्ति उक्तविशेषणत्वे सति युगपदिन्द्रियसम्बद्धत्वात् तद्धटवदिति। तत्राद्ये सिद्धसाधनम्। श्रोत्रस्यासंस्कार्यत्वाभ्युपगमात्। द्वितीये तु भागासिद्धिः। उपान्त्यादेरस्माकमसिद्धेः तत्र तव हेतोरसिद्धेश्च। तदेवं न वर्णनित्यत्वे कश्चिदपि बाधः सम्भवी।

Refutation of the view that the Āgamas other than the Vedas are also of non-human origin

Trans. : (If the Vedas, being Āgamas, are considered to be of non-human origin, then) the statement that the other scriptures (i.e., the Āgamas of the heretics) would also be taken to be of non-human origin is like the maxim of *gomayapāyasa* (which means that cow-dung is made of milk because it comes from the cow) as there is no such invariable concomitance between the Āgamas and the state of being of non-human origin (*na cāgamasyāpauruṣeyatvādinā tādṛśī vyāptiḥ*, ibid., p. 25). But the invariable concomitance between the Āgamas and the state of being of non-human origin is accepted in the case of the Vedas by the siddhāntin. The siddhāntin replies that it is also established in the case of the pūrvapakṣin that milk is the product of a cow (like cow-dung; so, according to him, cow-dung should be understood to be made of milk since it is a product of the cow, which is an absurd argument). However, the pūrvapakṣin's argument does not have any scope for application here as there is no valid means of knowledge to prove the contrary instance (that the Vedas are not eternal and that they are of human origin; cf. *pramāṇānugrāhako hi tarkaḥ. na cātrānugrāhyaṁ pramāṇamasti. ato viparyayāparyavasānādapi nāsya sattarkateti*, VV, p. 25). That there is no evidence to prove the contrary has already been demonstrated. (Since there is no accepted viable valid means to prove the contrary), the (contingency of) simultaneous cognition of all the varṇas gets explained thereby. How does the simultaneous cognition of all the varṇas come about? Is it because they simultaneously come in contact with the auditory sense organ? The siddhāntin does not accept this as this is not established. For the varṇas by themselves do not come into contact with the sense organ but through the adjunctival function of the sound (which manifests them) and the sound does have a sequence; this is our position. And the (following) syllogistic propositions do not occasion any contradiction of the view that the varṇas are eternal : 1. The auditory sense organ, being a sense organ like the eyes, does not undergo any change by the well-regulated refinements or modulations (helpful) in hearing the letter-sounds which are capable of being cognised by the same sense organ, which occur in the same space and which are invested with the same properties. 2. Or, the words, having the abovementioned qualifications, do not undergo any change by the well-regulated modifications, being simultaneously connected with the sense organ like the pot. In the first syllogistic proposition, the fault of proving that which has already been proved applies as we do not subscribe to the view that the auditory sense organ is subject to any modification. The second syllogism suffers from the fault of partial non-establishment of the dharmin (*bhāgāsiddhi*) as the letter-sounds proximate to the final one are non-existent for us (being only inferable) and, thus, there is a part of the dharmin in which the reason 'having the same qualification and connected with the sense organ' does not exist. Thus (after it has been demonstrated that the syllogisms of the pūrvapakṣin are not supported by any contradictory argument against the contrary instance, we can say that) there is nothing that contradicts the view that the varṇas are eternal.

Ann. : The pūrvapakṣin says that if the Vedas, being Āgamas, are of non-human origin then the other Āgamas should also be considered to be of non-human origin. The siddhāntin does not agree with the pūrvapakṣin on this point saying that to hold such a view is to follow the maxim of *gomaya-pāyasa* but it is absurd to think that cow-dung should be considered to be made of milk because it comes from the cow. In other words, the scriptures of the opponent cannot be equated with the Vedas simply because they are called Āgamas (cf. *na cāgamasyāpauruṣeyatvādinā tādṛśī vyāptiḥ. manvādivākyeṣu vyabhicārāt. na ca teṣvapi prasaṅga-sāmyaṁ kartṛsmṛtivirodhāt. tathā ca yathā gomayasya govikāra-tvena payovat pāyasasādhanatvamāpadyate tadvadāgamatvenā-pauruṣeyādisādhanaṁ pāṣaṇḍānāmiti*, VV, p. 25). The invariable concomitance exists between the Vedas and their being of non-human origin, and not between the Āgamas and their being of non-human origin because the scriptures composed by Manu, etc. are Āgamas but their having been authored by a human-being is evident since the authorship of such Āgamas is remembered. There is no such remembrance of any author with regard to the Vedas. So, the invariable concomitance between the Veda and its being of non-human origin does not suffer from any defect. On the other hand, if some objection is raised with reference to the position of the pūrvapakṣin, such as the remembrance of some author or the other with regard to his scriptures, he does not have any argument that would resolve the doubt raised against his point of view. That is the reason why the siddhāntin avers that the Vedas are of non-human origin and hence eternal. It is logically entailed from this view that the varṇas are eternal and also all-pervasive. As a result, the contingency of their being perceived simultaneously is incurred as, being all-pervasive, they should always be in contact with the auditory sense organ (*yadi varṇāḥ sarvagatā nityāśca niścīyante tadā sarvavarṇānāmaparyāyeṇa pratītiprasaktiriti*, ibid., p. 26). How this contingency is taken care of is explained in the following.

According to the Mīmāṁsakas, the varṇas by themselves are not apprehended by our auditory sense organ. It is actually the sound which manifests them. So, we hear the varṇas only through the adjunctival functions of the sound (*na ca śuddhā varṇāḥ śrū-yante. upahitānāmeva śravaṇādityarthaḥ*, ibid., p.26). The sound has a particular sequence. So, a varṇa also appears to be having a sequence. In this way the contingency of the simultaneous apprehension of all the varṇas can be taken care of.

The pūrvapakṣin uses two syllogisms to prove the contrary, to wit, the varṇas are simultaneously perceived. But these syllogisms are rejected by the siddhāntin. The two syllogisms are as follows : 1. (*śrotrasaṁskārapakṣa*) The auditory sense organ, being a sense organ like the eyes, does not undergo any change by the sequential modifications (helpful) in cognising the letter-sounds which are capable of being cognised by the same sense organ, when they have the same property and when they occur in the same space like the eyes which simultaneously perceive the objects capable of being apprehended by them when they have the same property and happen to be at the same place. In the same way the varṇas should also be heard simultaneously. 2. (*varṇasaṁskārapakṣa*) The letter-sounds (varṇas), having the same qualification, do not undergo any sequential modification, being simultaneously connected with the sense organ like a pot. Just as the pot connected with the visual sense organ is cognised by the eyes simultaneously. Likewise the varṇas ought to be cognised simultaneously. To ward off this undesirable situation, the siddhāntin points out the fallacies in the syllogistc propositions of the pūrvapakṣin. In the first syllogism, there is a defect of proving that which has already been proved as the siddhāntin does not subscribe to the view that the auditory sense organ undergoes any modification because of the production of letter-sounds. So far as the second inference is concerned, it suffers from the defect of partial non-establishment of the dharmin as the letter-sounds proximate to the final one are non-existent in the siddhantin's view. They are always inferable and in the inferable entities the reason 'connected with the sense organ' does not exist. This fallacy is known as *svarūpāsiddhi*. In this way these syllogisms fail to successfully prove the simultaneous cognition of the varṇas, which are eternal and all-pervasive according to the siddhānta view. Now the pūrvapakṣin is left with no such argument that can disprove the view that varṇas are eternal. The siddhāntin resolves the problem of simultaneous apprehension of the varṇas saying that they become manifest by virtue of the sound produced by the internal air. The sound, of course, has a sequence. That is why the varṇas also appear to be sequential when they are heard with the help of the sound. Thus there is no simultaneous apprehension of the eternal and all-pervasive varṇas.

वेदापौरुषेयत्वे श्रुतिस्मृतिवचोविचारः अनुमानप्रयोगाश्च

ननु वेदस्य कार्यत्वादि सृष्टिश्रुतेरेव सिद्धम्। न च 'अनादिनिधना नित्या वाक्' इत्यादिस्मृतिविरोधः। श्रुतेः प्राबल्याद् इति चेद्। न हि तावद्धैरण्यगर्भसर्गश्रुत्या वेदस्य कार्यत्वादिसिद्धिः। श्रुत्यन्तरविरोधस्योक्तत्वाद्। 'यो ब्रह्माणं विदधाति पूर्वम् यो वै वेदांश्च प्रहिणोति तस्मै' इति ह्युक्तम्। उक्तञ्च 'नाचिकेतमुपाख्यानमि'त्यादि श्रुत्यन्तरम्। एवं च सति हैरण्यगर्भसृष्टिश्रुत्या न स्मृतेर्विरोधोऽपि। तथा 'तस्माद्यज्ञात्सर्वहुतः। ऋचस्सामानि जज्ञिरे' इत्यादि परमात्मसृष्टिश्रुत्यापीति द्रष्टव्यम्। अन्यथोक्तश्रुत्यन्तरविरोधात्। वंशश्रुतौ च 'परमेष्ठी ब्रह्मणो ब्रह्म स्वयंभ्वि'ति ब्रह्मैव वेदरूपेणाविर्भवतीति श्रूयते। ब्रह्मसामानाधिकरण्यश्रुतेः। वेदस्योत्पत्त्यसम्भवश्चोक्तः। अतो वेदसृष्टिश्रुतिर्बाध्येत दर्शितश्रुत्या 'अनादिनिधना वागि'ति स्मृत्या च, यथा 'वेदं कृत्वा वेदिं करोती'ति श्रुतिः 'क्षुत आचमेदि'ति स्मृत्या। तस्मात् श्रुतिस्मृतिन्यायबलाद्वेदस्य नित्यत्वं निश्चीयते। दर्शिते हि श्रुतिस्मृती। प्रयोगस्तु — वेदोऽपौरुषेयः शरीरवृत्तीतरत्वे सति प्रलयस्थत्वादात्मवत्। हेतुसिद्धिस्तूक्तागमबलात्। नित्यत्वमस्माकमुपाधिरिति चेत्तत्किं सार्वकालीनत्वम् असार्वकालीनत्वविपर्ययः अथवा अविनाशित्वम्। आद्ये साध्याव्याप्तिः। काले साध्यभावेऽप्युपाध्यभावात्। द्वितीयतृतीययोरप्ययमेव दोषः। प्रागभावे साध्यवत्त्वेऽप्युपाध्यभावात्। अकार्यत्वं तर्ह्युपाधिरस्तु। न। तस्य तवासिद्धेः। कार्यत्वसिद्धितन्त्रा ह्यकार्यत्वसिद्धिः। कार्यत्वं च ते न सिध्यतीत्युक्तम्। एवमकारणत्वमप्यसिद्धं नात्रोपाधिः। उत्पत्त्यसिद्धौ हि तत्सापेक्षप्रागभाविकारणासिद्धेरकारणवत्त्वासिद्धिः। विपक्षे बाधकतर्कस्योक्तत्वात्। बाधकतर्काभावाच्च न शङ्कितोपाधिता। नापि विरुद्धता, हेतोः सपक्षवृत्तित्वात्। असाधारणताविरहस्त्वतिरोहित एव। सपक्षवृत्तेः स्पष्टत्वात्। नापि कालात्ययापदिष्टता। बाधाभावात्। सत्प्रतिपक्षता त्वनाशङ्कनीया। उक्तदिशा प्रतिप्रयोगासम्भवस्योक्तत्वात्। स्फुटो दृष्टान्तदोषविरहोऽपि। अत्र उक्तिदोषस्तु प्रमेयाविरोधीति निस्तरङ्गमेव वेदस्यापौरुषेयत्वानुमानम्।

Deliberation on the scriptural statements regarding the non-human origin of the Vedas and syllogisms

Trans. : The pūrvapakṣin's view that the Veda is a product, etc. is proved by the very Vedic evidence of creation (*sṛṣṭi-śruti*) and there is no contradiction of it by the smṛti 'The speech is eternal and has no beginning and end (Mahābhārata Śānti-parva, 231. 56)' because the Vedic evidence is stronger than the smṛti evidence. (The siddhāntin says) that the Veda is a product, etc. is definitely not proved by the Vedic evidence of creation by Hiraṇyagarbha as its contradiction by another Vedic evidence has already been mentioned : It is God who first brought forth Brahmā and then transmitted the Vedas to him. Another Vedic evidence (of the eternity of the Veda) has also been cited : This eternal anecdote as received by Naciketā and as told by Death. Given this, the Vedic evidence of creation by Hiraṇyagarbha would also not contradict the smṛti evidence. In the same manner it should be understood that there is no contradiction of the smṛti evidence by the (following) Vedic evidence : From the sacrifice in which Puraṣa identified with the whole universe has been offered as oblation, were born the hymns and Sāmans. Otherwise, there would be contradiction of the Vedic evidence cited (above). And in the Vaṁśa Brāhmaṇa of the Bṛhadāraṇyaka Upaniṣad, it is said that Parameṣṭhin (received vidyā) from Brahmā, that is from the Veda. Brahmā is self-born; this means it is Brahman who manifests Itself as the Veda since both Brahman and Veda are in apposition, having the same case-ending. It has already been mentioned that the Veda cannot be originated. Therefore, the Vedic evidence of the creation of the Veda is superseded by the Vedic evidence (*nāciketamupākhyānam*) already cited and by the smṛti (evidence) 'the speech has no beginning and end' in the same manner as the Vedic statement 'having prepared a brush of Darbha grass, he prepares the altar' is superseded by the smṛti injunction 'on sneezing he should sip water'. Hence taking into consideration the force of the statements of both the Veda and the smṛti, the eternity of the Veda has to be determined. (In this respect) the śruti (Vedic evidence) and the smṛti have already been cited. The syllogistic proposition, too, is as follows : The Veda is of non-human origin since it exists at the time of dissolution, being other than what exists in a body like the soul. The probans is established on the basis of the Āgama mentioned above. The opponent points out the existence of an upādhi: 'the state of being eternal'. What does this upādhi mean? Does it mean 'being existent at all times', or 'being the opposite of that which does not exist at all times' or 'being indestructible'? In the first alternative, there is no concomitance of the upādhi 'being existent at all times' with the major term (sādhya). Although the major term exists in time, the upādhi does not (*kāle khalvapauruṣeyatvamiṣyate na ca sarvakālīnatvaṁ tasya. svāsambandhāt*, VV, p. 30). So far as the second and third alternatives are concerned, the same fault is applicable, i.e. there is no concomitance of the upādhi with the major term. The pre-non-existence is of non-human origin but neither 'being the opposite of that which does not exist at all times' nor 'the state of indestructible' exists in the pre-non-existence (*prāgabhāva*). Then let 'the state of not being an effect' be an upādhi. No, as this is not well-known in your case. The reason is that 'the state of not being an effect' is dependent on the establishement of 'the state of being an effect' which you have not been able to prove (because of the fault of mutual dependence, see NRD, p. 16 and VV thereon). In this way 'the state of not having a cause' is also not established and, thus, this also is not an upādhi here (see VV, p. 31). When the concept of production has not been proved, depending on this, the cause preceding production also remains unproved and consequently, 'the state of not having a cause' remains unknown. The contradictory argument with respect to the contrary instance (that the Veda is of human origin) has already been cited. And in the absence of a contradictory argument against the view that the Veda is of non-human origin, there does not exist (even) a doubtful upādhi. (Moreover,) there is no fallacy known as *viruddha* as the reason resides in the illustration (*sapakṣa*). The absence of the fallacy known as *asādhāraṇa anaikāntika* too is obviously present as the reason evidently exists in the sapakṣa. Also the fallacy known as *kālātyayāpadiṣṭatā* does not apply as the reason is not stultified (i.e., there is no stronger evidence which can prove the absece of the probandum). That the probans has the counterprobans should not even be doubted as the impossiblity of the counter-syllogism has already been shown in the foregoing (see supra p. 26). The absence of faults in the illustration too is obvious.

Here, the fault relating to the statement (of the illustration, see VV, p. 31) also does not go against what is to be proved. Therefore (it can fairly be concluded that) the syllogistic proposition used in proving the non-human origin of the Vedas does not suffer from any defect.

Ann. : In the present passage, the problem relating to the non-human origin of the Vedas is the pivotal point. The account given here seems to be a precursor of what has been discussed in the Citsukhī in this regard. There are conflicting statements in the Vedic scriptures (śruti) regarding whether the Vedas are a product or they are eternal. The Vedic statement (*idaṁ sarvam asṛjata*, ibid., p. 28) relating to the creation by Hiraṇyagarbha (*Hiraṇyagarbhasṛṣṭiśruti*) clearly says that the creation inclusive of the Vedas was a product of Hiraṇyagarbha. Hence, the Vedas are a product; they are not eternal. On the other hand, the Vedic statements 'It is God who first brought forth Brahmā and then transmitted the Vedas to him', 'This eternal anecdote as received by Naciketā and as told by Death' and 'Brahmā is self-born, which means it is Brahman who manifested Itself as the Veda' support the view that the Vedas are not a product (cf. *kiṁ ca bṛhadāraṇyake vaṁśabrāhmaṇe parameṣṭhī (virāṭ) brahmaṇo vedākhyādvidyāmāpede. brahma tu vedākhyaṁ svayambhu svayameva paramātmā tadrūpeṇa bhavatīti vyutpatteriti brahmaṇo vedātmanāvirbhāvaḥ śrutaḥ*VV, p.28). However, the first śruti statement given here can be interpreted in favour of both the views. In such a situation, it is essential that these conflicting statements should be properly examined to arrive at a cogent conclusion.

Manifestation can also be construed as creation. If the Vedas are accepted as eternal, then it can fairly be held that they are made manifest at the beginning of each cycle. Following this line of argument, it can be said that the Vedas are of non-human origin. Ānandānubhava has discussed a significant point relating to the contradiction between the śruti and the smṛti literature. He quotes a smṛti verse and says that sometimes an injunction of the smṛti supersedes that of the śruti. He illustrates this point by quoting the śruti injunction 'having prepared the brush of darbha-grass, he prepares the altar.' There is a sequence between two acts as enjoined by this śruti injunction. The act of preparing the brush of darbha-grass is to be immediately followed by the act of preparing the altar. There should not be any intervention between the two. However, the smṛti statement '*kṣuta ācamet*', enjoining the sipping of water before the preparation of the altar if there is sneezing just after the preparation of the brush of darbha-grass, overrules the order enjoined by the śruti (*vedaṁ kṛtvā vediṁ karoti*). In this particular instance, there is a conflict between the injunction of the śruti and that of the smṛti. The latter overrules the order enjoined by the śruti injunction in case there is sneezing. Otherwise the smṛti injunction would have no scope of application. In the same way, the smṛti statement 'the speech has no beginning and no end; it is eternal' will supersede the śruti statement which says that the Vedas are a product. The reason is that the śruti statements to the effect that the Vedas are eternal and that they are of non-human origin are greater in number than those which mention the product view. So the contradiction between two śruti statements is resolved by construing the product view as the manifestation view. Thus, the smṛti statement relating to the eternal nature of the Vedas is to be preferred to the product view of the śruti.

Ānandānubhava then presents a syllogistic proposition to prove the eternity and non-human origin of the Vedas. The syllogism reads as follows : The Veda is of non-human origin since it exists at the time of dissolution being other than what exists in a body like the soul. He says that the reason (*hetu*) given in the syllogism is on the basis of the Āgamas and the śruti statements '*dhātā yathāpūrvam akalapayat*' and the like. The justification to keep the term 'existing at the time of dissolution' is to ward off over-extension of the probans to a pot, etc. Although a pot is other than what exists in a body, it does not exist during dissoution (*pralaya*). Dharma, impressions, etc. do exist in the individual self even at the time of dissolution but they are excluded by the expression 'other than what exists in a body.'

He discusses several possible interpretations of 'eternity' which has been used by the pūṛvapakṣin as an imposed property (*upādhi*) to show that the reason (*hetu*) is fallacious. There are three possible meanings of 'eternity' : It may mean 'the state of existing at all times', or 'being the opposite of that which does not exist at all times' or 'the state of not being destructible'? In the first alternative, there is no concomitance of the upādhi consisting in 'the state of existing at all times' with the major term (*sādhya*). Although the major term exists in time, the upādhi does not exist in it since time cannot exist in time in terms of which the first alternative interpretation has been construed (*yad apauruṣeyaṁ tatsarvakālīnam iti na vyāptiḥ. kāle khalvapauruṣeyatvamiṣyate. na ca sarvakālīnatvaṁ tasya. svāsambandhāt. kālāntarasya cābhāvāt. tato na sarvakālīnatvamapauruṣeyatvopādhiriti*, VV, p. 30). So far as the second and third alternatives are concerned, the same fault remains applicable, i.e. there is no concomitance of the upādhi with the major term (sādhya). There is pre-non-existence of non-human origin but there is neither 'being the opposite of that which does not exist at all times' nor 'the state of not being destructible'. After this signification of the upādhi has been analysed and discarded, the author takes up another interpretation of the upādhi. It consists in 'the state of not being an effect.' This is also not accepted by the siddhāntin as it could not be proved in accordance with the view of the opponent. The reason is that 'the state of not being an effect' (*akāryatva*) is dependent on 'the state of being an effect' which the pūrvapakṣin has not been able to prove (because of the fault of mutual dependence. Cf. *utpattyādimattvaṁ ca sādhyaṁ te durghaṭam. utpattimattvaṁ hi tvatpakṣe prāgasataḥ sattāyogitvam. taccāprasiddham prāktvotpattyoranyonyāśrayatvāt*, NRD, p. 22). This has already been discussed. In this way 'the state of not being an efffect' also remains unproved and, so, this cannot be used as an upādhi. In the absence of the concept of production, the cause preceding production and depending on it also remains an unsubstantiated entity. As such, 'the state of not being a cause' also cannot be taken as an upādhi.

The siddhāntin further brings forth an argument which stultifies the contrary instance, that is, the view that the Vedas are not eternal and that they have been authored by a human being. The argument runs like this : The pūrvapakṣin has not been able to clarify and establish what an effect is because of the defect of mutual dependence as has been pointed out in the foregoing paragraph. The argument in favour of the eternity of the varṇas, which has been discussed elaborately and conclusively proved, endorses the view that the Vedas are of non-human origin (*apauruṣeya*). Discussing the present syllogistic proposition, the siddhāntin further analyses the possible fallacies of reason, namely, *viruddha, asādhāraṇa anaikāntika, bādhita* and *satpratipakṣa* (hetu). He discusses them, proves their untenability and concludes that the following syllogism is flawless : The Veda is of non-human origin since it exists at the time of dissolution being other than what exists in a body like the soul (also cf. VV, p. 31).

किञ्च कल्पादौ वेदाध्ययनं गुर्वध्ययनपूर्वकं वेदाध्ययनत्वाद् इदानीन्तन-वेदाध्ययनवत्। एवमयमनादिरनन्तो वेदाध्ययनसन्तानः। अन्यथोक्तनीत्या वेदस्योत्पत्त्यसम्भवादध्ययनसन्तानाभावप्रसङ्गः। भारतादेश्चोत्पत्तिसम्भवान्नाति-प्रसङ्गः। दोषान्तरासम्भवोऽत्राप्युक्तदिशा दर्शनीयः। तस्मान्नित्याः अनाप्त-प्रणीताश्च वेदाः। यदप्यनाप्तवाक्यत्वेन वेदस्याप्रामाण्योद्घोषणं, तन्निरस्तं पुरस्तात्। नित्यत्वेऽपि च वेदस्यानपेक्षत्वात् किमिति न प्रामाण्यम्? किमिति वा न स्वत एव यच्चक्षुर्वद्वेदः प्रमाणं न स्यात्। प्रपञ्चितं च वेदस्यानपेक्षत्वं नित्यत्वमपौरुषेयत्वं च बहुभिरगाधबुद्धिभिरित्युपरम्यते।

Trans. : Moreover, the study of the Veda in the beginning of the kalpa was preceded by the preceptor's study of the Veda since it is a study of the Veda like a study of the Veda now-a-days. In this way, the series of the study of the Veda has no beginning and no end. Otherwise on account of the impossibility of the production of the Veda according to the principle discussed above, the contingency of the absence of the continued series of the study of the Veda would be incurred. This would not over-extend to the works such as Mahābhārata, etc. because of the possibility of their production. The absence of other faults should be understood in the aforesaid manner (i.e. as in the context of the syllogism used to prove the eternalness and non-human origin of the Vedas). Therefore, the Vedas are eternal and are not authored by any trustworthy person. The proclamation that the Vedic sentence, not being a sentence of a trustworthy person, is not valid has already been repudiated. Also being eternal and independent (not requiring anything for its authenticity), does the Veda not bear validity? Is it not self-valid like the eyes? The eternalness and independence of the Veda and its being of non-human origin have elaborately and conclusively been discussed by many persons of profound intellect. Hence we stop here.

Ann. : The siddhāntin says that if the study of the Veda at the beginning of the creation is not accepted, then the continuity of the tradition of Veda's study cannot be maintained. But its continuity is admitted in the tradition and so the beginningless series of the study of the Veda implies the eternalness of the Veda and also its non-human origin. The impossibility of the production of the Veda could presuppose the absence of the series of the study of the Veda. To explain, the absence of the Veda, i.e. the absence of the cause, would incur the absence of the continuity of its study. The continuity of the study of the Veda thus proves the eternalness of the Veda. There is no over-extension of eternalness to the Mahābhārata since its authorship is rememberred that it was composed by Vedavyāsa and, hence, it is not eternal. The absence of other faults in the present syllogism is to be explained in consonance with the aforesaid direction (*asādhāraṇavirahastvatirohita eva,* see supra p. 49). Thus we arrive at the conclusion that the Vedas are eternal and they were not authored by any trustworthy person. Here an objection could be raised that the Veda, not being a sentence of a trustworthy person, is liable to being bereft of authenticity. But such an objection has already been discussed and discarded.

Now the author takes up the question relating to the validity of the Veda. Does the Veda being eternal and not requiring any other evidence for its own authenticiy possess validity? The question has been raised to lay emphasis on the fact that the validity of the Veda is unquestioned. The second question raised by him concerns the intrinsic or extrinsic nature of this validity.

Although the problem relating to the intrinsic or extrinsic validity of the Veda has been elaborately debated by the scholarly persons, the author now discusses this issue in the right earnest.

वेदस्य परतःप्रामाण्यवादपूर्वपक्षः

नन्वस्तु वेदस्य प्रामाण्यं, स्वत इति तु न क्षम्यते। तत्प्रमाणाभावात्। स्वतस्त्वं हि प्रामाण्यस्य ज्ञानहेतुमात्राधीनत्वं ते विवक्षितम्। न चात्र प्रमाणमस्ति। यत्तु प्रमाणम् — [प्रमाणं ज्ञानहेतुजन्यमात्रवृत्ति दोषाजन्यज्ञानैकधर्मत्वात् इति। तदसत्। अतिप्रसङ्गात्। ननु अप्रामाण्यं ज्ञानसामग्रीजन्यमात्रवृत्ति प्रामाण्येतरत्वे सति ज्ञानैकधर्मत्वाद् ज्ञानत्ववद् इति प्रतिप्रयोगः स] नोपपद्यते, अप्रामाण्यस्य दोषहेतुताया अवश्याभ्युपेयत्वात्। अन्यथातिप्रसङ्गात्। एवं तर्हि भवत एवैवमनुमानमस्तु। दोषान्वयव्यतिरेकयोश्च गुणान्वयव्यतिरेकयोरिव प्रतिबन्धविरोधिविषयतयान्यथासिद्धिः। न चापसिद्धान्तता। प्रमाणवत्त्वेनैवास्य सिद्धान्ततापत्तेः न च प्रामाण्यपरतस्त्वे बाधः कश्चित्। अनुमानान्तरेऽप्येवमूहनीयम्। प्रमापरतस्त्वेऽनुमानम् — प्रमा न ज्ञानहेतुमात्राधीना ज्ञानविशेषत्वाद् अप्रमावदिति।

ज्ञानविशेषत्वहानिर्विपक्षे बाधः। दोषान्तराभावश्च यथासम्भवमूहनीयः। तथा प्रमा प्रमाणाप्रमाणसाधारणकारणातिरिक्तजन्या कार्यत्वाद् घटवदिति प्रयोगः। दोषासम्भवोऽत्रापि यथायोगमूहनीयः।

Extrinsic validity of the Veda : Pūrvapakṣa

Trans. : Let the Veda be a valid means of knowledge but its self-validity is not acceptable since there is no evidence to this effect. According to you, self-validity of knowledge is that which depends only on the causal conditions and in this respect there is no evidence. If there is an evidence : [Validity exists only in a cognition that is produced by its causal factors since it is a property only of the cognition which is not generated by a defect, then this is not true as it suffers from the fault of over-extension. (For the Buddhists subscribe to the view of the intrinsic nature of invalidity, see VV, p. 34 :) Invalidity resides only in that (cognition) which is produced by its causal conditions since, being other than validity, it is a property only of the cognition like the state of being a cognition (*jñānatva*). However, this counter-syllogism] does not seem to be based on reason as it should necessarily be admitted that invalidity is caused by a defect (besides the causal conditions). Otherwise it would lead to over-extension (for this see ibid., p. 34). If this is the case, then let only your syllogism (presented above) be accepted in this respect. (But) like the positive and negative concomitance of a guṇa (in the production of a valid and an invalid cognition in a respective manner), the positive and negative concomitance of a defect (in the generation of an invalid and a valid cognition respectively) is established differently (*anyathāsiddha*) since a defect (*doṣa*) is contrary to guṇa (which is instrumental in producing a valid cognition). And there is no falsification of an accepted principle (of Mīmāṁsā which accepts invalidity as extrinsic, whereas the Buddhist proves it to be intrinsic by divesting the defect of its causality) since a theory derives its essence when it is based on an evidence (which is inference in this case). (Therefore, *doṣa*, being anyathāsiddha, ceases to be a cause. Consequently, invalidity can be accepted as intrinsic by the Buddhists). (The Buddhist further points out :) Also there is no contradiction of the view-point regarding the extrinsic nature of the validity of a cognition. (Apprehending another syllogistic proposition by the Mīmāṁsaka to endorse the view of the intrinsic nature of validity, the Buddhist extends to it the defect consisting in the incapability of the reason to prove the probandum, i.e. *śaṅkitā-prayojakatā* saying that) the same line of thinking should be adopted in respect of the other syllogism. The syllogism to prove the extrinsic nature of the validity of a cognition is as follows : A valid cognition is not dependent only on its causal conditions since it is a cognition invested with a special characteristic like an invalid cognition. Loss of the special characteristic of a valid cognition is a deterrent to the contrary view-point. The absence of other faults (in respect of the extrinsic nature of validity) is to be considered in all possible manners. In the same way (there is another syllogism to prove the extrinsic nature of the validity of a cognition) : A valid cognition is produced by the factors other than those which are common to the means of both valid and invalid cognitions since it is a product like a pot. Here also the absence of faults should be considered as the context requires.

Ann. : The problem of intrinsic and extrinsic nature of validity has been extensively debated in the Indian philosophical systems. The Mīmāṁsakas and the Vedāntins hold that the validity of a cognition is intrinsically conditioned. On this issue, however, they differ in respect of details. So far as the invalidity of knowledge is concerned, they hold that it is determined extrinsically. According to the Buddhists, invalidity is intrinsic and validity is extrinsic as they hold that all knowledge is invalid by nature. The Naiyāyikas view that both validity and invalidity of a cognition are extrinsically conditioned since guṇa and doṣa are instrumental in the generation of a valid and an invalid cognition in a respective manner. These factors (guṇa and doṣa) are construed as different from the causal conditions of a cognition. It is in this background that the author of the Nyāyaratnadīpāvali discusses the problem of the intrinsic nature of the validity of the Vedic testimony.

The siddhāntin's view is that the Veda is of non-human origin. This leads to the view of the intrinsic nature of the validity of the Vedic testimony. The pūrvapakṣin does not accept the intrinsic nature of the validity of the Vedic testimony because, according to him, there is no proof in this regard. In order to demonstrate the absence of proof with regard to the view that the Veda is self-valid, the pūrvapakṣin presents the siddhāntin's concept of the intrinsic nature of validity : The intrinsic nature of the validity (of a cognition) in general consists in its being dependent on the causal conditions which produce the cognition itself. The commentator of NRD throws light on the view as follows : The intrinsic nature of validity consists in its residing in a cognition which is produced only by its causal factors. However, the pūrvapakṣin points out that validity cannot at all be produced, let alone its being generated by the same causal conditions. The reason is that validity, being either a universal or an upādhi in the form of absolute absence of the sublation of a cognition not residing in a locus of memory, cannot be produced. Only on being a product of the same causal factors as are responsible for the production of a cognition, the validity of that cognition can be regarded as intrinsically valid (*jñānasāmagrīmātrajanyavyaktivṛttitvaṁ prāmāṇyasya svatastvam. na ca tajjanyatvaṁ prāmāṇyasya. smṛtitvānadhikaraṇajñānagatabādhātyantābhāvarūpopādhitve jātitve ca janmāyogāt. jñānasāmagrīmātrajanyatve ca jñānavattadharmatāsambhavāditi bhāvaḥ*, VV, p. 33). In such a situation, how can validity be proved to be intrinsic? The pūrvapakṣin further adds that there is also no evidence for the intrinsic view-point of validity. Apprehending the untenability of the absence of evidence in respect of self-validity, the pūrvapakṣin restates the syllogism intended to be put forward by the other side to keep the discussion going on (*pramāṇābhāvasyāsiddhim āśaṅkya parābhipretaṁ pramāṇam anuvadati*, ibid., p. 33) : Validity resides in that (cognition) which is produced only by the causal conditions since it is a property belonging only to the cognition which is not produced by a defect (*doṣa*). The pūrvapakṣin says that this is not true as it suffers from the fault of over-extension (*tadasat. atiprasaṅgāt.* NRD, p. 34). The overextension is in the form of the counter-syllogism which supports the view of the intrinsic nature of invalidity, which is held by the Buddhists. The counter-syllogism of the Buddhist reads as follows: The intrinsically conditioned nature of invalidity consists in its existing only in a cognition which is produced by its causal factors since, being different from validity, it is the property that resides only in a cognition like the state of being of a cognition (Cf. *aprāmāṇyaṁ jñānasāmagrījanyamātravṛtti prāmāṇyetaratve sati jñānaika-dharmatvāt jñānatvavat iti,* NRD, p.34). The siddhāntin does not accept the viability of the counter-syllogism. He says that if a defect is not accepted as a causal factor in the generation of an invalid cognition, then it would suffer from the defect of over-extension. This is explained by Ānandajñāna as follows : If invalidity is accepted to reside only in a cognition generated by its causal conditions, and not in a cognition which is generated by a defect, then the cognition of the silver being internal would also become liable to be termed erroneous like the cognition of the silver being external (*yadyaprāmāṇyaṁ doṣajanyajñānāvṛttijñānamātrahetu-janyāśritam iṣyate tadā rajatāderdoṣakṛtabahiṣṭvadṛṣṭivadāntaratva-pratīterapi karaṇadoṣamantareṇāpramāṇatvaprasaktirityaprāmāṇya-sya doṣahetutāyāḥ svīkartavyatve sūcitām āvaśyamityupapattim eva viśadayati,* VV, p. 34). The cognition of the silver being external is by nature erroneous as per Vijñānavāda, whereas the cognition of the silver being internal is true.

For the sake of argument, the Buddhist accepts the positive concomitance of a defect for the generation of an invalid cognition but contends that the defect (*doṣa*) would not be construed as a cause like a *guṇa* which is not considered to be a cause of a valid cognition over and above the causal conditions according to the Mīmāṁsakas. As per the Buddhist view, the defect is considered to be anyathāsiddha since the positive and negative concomitance only cannot invest it with the nature of a cause as the function of a defect gets exhausted in obstructing the effectiveness of a guṇa (*sati kāraṇaguṇe pramāṇajñānaṁ jāyate nānyathetyanvayavya-tirekayoḥ pramāṇajñānapratibandhabhūtadoṣavirodhiguṇaviṣaya-tayā'nyathāsiddhivad doṣānvayavyatirekayorapyapramāṇaprati-bandharūpaguṇavirodhidoṣaviṣayatvenānyathāsiddhisambhavānna doṣānvayavyatirekābhyām aprāmāṇyasvatastvasādhanabādhana-sambhāvaneti bhāvaḥ,* ibid., pp. 34-5). This leads to the Buddhist view of self-validity of an invalid cognition which renders false the Mīmāṁsaka's view of the extrinsic nature of an invalid cog-nition. However, the pūrvapakṣin says that the Mīmāṁsaka should not consider the self-validity of an invalid cognition as a falsification of his view as that which is proved by an evidence should be accepted as a valid principle. According to the Buddhist, the syllogistic proposition presented by him is an evidence for the extrinsic nature of invalidity. Moreover, there is no contradiction of the view of the extrinsic nature of a valid cognition and the syllogistic proposition to this effect is as follows : A valid cognition is not dependent only on the causal conditions since it is a special cognition like an invalid cognition. The loss of the special character of a valid cognition is a deterrent to holding the contrary view. Another syllogism reads as follows : A valid cognition is produced by the factors other than those which are common to the means of both valid and invalid cognitions since it is a product like a pot. Just as something other than that which is common to both the valid and invalid instruments of cognition is required as in the case of a pot since it is a product, in the same manner a valid cognition, being a product, requires special conditions other than the causal ones. As explained in the foregoing, the extrinsic nature of a valid cogntion has been accepted by the Naiyāyikas and the Buddhists. This is the pūrvapakṣa view regarding the extrinsic nature of the validity of a cognition.

परतःप्रामाण्यनिरसनम्

उच्यते — न तावत् प्रमापरतस्त्वे आद्यः प्रयोगो मानम्। प्रत्यक्षादिना ज्ञानविशेषेण व्यभिचारात्। ननु सोऽपि प्रमाणत्वाद्धर्मी। अतः कथं व्यभिचारः? इत्थं – तत्र हि किं ज्ञानव्यक्तेः प्रमाव्यक्तितोऽस्ति विशेषः किं वा प्रमाव्यक्तिरेव ज्ञानव्यक्तिः? आद्ये — प्रत्यक्षज्ञानव्यक्त्या स्फुटो व्यभिचारः। द्वितीये तु जन्यापि ज्ञानरूपा प्रमा ज्ञानहेत्वधीना न भवतीत्युक्तं भवेत्। अतः स्फुटो बाधः। प्रत्यक्षान्यत्वं च विशेषणं ते व्यर्थम्। न चात्र विपक्षे बाधः कश्चित्। ज्ञानविशेषत्वं तु तटस्थोपाधिवशादुपपद्यत इति वक्ष्यते। अतिप्रसङ्गः कल्पनागौरवप्रसङ्गश्च प्रमापरतस्त्वे बाधकः। तस्मादाद्यः सावद्यः प्रयोगः। द्वितीयप्रयोगेऽपि बाधकतर्कसद्भावो विपक्षे बाधकतर्काभावश्च तुल्यः। भवत्पक्ष एवेश्वरप्रमायां प्रतिज्ञाबाधो हेत्वसिद्धिश्चोक्ता। अथैतत्परिजिहीर्षया किंचिद्विशेषणमुपाददीत तदापीतरपक्षे व्यर्थविशेषणतैव। तं वारयेद्विवादपदं ज्ञानं धर्मीति चेन्न, वक्ष्यमाणदिशा प्रत्यक्षज्ञानभागे बाधप्रसङ्गात्। एतेनैतदपि परास्तम्।

Refutation of the view of extrinsic nature of validity

Trans. : The siddhāntin explains : The first syllogistic proposition too fails to establish that the validity of a cognition is extrinsic as the reason, consisting in a cognition having a special characteristic, suffers from deviation as regards the perceptual cognition, etc. The pūrvapakṣin replies that the perception, etc., being pramāṇas, can also be classified as dharmin (*pakṣa*). In that case how can there be any violation in respect of the perceptual cognition (since, being dharmin, a perceptual cognition ceases to be the vipakṣa)? The siddhāntin explains the incidence of deviation by putting forward two alternatives: 1. Does a cognition in general differ from a valid cognition ? Or, 2. Is the valid cognition identical with a cognition in general? In the first alternative, there is an evident deviation of the reason in respect of a perceptual cognition (as it has a special characteristic but it is not dependent on conditions other than those which have produced it). In the second alternative, it comes to be stated as follows : Being also a product, the valid cognition of the form of a cognition in general is not dependent on its own causes. So, the bādha fallacy is evident. Also the qualification 'other than perception' used by you is redundant. Besides, there is no contradiction of the contrary view (that validity of a cognition is intrinsic). So far as the special characteristic of a cognition is concerned, it may be explained by invoking an indifferent qualification (*taṭastha upādhi*, that is, by construing the specific nature of a valid cognition as 'having an unknown content'). The defects of overextension and laxity in postulation are deterrent to the view of extrinsic nature of validity. Hence, the first syllogistic proposition is violative in nature. The second syllogistic proposition (*kāryatvānumāna*, see VV, p. 37) also equally suffers from *śaṅkitāprayojakatva* since there exists a contradictory argument (against the extrinsic nature of the validity of a cognition), whereas there is no such argument in respect of the contrary instance (that validity is intrinsic). In your case there is a contradiction (*bādha*) of the premise in the form of God's valid cognition (since it is not a product) and also there is a fallacy of reason known as *svarūpāsiddhi* (as the state of being a product does not exist in God's cognition). And if, in order to avoid this stance, some qualification (like other than God's cognition, etc.) is sought to be brought in, then also it would be rendered infructuous in respect of the other view (which has no place for God). In order to tide over this undesirable situation, if a cognition is made the subject of dispute, then also this fails to deliver as the perception part would be liable to be contradicted in the manner which is going to be explained. The other syllogistic proposition also stands dismissed thereby (see VV, p. 38).

Ann. : The siddhāntin now takes upon himself the task of analysing the arguments, adduced by the pūrvapakṣin in support of the view that the validity of a cognition is extrinsic, that is, it depends on the conditions other than those which generate it. The pūrvapakṣin has put forward two syllogistic propositions to prove his viewpoint : 1. A valid cognition is not dependent only on its causal factors since it is a cognition invested with a specific property like an invalid cognition. 2. The valid cognition is produced by the factors other than those which are common to both valid and invalid means of cognition since it is a product like a pot.

The siddhāntin does not accept that the first syllogistic proposition is capable of proving the extrinsic nature of a valid cognition since the reason 'cognition invested with a special characteristic' is fallacious as it resides in a perceptual cognition which does not have the absence of depending only on the causal conditions of a cognition, i.e. it depends only on its causal conditions. In other words the reason or the middle term exists in a perceptual cognition where the major term (*sādhya*) does not. (cf. *pratyakṣādau jñānaviśeṣatvamasti. na ca jñānahetumātrādhīnatvābhāvaḥ*, ibid., p. 36). When the second syllogism is taken into consideration, a valid cognition, identical with a cognition in general, does not remain a product of its causal factors alone as it is said to be brought into existence also by the conditions other than its own causal factors. Thus the absence of the sādhya comes to reside in the pakṣa. This is nothing but the stultification of the sādhya residing in the pakṣa. To escape this defect of sublation, if the qualification 'other than a perceptual cognition' is used, it does not serve any purpose as cognitions other than perception such as inferential cognition, verbal cognition, etc. are also invested with a special characteristic. So, the situation would continue to remain unaltered.

The siddhāntin continues to buttress the view that the validity of a cognition is intrinsically conditioned because there is no contradictory argument against it. So far as the specific character of a valid cognition is concerned, this can be explained by taking recourse to an indifferent qualification (*taṭastha upādhi*, that is, by construing the specific nature of a valid cognition as 'having a content not known before'. Cf. *pramāyā jñānahetumātrādhīnatve hetuviśeṣāt jñānaviśeṣatvābhāve'pyajñātārthaviṣayatvena tadupapattir uttaratra vyaktībhaviṣyatītyarthaḥ*, VV, p. 37).

The siddhāntin puts forward two more arguments against the view that validity is extrinsic : 1. Over-extension and 2. Laxity in postulation. According to Ānandajñāna, the first argument is deterrent to the syllogistic proposition put forward to prove the extrinsic nature of validity in the following way : If the special character of a valid cognition is attributed to the indifferent condition (*taṭastha upādhi*) as explained above, the contrary instance ceases to be contradicted. This constitutes over-extension as the same reason would be proving the contrary instance of the syllogistic proposition under consideration. The second argument against the extrinsic view of a valid cognition consists in laxity in the postulation of factors other than the causal ones in the production of a valid cognition when the production of a valid cognition can be explained only in terms of the causal conditions. Hence, postulating other conditions results in laxity (*jñānahetumātrādeva pramotpattisambhave tadanyaguṇādestaddhetutvakalpane gauravaṁ prasarediti bādhakāntaramāha*, ibid., p.37). On the basis of these arguments, the view that validity is extrinsically conditioned does not hold good. So far as the second syllogistic proposition is concerned, there is a defect of *śaṅkitāprayojakatva* because a contradictory argument exists against the view of the extrinsic nature of validity, whereas no such argument is available against the view that validity is intrinsic. Because of this fault, the reason is rendered incapable of proving the probandum for which it has been used. Moreover, the premise (*pratijñā*) would stand stultified if God's valid cognition is made the minor term and the fallacy of the reason known as *svarūpāsiddhi* would become applicable. To explain, God's cognition is eternal. Therefore it is neither a product nor is it dependent on other factors much less on causal ones. Thus the very premise (*pratijñā*) of the syllogistic proposition would remain partially contradicted for the reasons just mentioned. If, to escape this undesirable stance, some qualification such as 'other than God's cognition' is sought to be brought in, then also it would be rendered infructuous in respect of those who do not subscribe to the view that God exists. Again to tide over this situation, if 'cognition is made the subject of dispute', then the perception part of the pakṣa would still be contradicted as it is a cognition which has a specific characteristic while it has not been generated by conditions other than the causal ones. Consequently, it is of little use revising the minor term. Taking into consideration the points discussed here, it may be concluded that the syllogistic proposition using the state of being a product (*kāryatvahetu*, see supra pp. 56 and 59) stands rejected.

यदाहोदयनः — 'प्रमा ज्ञानहेत्वतिरिक्तहेत्वधीना कार्यत्वे सति ज्ञानविशेषत्वाद् अप्रमाव'दिति। अत्रापि हि प्रत्यक्षादिना व्यभिचारः। ईश्वराश्रयप्रमायां च बाधोऽविशिष्टः। हेत्वसिद्धिश्च तुल्या। अस्तु तर्हि प्रामाण्यम् ज्ञानहेत्वतिरिक्त-हेत्वधीनाश्रयं ज्ञानत्वन्यूनवृत्तित्वाद् अप्रामाण्यवदिति प्रयोगः। न। प्रत्यक्ष-त्वादिना व्यभिचारात्। नन्विन्द्रियाद्येव तदाश्रयस्यातिरिक्तं कारणम्। कियत्तर्हि ज्ञानं प्रति प्रयोजकम्। आत्ममनस्संयोग इति चेन्न। सुखादेरपि ज्ञानत्वप्रसङ्गात्।

Trans. : Udayana says, "A valid cognition is dependent on factors other than its causal ones since, being a product, it is invested with a special property like an invalid cognition." Here also there is a fallacy in respect of perception, etc. Also the contradiction (*bādha*) of the sādhya existing in the valid cognition of God is the same and same is the asiddhi fallacy of the reason (since, being eternal, it is not a product). (To avoid this), let then the syllogistic proposition be as follows : Validity exists in that (valid cognition) which is dependent on factors other than the causal ones as it exists in fewer loci than the state of being a cognition like invalidity. This syllogism does not help because it suffers from violation in respect of the universal property existing in a perceptual cognition, etc. (*pratyakṣatvādinā vyabhicārāt*, NRD, p. 38). In case the senses, etc. are to be construed as being other than the causal factors, then what is that which would occasion a cognition (in general)? If the contact of the soul with the mind is construed as being the cause of a cognition (in general), then the contingency of pleasure, etc. falling under the category of cognition would be incurred. (Hence, the defect of deviation in respect of the state of being a perceptual cognition remains as it is and the revised syllogistic proposition put forward by Udayana to prove the extrinsic nature of validity from the generation point of view does not succeed in proving the probandum.)

Ann. : Udayana in the Nyāyakusumāñjali uses a syllogistic proposition to prove the extrinsic nature of a valid cognition : A valid cognition depends upon causes other than those which produce the cognition since, being a product, it is also invested with a special characteristic like an invalid cognition. A defect (*doṣa*) accompanies the causal conditions of an invalid cognition just as the causal conditions of a valid cognition are accompanied by some merit (*guṇa*). Hence a valid cognition is extrinsic since it comes into existence because of *guṇa* which is over and above the conditions which generate a cognition in general. The siddhāntin does not agree with Udayana since there exists violation with regard to the perceptual cognition. The reason is that the perceptual cognition is generated only by its causal conditions but it is regarded as a special cognition. This means that the reason exists in perception, which may be valid, but the sādhya is absent in it. This is the fallacy known as *sādhāraṇa anaikāntika*. Moreover, the sādhya is also partially contradicted in the case of the valid cognition of God since, being eternal, it does not depend upon causal conditions much less having been produced by something other than its causal factors. The substantive part of the reason also does not exist in it as it is not subject to variation because of some additional property introduced into it. The revised form of the syllogistic proposition in which validity is made the minor term to prove its exrinsic nature would meet the same fate. The major term in this syllogism is validity which has a locus (valid cognition) dependent on conditions which are other than the causal ones (*jñānahetvatiriktahetvadhīnāśrayam*). The reason consists in 'existing in fewer loci than the state of being a cognition' (*jñāna-tvanyūnavṛttitvāt*). The illustration is the same, that is, invalidity. This syllogism also suffers from the defect of deviation. The state of being a perceptual cognition is located in the perceptual cognition which requires nothing more than its causal factors for its production. It exists in fewer loci than the state of being a cognition.

Thus the major term is absent in the perceptual cognition, whereas the reason resides in it. Thus the reason suffers from the fallacy known as *sādhāraṇa anaikāntika* since it is not concomitant with the sādhya. In order to maintain that there is a defect of deviation, the siddhāntin raises a query : If the sense organs, etc. are taken as constituting the extracausal conditions to bring about a cognition, then what is that which generates the cognition in general (*vyabhicāraṁ sādhayituṁ śaṅkate*, VV, p. 38)? If the contact of soul with the mind is construed as an occasioner (*prayojaka*) of a cognition in general, then even pleasure, pain, etc. would fall under the category of cognition, which is obviously not desirable. So, the senses, etc. should be included in the causal apparatus of a perceptual cognition and the fallacy known as *sādhāraṇa anaikāntika* as regards the perceptual cognition remains as it is. Consequently, the revised syllogistic proposition put forward to prove the extrinsic nature of validity from the cognition point of view is incapable of proving it.

यदपि कुसुमाञ्जलौ प्रमाज्ञप्तिपरतस्त्वे मानमुक्तम् 'प्रामाण्यं परतो ज्ञायते अनभ्यासदशायां सांशयिकत्वाद् अप्रामाण्यवदि'ति । विपक्षे च प्रामाण्यसंशयो न स्यादिति बाधः । ज्ञाननिश्चायकादेव तन्निश्चयप्राप्तेः, तदपि वार्तम् । धर्मिहेत्वोरसिद्धेः । आनुमानिक एव हि ते प्रामाण्यनिश्चयः, तन्निश्चयश्च तत्संशयपूर्वकः, अन्यथा सिषाधयिषाभावादनुमानासम्भवात् । संशयश्च निश्चयपुरस्सरः प्रसिद्धः । अतः प्रामाण्यसंशयनिश्चययोरन्योन्याश्रयत्वादनवस्थानाद्वा नैकमपि सिद्ध्यति ।

स्यान्मतं लोकसिद्धमेव प्रामाण्यम् , अतः क्वचित् संशयनिश्चयोपपत्तिः । अन्यथा तवाप्यप्रामाण्ये संशयनिश्चयानुपपत्तिस्तुल्या स्यात् । न । त्वया हि प्रमाणसिद्धमेवानुमानमङ्गीक्रियते । न च लोकाख्यमनुमानाद्यतिरिक्तं किञ्चिन्मानमस्ति । न च मानं विना ते किञ्चित् सिध्यति । अप्रामाण्यं त्वस्माकम् स्वरूपतो लोकप्रसिद्धं धर्मिविशेषे अनुमेयमिति नास्य प्रतिबन्दिता । किञ्च अर्थविशेषितमेव ज्ञानं प्रतीयते । तद्विशेषितत्वञ्च किञ्चित्सन्दिग्धम् । कुम्भोपलम्भस्याम्भो विषय आसीद् नवेत्यतो व्यभिचारो दुर्वारः । अनभ्यासदशायामिति च विशेषणं व्यर्थम् । असिद्धिपरिहारार्थं तदिति चेन्न, व्यभिचारनिवृत्यर्थत्वाद्धेतुविशेषणस्य यथाहुः - 'सम्भवे व्यभिचारे च विशेषणमर्थवदि'ति । असिद्ध्यसम्भवाच्चात्र न तत्परिहारो युक्तः । एकमेव हि ते प्रामाण्यं तच्चेत् क्वचित्सन्दिग्धं कथं तस्य तथात्वमसिद्धम् ।

Trans. : In Nyāyakusumāñjali a syllogism to prove the extrinsic nature of the cognition of validity has been given as follows : Validity is known extrinsically (*parataḥ*) since it is subject to doubt in an unfamiliar state (*anabhyāsadaśāyām*) like invalidity. The contradictory argument in respect of the contrary instance is : Validity is not subject to any doubt because that which ascertains a cognition also ascertains its validity. This also is not tenable as (in this way) the minor (*pakṣa*) and middle (*hetu*) terms would not be possible. Your certitude about the validity of a cognition is obtained from a syllogistic proposition. The certitude about validity is preceded by the doubt about it. Otherwise, in the absence of a desire to infer (*siṣādhayiṣā*) (or in other words, in the absence of the pakṣa), no syllogistic proposition would be possible. And it is well known that doubt is preceded by certitude. So, neither certitude nor doubt about validity would get established because of their mutual dependence or infinite regress.

In case only (that) validity which is current among people (*lokasiddha*) is taken (as the minor term), then doubt and certainty with respect to it could somehow be entertained. Otherwise doubt and certainty with regard to invalidity would be equally impossible also in your case. (The siddhāntin says :) No, you accept only the logically established syllogism. And there is no evidence (means of a valid cognition) known as *loka* (people) other than inference, etc. And you do not accept anything unless it is established by evidence. However, we do accept invalidity as it is current among the people and that becomes a specific pakṣa (*dharmiviśeṣa*) in which an inferable property exists. Therefore, this is not liable to contradiction. Moreover, only a cognition qualified by the content is known and the property that resides in that qualified cognition may somehow be taken as doubtful. When a pot is known, there exists a doubt whether water is contained in it or not. Hence deviation (with respect to the invariable occurrence of a pot with water) cannot be avoided. The qualification 'in a state of unfamiliarity' (*anabhyāsadaśāyām*) is redundant (whether this qualification belongs to the reason or to the statement of the proposition). If it is said that it is added in order to avoid the (partial) non-establishment (*bhāgāsiddhi*), then this is not proper since the purpose of adding a qualification is only to do away with (some kind of) deviation (*vyabhicāra*) as it has been said, "When there is a possibility of some violation, the qualification becomes meaningful." (Moreover,) there is no *asiddhi* fallacy here. Consequently, its removal is not required. There is only one validity according to your view and if that is in some respect doubtful, how can it not be same (i.e. how can it be definite in some other respect when, being single, it has no division).

Ann. : In this portion, the focus is on whether validity can be used as the minor term (*pakṣa*) or not. The siddhāntin takes up the syllogism of Udayana for discussion, adduces arguments and demonstrates that validity (*prāmāṇya*) cannot be used in the form of a minor term as the validity of a cognition is never in doubt. So, when validity cannot be taken as the minor term, how can its extrinsic nature be inferred? So far as the inference of the extrinsic nature of invalidity is concerned, the siddhāntin accepts invalidity as it is current among the people and says that it can be used as the minor term in order to infer its extrinsic nature. The following discussion centres round this issue.

The syllogistic proposition which Udayana has put forward in Nyāyakusumāñjali to prove the extrinsic nature of the cognition of validity is as follows : Validity is extrinsically known since there is a doubt about it in an unfamiliar situation (*anabhyāsadaśāyām*). If the validity of a cognition were known intrinsically, there would not be any doubt about it. But we encounter doubt regarding our own cognition whether it is true or not. Consequently, the validity of a cognition is not known intrinsically. As per the view of self-validity, what produces a cognition also ascertains its validity. Hence, there is no room for doubt and in the absence of a doubt, there would not be any pakṣa and hence no syllogistic proposition to infer its extrinsic nature. Moreover, the certitude which is obtained with the help of a syllogistic proposition is obviously preceded by a doubt and it is well-known that the doubt is also preceded by certitude as in the man-post illustration. In this way, both doubt and certitude are mutually dependent and thus neither of them gets established. Thus in the absence of the necessary conditions of a syllogistic proposition, there is no possibility of inferring the extrinsic nature of validity.

In order to tide over this hurdle, if validity current among the people (*lokasiddha prāmāṇya*) was taken as the subject of dispute, then a doubt about it could somehow be entertained. Otherwise, the pūrvapakṣin points out, certitude and doubt would equally be untenable in respect of invalidity, which the siddhāntin holds to be extrinsic because of its having been brought about by a defect over and above the causal factors. The siddhāntin, however, drives home his point of view saying that, although a case of syllogistic proposition with regard to invalidity is possible, it is not possible with regard to validity as the pūrvapakṣin does not subscribe to anything that is not proved by an evidence. Despite this, if validity current among the people is taken recourse to, then it could be included either in perception or in inference or in verbal testimony (cf. *lokasya pratyakṣāntarbhāve prāmāṇyasya pratyakṣatve tatprāmāṇyasyāpi pratyakṣāntaraviṣayatvenānavasthā. anumānāntarbhāve ca prāmāṇyasyānumeyatve parasparāśrayatvāditadavasthameva. vākyāntarbhāve prāmāṇyasya tadgamyatve tatprāmāṇyasyāpi vākyāntaragamyatvādanavasthaiveti bhāvaḥ*, VV, p. 40). However, due to the fault of infinite regress or mutual dependence as pointed out in the Vedāntaviveka, the loka as the means of a valid cognition, to wit, *prāmāṇa* cannot be regarded as tenable. In the absence of that, validity cannot be construed as the minor term (*pakṣa*) and hence no syllogistic proposition is possible to prove the extrinsic nature of validity.

However, the pūrvapakṣin says that, even on the view of self-validity, a case can be made out for a syllogism as the property existing in a cognition qualified by the content could be taken as doubtful even though it is comprehended with the same causal apparatus by which the cognition of that content is comprehended (*ghaṭajñānaṁ paṭajñānamiti jñānasvarūpamavagamyate tathā ca ghaṭādyarthaviśeṣitatvaṁ jñānadharmo jñānajñāpakasāmagrīmātrajñāpyaḥ*, ibid., p. 41). To illustrate : When one sees a pot full of water, the water is cognised with the help of the same causal conditions by which the pot has been cognised. Even then one person may be sure about water in the pot and the other may not be so. (*ambhasaḥ kumbhagrāhakasāmagrīgrāhyatvāniyame'pi pūrṇakumbhopalambhe kumbhāmbhasa uktasāmagrīgrāhyatvaniyamāt. ekasya pūrṇakumbholambhe tanniyame'pyanyasyasaṁśayadarśanāt*, ibid., p. 41). In the same way, validity can also be taken as being subject to doubt and consequently, a syllogistic proposition can legitimately be formulated to prove the extrinsic nature of validity. However, the siddhāntin says that the property existing in the qualified cognition of a pot full of water cannot be put on a par with the validity of a cognition as the water in a pot is not necessarily known with the same causal conditions by which the pot is known (*ambhasaḥ kumbhagrāhakasāmagrīmātragrāhyatvānaṅgīkārāt*, CS, p. 210).

Thus having dismissed the contention of the pūrvapakṣin that validity can be taken as the minor term, the siddhāntin accepts invalidity as it is current among the people. This, however, is not to be construed as an argument binding on the pūrvapakṣin to accept validity on the basis of the loka evidence to prove its extrinsic nature. The reason is that, according to him, only that which is logically established is acceptable. The siddhāntin makes short work of the very basis of a syllogistic proposition which the Naiyāyika uses to prove the extrinsic nature of validity by pointing out the fault of mutual dependence with regard to doubt and certainty as explained above. In the absence of a doubt there would not be any syllogism because, without a doubt, there would not be any pakṣa, the very basis of a syllogistic proposition.

The Naiyāyika subscribes to that which is logically obtained. On the other hand the siddhāntin accepts the popular view about invalidity. According to him, the popular belief can become the basis of a syllogistic proposition as it does not confer definite status on invalidity. Thus, the possibility of a doubt being there, a case for inference can be made out to infer the extrinsic nature of the invalidity of cognition.

The siddhāntin continues to criticise the syllogistic proposition presented by Udayana. He points out that the use of the expression *anabhyāsadaśāyām* as a qualification of the reason is used to do away with the asiddhi of the reason as there is no doubt about the definite knowledge of a pot, etc. In this situation, to establish the residence of the hetu in the pakṣa, the qualifying term *anabhyāsadaśāyām* (*abhyāsadaśāpannaghaṭādijñāneṣu sāṁśayikatvābhāvena hetorasiddhitā tannirāsārthaṁ viśeṣaṇam*, VV, p. 41). The siddhāntin says that the use of the qualifying term *anabhyāsadaśāyām* to escape the partial non-establishment of the minor term is not justified (cf. *bhāgāsiddhiparihārārthaṁ hetuviśeṣaṇamanucitam*, ibid., p. 41) as the qualifying term is used only to do away with some deviation (*vyabhicāra*) as it has been said so by the elders : When there is a possibility of some deviation, the use of a qualifying term assumes significance. (See *sambhave ca vyabhicāre viśeṣaṇamarthavat*, NRD,

p. 41). As such, to avoid the fault of partial non-establishment, to wit, *bhāgāsiddhi* is not a substantial ground for the use of a qualification. However, to buttress his position, the pūrvapakṣin presents a situation in which a qualification is said to be used to dispense with the fault of asiddhi : The eyes are born of the fire since, being a substance, they manifest only the colour among the qualities colour, etc. like a lamp (*cakṣustaijasaṁ rūpādiṣu madhye rūpasyaiva vyañjakadravyatvāt pradīpavadityatra.....hetuviśeṣaṇam asiddhinivārakam*, VV, p. 41). The eyes can perceive a substance besides the colour. So, if the hetu was given as *rūpasyaiva vyañjakadravyatvāt*, then it would not be there in the pakṣa, that is 'the eyes'. To avoid this fallacy of asiddhi, the qualifying phrase *rūpādiṣu madhye* has been included. But such is not the case in the present context as there is no asiddhi. So, in the absence of any asiddhi, the use of the qualifying term *anabhyāsadaśāyām* to do away with that is not at all required (*prakṛte cāsiddherasambhavānna tannivṛttyarthaṁ viśeṣaṇamityarthaḥ*, ibid., p. 42). So, the qualifying term having been proved redundant, the syllogism put forward by Udayana gets further weakened.

अथेदं प्रतिज्ञाविशेषणं तदापि व्यर्थमेव तत्। सर्वत्रैव हि ते प्रामाण्यं परतो ज्ञायते। न त्वनभ्यस्तस्थल एव। न चात्र विपक्षे बाधः कश्चित्। प्रामाण्यस्य हि ज्ञानसमानज्ञापकत्वेऽपि दोषात् संशयोपपत्तिः ज्ञानस्यार्थविशेषितत्वस्येव, तस्मात् प्रमाज्ञप्तिपरतस्त्वेऽपि न किञ्चिन्मानमस्ति। एवं व्यवहृतिपरतस्त्वमपि विमानमेव। अथ मानं प्रामाण्यं परतो व्यवहारगोचरः ज्ञानत्वेतरत्वे सति ज्ञानधर्मत्वाद् अप्रामाण्यवद्। न। ज्ञानस्यार्थविशेषितत्वेन व्यभिचारात्। तदन्यत्वविशेषणेऽपि ज्ञानस्यार्थविशेषणत्वेन व्यभिचारस्तुल्यः। अतः सर्वतः प्रामाण्यपरतस्त्वं मानाभावादसम्भवि।

Trans. : If the expression *anabhyāsadaśāyām* is to qualify the statement of the proposition (i.e. *pratijñā*), then also it is redundant since, according to you, validity everywhere is known extrinsically, and not only in a state of non-familiarity (*anabhyastạsthale*). And there is no deterrent here to the contrary view. Even if it is accepted that validity is known by the same conditions that make the cognition known (that is, if validity of a cognition is known intrinsically), then also the existence of doubt about it may be justified because of some defect as in the case of the property residing in a cognition qualified by its content (as explained in the foregoing section). Therefore, it may be accepted that there is also no evidence for the extrinsic nature of the cognition of validity. In the same way, there is no evidence for the extrinsic view of the use of validity (i.e. that validity is extrinsic from vyavahāra point of view). And if a syllogism is adduced – validity becomes an object of vyavahāra extrinsically since it is a property of a cognition at the same time being different from the state of being a cognition like invalidity – then this evidence does not help because it suffers from deviation in respect of the property residing in the cognition qualified by the content. If the reason is qualified by 'other than the state of being a cognition qualified by its content', the same fault of deviation becomes applicable in respect of the cognition having the state of being a qualifier of the content. Therefore, from all the points of view, the extrinsic nature of validity is not possible because there is no evidence to this effect.

Ann. : After the siddhāntin has proved that the qualification 'in a state of unfamiliarity' of the reason is redundant, he further criticises the pūrvapakṣin by pointing out that the term 'in a state of unfamiliarity' (*anabhyāsadaśāyām*) also does not serve any purpose when it is made to qualify 'the statement of the propositioin' in the syllogism presented above. The reason is that this qualification lacks justification since, according to the Naiyāyika, validity is known extrinsically in all situations, and not only in a particular unfamiliar situation. The qualification has significance only when it performs the function of dispensing with some kind of deviation but there is nothing of this sort in the present case. Moreover, there is no contradictory argument against the contrary viewpoint. In other words the view of the intrinsic nature of validity remains uncontradictable. Although validity is known from the same conditions by which a particular cognition is known, still there can be doubt about it because of some deficiency in the causal conditions. Hence the extrinsic nature of validity from the cognition point of view is not possible as there is no evidence in this respect. The author now touches upon another aspect. He says that just as a cognition and its validity are intrinsic in respect of their comprehension in the same manner a cognition and its validity are also intrinsic in respect of their practical usage. It means that the conditions which are responsible for using a cognition are also instrumental in the use of the validity of that cognition. When the pūrvapakṣin uses a syllogistic proposition to prove the extrinsic nature of the use of a cognition and its validity, the siddhāntin shows that it is deficient. The syllogism used by the pūrvapakṣin is as follows : Validity becomes an object of practical use extrinsically since it is a property of cognition, at the same time being different from the state of being a cognition like invalidity. This syllogism is not faultless. It suffers from deviation in respect of the property residing in a cognition qualified by its content since it is not extrinsic as has been explained in the foregoing section. Whether the cognition is qualified by the content or whether it is made to qualify the content; in both the cases the property residing in the cognition suffers from the *anaikāntika* fallacy. To explain, the property of the cognition qualified by the content (*arthaviśeṣitatva*) is also a property that inheres in a cognition (*jñānadharma*) which is different from the state of being a cognition (*jñānatvetara*) but the sādhya (being extrinsic from vyavahāra point of view) does not exist in it. Hence the fallacy known as *anaikāntika* exists. In the same manner the same fallacy becomes applicable even when the cognition is made to qualify the content. The state of being a qualifier (*arthaviśeṣaṇatva*) is also a property of the cognition which is different from the state of being a cognition but it does not have the sādhya in it as explained just now (cf. *jñānasya arthaviśeṣaṇatvena vyabhicārastulyaḥ*, VV, p. 43). Hence the syllogism adduced to prove the extrinsic nature of validity from vyavahāra point of view is not well-equipped to prove the probandum. So, the extrinsic nature of validity from the point of view of practical activity based on it remains unsubstantiated.

प्रामाण्यस्य उत्पत्तिस्वतस्त्वे प्रयोगाः

प्रामाण्यस्य स्वतस्त्वेऽनुमानम् — प्रामाण्यं ज्ञानहेतुमात्रजन्याश्रयम् अप्रामाण्येतरत्वे सति ज्ञानैकधर्मत्वाद् ज्ञानत्ववत्। दोषजत्वेन व्यभिचारो मा भूदिति ज्ञानैकधर्मत्वमुक्तम्। तद्धि व्याधेरपि धर्मः। तथा प्रामाण्यम् उक्तविधम् अप्रामाण्येतरत्वे सति ज्ञानत्वन्यूनवृत्तित्वात् प्रत्यक्षत्ववत्। प्रत्यक्षं हि ज्ञान-हेतुमात्रजन्यमित्युक्तम्। तेन नात्र दृष्टान्ते साध्यविरहः।

Syllogisms to prove the intrinsic nature of validity

Trans. : The syllogistic proposition to infer the intrinsic nature of validity is : Validity inheres in that (cognition) which is generated only by its causal conditions since it is a property of the cognition only, being at the same time different from invalidity like the state of being a cognition (*jñānatva*). The inclusion of the expression 'property of cognition only' is to do away with deviation in respect of 'that which is produced by faults' since the property, which is caused by faults, i.e. deficient humours, exists in a disease also. Thus (another syllogism to prove the intrinsic nature of validity is) : Validity is of the said kind (that is, *jñānahetumātrajanyāśrayam*) since it is different from invalidity and at the same time is less extensive than the state of being a cognition (*jñānatva*) like the state of being a perceptual cognition (*pratyakṣatva*). For it has been already said that a perceptual cognition is produced only by its causal conditions and hence the sādhya is not absent in the illustration.

Ann. : After rejecting the view of the pūrvapakṣin that validity is extrinsic from generation, cognition and usage points of view, the siddhāntin now puts forward syllogistic propositions in support of the intrinsic nature of validity from the generation point of view lest his view of the intrinsic nature of the validity of a cognition should meet the same fate (*svapakṣasyāpi parapakṣavadupekṣaṇīyatvaśaṅkāṁ śithilayati — prāmāṇyamiti,* VV, p. 43). To escape the fault of proving that which has already been proved (*siddhasādhyatā*), the term *mātra* has been inserted in the probandum as the locus of that which has been generated by the causal conditions of a cognition accompanied by the absence of demerits is also a locus of that which is produced by the causal conditions of a cognition (*doṣābhāvādisahakṛtajñānahetujanyāśrayatve'pi prāmāṇyasya jñānahetujanyāśrayatvamastīti siddhasādhyatā. sā mā bhūditi mātrapadam,* ibid., p. 43). This is the reaon why validity has been mentioned to inhere in a cognition which is produced only by its causal factors. So 'having the locus which is produced only by its own causal apparatus' is the major term (*sādhya*). The reason has two parts. One is that it is a property only of cognition and the second is that it is different from invalidity since invalidity, according to the siddhāntin, is extrinsic in nature. If this was not mentioned, then the reason would also over-extend to invalidity which is also the property of a cognition, though opposite to validity. The very mention that validity is the property of a cognition only helps save the fault of over-extension of the reason to a disease which is produced by some disorder in humours, but which is not the property of a cognition. The second syllogistic proposition also proves the intrinsic nature of validity. Validity resides in that which is produced only by its causal factors, being different from invalidity (which is caused by some demerit in addition to the causal factors and hence extrinsic) and at the same time existing in fewer loci than those in which the state of being a cognition resides (*jñānatvanyūnavṛtti*). It has already been mentioned before that perception, though being a special kind of cognition, is held to be produced only by its causal factors. This is the reason why the property of being a perceptual cognition (*pratyakṣatva*) has been given as an illustration since it does not suffer from the defect of the sādhya being absent in it. A proper illustration is essential to prove the sādhya, that is, the intrinsic nature of validity.

अप्रामाण्यस्य स्वतस्त्वनिराकरणम्

नन्वेवमप्रामाण्यस्य स्वतस्त्वंप्राप्तिप्रसङ्गः, न। परस्यैवं प्रयोगासम्भवात्। बौद्धेन हि दोषो ज्ञानहेत्वतिरिक्तो बुद्धिरूपस्य बहिष्ट्वभाने हेतुरेष्टव्यः। अन्यथातिप्रसङ्गात्। अतः कथं तद्वैपरीत्यं तेन साध्यते।

ननु दोषोऽप्रमाणज्ञानस्य हेतुः चक्षुरिव प्रत्यक्षज्ञानस्य। न। दोषस्य ज्ञानाहेतुत्वेऽनुपपत्त्यभावात्। चक्षुषस्तथात्वे तूक्तो दोषः, सुखादेरपि ज्ञानत्वप्रसङ्ग इति। यच्चोक्तं भवत एवैवमनुमानमस्त्विति, तदपि दोषस्य ज्ञानाहेतुत्वोपपादनेन निरस्तम्। ज्ञानहेतुमात्रजन्यत्वसाधने च भ्रमस्य दोषजन्यत्वप्रसिद्धिबाधः। विपर्ययापर्यवसानाच्च नायं प्रसङ्गः। उक्तश्च प्रमापरतस्त्वेऽनुमानासम्भवः। अत एव न बाधप्रतिरोधौ शङ्कनीयौ।

Refutation of the view of intrinsic nature of invalidity

Trans. : Thus invalidity would become liable to be intrinsic in nature. No, since the other (pūrvapakṣin) cannot use a syllogistic proposition in this way. The reason is that the Buddhist would have to postulate a defect besides the causal factors of a cognition to explain the external appearance of the object that has the form of consciousness (*buddhirūpasya*). Otherwise, this would incur the fault of over-extension (i.e. the internal apprehension of the silver would be rendered erroneous, see *āntarasyāpi rajatapratibhāsasya tathātvaprasaṅgāt*, VV, p. 45). So, why is then the opposite (the extrinsic nature of an invalid cognition because of the postulation of a defect as a cause) being proved by him?

Let (then) a defect be the cause of an invalid cognition just as the eyes are of a perceptual cognition. No, this is not so as there is no impropriety in assuminng that a defect does not constitute a cause in the generation of a cognition. But if the eyes are not accepted as a cause, then this would be tantamount to a defect, which is that pleasure, etc. would have to be understood as a cognition. And the statement 'let your syllogism remain as it is' (see NRD, p. 34) has been discarded by explaining that a defect does not constitute a cause in the generation of a cognition. If an invalid cognition is sought to be proved as produced only by the causal factors of a cognition, then this would contradict the established fact that an erroneous cognition is generated by a defect. This would not lead to a contingent situation (*prasaṅga*) as this does not result in an opposite view (that validity is extrinsic). It has already been made clear that no syllogism is possible in support of the view that a valid cognition is extrinsically conditioned. Therefore, neither the fault of contradiction nor that of having a counter-syllogism should be apprehended against the intrinsic view of the validity of a cognition.

Ann. : The Buddhist holds the view that the invalidity of a cognition is intrinsically conditioned. In this context the syllogism put forward by him is as follows : Invalidity resides in that cognition which is generated only by its causal conditions since, being different from validity, it is the property of a cognition only, like the universal that resides in a cognition (cf. *aprāmāṇyam jñānasāmagrīmātrajanyavṛtti prāmāṇyetaratve sati jñānaikadharmatvāj jñāna*[*tva*]*vat*, ibid., VV, 44). Two alternatives are possible in respect of this syllogistic proposition of the pūrvapakṣin. Either it is to prove his own point of view or it is to land the other in an undesirable situation (*kimidaṁ svapakṣasādhanaṁ kiṁ vā parasyāniṣṭāpādanamiti*. VV, pp. 44-5). The first alternative is simply not possible because he cannot use such an argument in his own favour. According to him, the internal object which is of the form of consciousness appears as external. The consciousness externalises the internal object owing to some defect and as a consequence it has to be construed as erroneous. If it is accepted that this is generated only by the causal factors, then all instances of cognition would be rendered erroneous. The Buddhist holds that the cognition having an external content is not valid. If a cognition which is generated by its causal factors is accepted as invalid, then the internal cognition of an object (say silver) would be invalid too (cf. *jñānasāmagrīmātrajanyasyāpi bahiṣṭvajñānasyāprāmāṇyābhyupagamāt. na caitadiṣṭam. āntarasyāpi rajatapratibhāsya tathātvaprasaṅgāt*, ibid., p. 45). In this way there is an argument against the Buddhist view, but the intrinsic nature of an invalid cognition is not at all supported by a substantial argument. If a defect is accepted to be a causal factor in the generation of an invalid cognition, then the opposite of what the Buddhist holds would be proved. Moreover, a defect cannot be put on a par with the sense organs as, the pūrvapakṣin suggests, in the case of a perceptual cognition. The pūrvapakṣiṅ's view is that there is no impropriety in holding that a defect is non-causal with regard to a cognition even though such a status has been denied to the eyes. To expain, if the eyes are said to be non-causal with respect to a visual perception, in other words, if the sense organs are not accepted to constitute the causal apparatus of respective cognitions, then only a contact of the mind with the soul would constitute the cause of all cognitions (NRD, P. 39). In that case, pleasure, pain, etc. also would have to be understood as having the property of a cognition (cf. *doṣasya jñānāhetutve 'nupapattyabhāvāt. cakṣuṣastathātve tūkto doṣaḥ sukhāderapi jñānatvaprasaṅga iti*, ibid., p. 45). The second alternative is also not possible. To explain, by construing a defect as non-causal, if the Buddhist seeks to prove the intrinsic nature of an invalid cognition, then he is not justified in holding such a view since a defect has to be accepted as a cause of an invalid cognition by virtue of the principle of positive and negative concomitance (cf. *anvayavyatirekābhyāṁ doṣasya taddhetutvādhigamāt*, VV, p. 45). Consequently, a defect cannot be treated on a par with the causal factors such as the sense organs, etc. It has to be a factor over and above the causal factors of a cognition. The siddhāntin further points out saying that, if it is said that an erroneous cognition is produced only by the causal factors of a cognition, then the established fact that an erroneous cognition is caused by a defect has to be abandoned. Since this does not culminate in the opposite standpoint that validity is extrinsic, the intrinsic view of invalidity would remain unestablished (*prāmāṇyaṁ svataścedaprāmāṇyamapi svataḥ syāditi prasaṅgasya prāmāṇyaparatastve paryavasānābhāvāt prasaṅgābhāsatvamiti,* VV, p. 46). It has already been made clear that there is no possibility of using a syllogistic proposition to prove the extrinsic nature of a valid cognition (see NRD. p. 43). The siddhāntin concludes saying that there is neither the fault of contradiction nor that of having a counter-syllogism against the view that the validity of cognition is intrinsically conditioned.

न च हेत्वसिद्धिः । तत्पक्षधर्मतायाः स्पष्टत्वात् । न चान्यथासिद्धता । उपाधेरसम्भवात् । अथ प्रमाणाप्रमाणसाधारण्यमुपाधिः । न चास्य साधनव्यापकता, प्रामाण्ये साधनभावेऽप्युपाधेरभावात् । साध्यसमव्याप्तिता तु ज्ञानत्व एवातिस्पष्टेति । न । साध्याव्यापकत्वात् । प्रत्यक्षत्वं ह्युक्तनीत्या साध्ययुक्तम् । न च तत्रायमुपाधिरस्तीति साध्याव्याप्तिः ।

न च शङ्कितोपाधिता । बाधकतर्काभावाद् । विपक्षे बाधकतर्कस्याभिहितत्वाच्च । ननु प्रमायां ज्ञानहेतुमात्रजन्यत्वे कथं ज्ञानविशेषता? तटस्थोपाधिवशादिति ब्रूमः । उपाधिश्चाज्ञातोऽर्थः । हन्त गतं धारावाहिकज्ञानानां प्रामाण्येन, न हि तेषामर्थभेदोऽस्ति । एतेन प्रमाणसंप्लवो व्याख्यातः । स इत्यज्ञातविषया स्मृतिश्च प्रमाणं स्याद् । न । पूर्वज्ञानविषयस्याप्युत्तरकाले अज्ञातत्वात्तद्ग्राहिणः प्रामाण्योपपत्तेः । संप्लवस्तु प्रलीयत एव । मानानामज्ञातविषयभेदात् संप्लवासम्भवात्, क्वचिन्न प्रलीयते । वह्न्यादिमात्रावलम्बनाभेदात् स्मृतेश्च नाज्ञातार्थता सम्भवेत् । संस्कारमात्रजत्वात् । स इत्याकारस्य गत्यन्तरं परेणापि वर्णनीयम् ।

Trans. : And the reason does not suffer from the fallacy of svarūpāsiddhi because its residence in the *pakṣa* is obvious. And the reason is not a different kind of asiddha, that is *vyāpyatvāsiddha* since there is no upādhi. Let then the state of being common to both the means of valid and invalid cognitions be an upādhi. It (upādhi) does not have the state of being concomitant with the reason since the reason exists in validity (*pakṣa*) whereas the upādhi does not. Its (*upādhi*'s) state of being concomitant bothways (*sama*) with the sādhya is evident only in the cognition-universal (*jñānatva*). No, this is not so since it is not concomitant with the sādhya. The state of being of a perceptual cognition (*pratyakṣatva*) is connected with the sādhya in accordance with the principle already mentioned. And the upādhi does not exist there. Hence it is not concomitant with the sādhya.

There is no ground for doubting the existence of an upādhi because there is no contradictory argument (against the sādhya in the pakṣa) and because a contradictory argument against the contrary view has already been mentioned.

When a valid cognition is accepted as having been generated only by the causal factors of a cognition, how can its specific character be accounted for? (The siddhāntin says that) we can explain it on the basis of an indifferent associate condition (*taṭastha upādhi*) of the form of an unknown content (of a cognition). Oh! Then the validity of a continuous series of cognitions would just vanish since there is no difference in the contents of the cognitions which take place in a cotinuous succession. This explains the mixture theory of the means of valid cognitions (*pramāṇasaṁplava*). And (then) the memory having an unknown content in the form of 'that' would be construed as valid. No, the content of the past cognition remains unknown in the succeeding moments and, therefore, the validity of the cognition having 'that' as its content could be taken as such. The mixture theory also does tend to disappear since there is no possibility of mixture because the unknown contents of the means of valid cognitions are different. In some cases it does not disappear since fire, etc. do not differ (while becoming the content of different means of cognition); and there is no possibility of an unknown content in memory since it is generated only by impressions. The other aspect of the the content in the form of 'that' should be explicated by the other (disputant).

Ann. : The siddhāntin gives a reply to the objections raised against the syllogism which he has put forward to prove the intrinsic nature of the validity of a cognition. He says that neither of the reasons suffers from the svarūpāsiddhi fallacy as both the hetus (1) *aprāmāṇyetaratve sati jñānaikadharmatvāt* and (2) *aprāmāṇyetaratve sati jñānatvanyūnavṛttitvāt* exist in validity (*prāmāṇya*) which constitutes the minor term (*pakṣa*). The reason also does not suffer from the fallacy of vyāpyatvāsiddhi as there is no upādhi to vitiate it. The pūrvapakṣin makes an attempt to defend his position by invoking an upādhi in respect of the reasons used in the syllogistic propositions put forward to prove the intrinsic nature of validity. He further clarifies saying that the state of being that which is common to the means of valid and invalid cognitions fulfils the criterion of an upādhi since it is not concomitant with the reason as the upādhi does not exist in validity, whereas the reason exists in it. The concomitance of the upādhi with the sādhya bothways (*samavyāpti*) is obvious in the state of being a cognition (*jñānatva*). In other words, the upādhi is concomitant with the sādhya and vice versa (*yatra jñānahetujanyāśrayatvaṁ tatra pramāṇāpramāṇasādhāraṇatvaṁ yatra cāyamupādhistatredaṁ sādhyamiti vyāptiḥ jñānatvādāvativyaktetyarthaḥ,* VV, p. 46). The siddhāntin does not accept this since the proposed upādhi does not fulfil the criterion of being an upādhi as there is no concomitance of the proposed upādhi with the sādhya. To explain, the state of being a perceptual cognition is associated with the sādhya in consonance with the principle as discussed by Ānandajñāna but the upādhi does not happen to be there. The reason is that Ānandajñāna interprets the perceptual cognition as an immediate valid experience in which the assumed upādhi (*pramāṇāpramāṇasādhāraṇatvam*) obviously cannot exist (cf. *samyagaparokṣānubhavaḥ pratyakṣam,* ibid., p. 47). Hence, obviously there is no concomitance of the upādhi with the sādhya. So, this ceases to be an upādhi. Moreover, there is no ground for even doubting the existence of an upādhi because of the absence of a contradictory argument against the view of the intrinsic nature of validity and because it has already been mentioned that there is a contradictory argument against the contrary view that validity is extrinsic. In this case neither of the unfavourable conditions mentioned above is available (*prakṛte tu nobhayamasti,* ibid., p. 47). On the contrary there is no contradictory argument against the siddhāntin's position and also there exists a substantial argument against the contrary view of the pūrvapakṣin. Hence the reason is well-equipped to prove the intrinsic nature of validity.

The pūrvapakṣin now raises an objection against the special characteristic of a valid cognition that it is generated only by the causal conditions of a cognition. The siddhāntin replies that the special nature of a valid cognition can be explained on the basis of an indifferent associate condition, to wit, *taṭastha upādhi,* which is nothing but the state of being an unknown content of a valid cognition. However, on this view, it would be difficult to explain the validity of the continuous perceptual cognitions (*dhārāvāhikajñāna*) since there is no difference in the contents of these continuous series of perceptual cognitions. Nevertheless, a continuous series of cognitions is admitted to be valid since the cognition of a succeeding moment has an unknown content as it is qualified by its being present in the succeeding moment. Hence, the content of the succeeding moment can be construed as being unknown and the validity of the cognition belonging to the succeeding moment could remain intact. If we do not accept difference among the contents of the continuous series of cognitions, then the mixture theory (*pramāṇasaṁplava*) would become applicable but, since the content of every member of the series of cognition is new, there is no incurrence of such a contingency.

An objection can be raised that memory may have an unknown content and, thus, it could be construed as a valid cognition. None-theless, the memory may be accepted as true but it cannot be accepted as a valid cognition since its content does not exist at the moment when memory is generated by the impressions of the experience of something in the past and it is often in the form of 'that'. How can the content in the form of the unknown 'that' be apprehended in memory? This problem is referred to here in *sa ityākārasya gatyantaraṁ pareṇāpi varṇanīyam* (NRD, p. 48). Ānanda-jñāna discusses various aspects of the nature of this content and by the process of elimination concludes that this unknown content of the past is made manifest by the witness consciousness (*pūrva-kālaviṣayo'yaṁ sākṣyavabhāsa iti,* VV, p. 48).

गुणस्य दोषाभावस्य च प्रमाहेतुत्वनिराकरणम्

नन्वौपाधिकत्वे प्रमाया उपाधिजन्यत्वात् परतस्त्वापत्तिः। न। तस्यास्तज्जन्य-त्वाभावात्। तर्ह्युपाधिर्व्यर्थः। न। प्रमाभेदे तच्छब्दप्रवृत्तौ च निमित्तत्वात्। अतो न प्रामाण्यस्वतस्त्वे विरोधगन्धोऽपि। विरुद्धत्वासाधारणत्वे हेतोः सपक्षवृत्त्या निरस्ते। नापि साधारणानैकान्तता। व्यभिचाराभावात्।

Refutation of the view that merit and absence of defects are the causes of a valid cognition

Trans. : If an upādhi has a role to play in the generation of a valid cognition, then having been generated by an upādhi, the valid cognition would be taken as extrinsically conditioned. (The siddhāntin says :) No. A valid cognition is not generated by an upādhi. Then the postulation of an upādhi would serve no purpose. (The siddhāntin says :) No, (it is not without any purpose) since the upādhi is a cause for the use of the term pramā for a cognition in order to distinguish it from an invalid cognition. Therefore, not even an iota of contradiction exists so far as the intrinsic nature of validity is concerned. The fallacies, viruddhatva and asādhāraṇatva are discarded on account of the reason being present in the sapakṣa. The reason also does not suffer from the fallacy known as *sadhāraṇa anaikāntika* as it does not deviate from the sādhya.

Ann. : This has already been discussed that a valid cognition has a specific characteristic and therefore it should have come into existence on account of some specific quality existing in the causal factors. The Naiyāyika attributes this to the merit of the causal conditions and subscribes to the view that the character of a valid cognition is extrinsic. It is in this background that the pūrvapakṣin's view has been presented in the following manner : The valid cognition is due to an upādhi which consists in the being of an unknown content. The pūrvapakṣin says that the generation of a valid cognition is dependent on this unknown content which is responsible for designating a particular cognition as valid. Hence its generation should be accepted as extrinsically conditioned. The siddhāntin does not agree and says that the upādhi in the form of an unknown content does not constitute causality since the valid cognition is not generated by it (*tasyāstajjanyatvābhāvāt*, NRD, p. 49). Since the unknown content is not accepted as a casue, it does not mean that the upādhi is rendered purposeless. The reason is that it serves the purpose of using the term 'valid' with reference to the cognition that has an unknown content. In this way a valid cognition, though generated by its own causal conditions, is still regarded as a valid cognition because of its unknown content and hence its character as a valid cognition remains intrinsic. There is absolutely nothing to assume that a valid cognition has the property of being extrinsically condtioned because there is no substantial argument against the intrinsic nature of the validity of a cognition. The fallacies of the reason known as *viruddhatva* and *asādhāraṇa anaikāntikatva* do not exist at all since the reason itself exists in *jñānatva* and *pratyakṣatva* which are given as illustrations in the syllogistic propositions. The *sādhāraṇa anaikāntika* fallacy also does not exist since the reason remains concomitant with the sādhya. In other words, the state of being a property only of a cognition, which is at the same time different from invalidity, exists in validity (*pakṣa*). Likewise in the other syllogistic proposition, the probans, which consists in being different from invalidity and in being less extensive than the state of being a cognition, also resides in the pakṣa. Thus the reasons are well-equipped to prove that validity is intrinsic.

नन्वेवमपि गुणान्वयव्यतिरेकबाधो दुर्वारः । न । तयोरन्यथासिद्धत्वात् । दोषो हि प्रामाण्यप्रतिबन्धकः, तद्विरोधी च गुणः, अतस्तदन्वयव्यतिरेकावन्यथासिद्धौ न गुणं कारणतयोपस्थापयतः । हन्तैवं गुणस्य कारणताऽऽपद्यते । तथा हि — विशेषाग्रहः प्रमाणस्य प्रतिबन्धकः तदभावश्च विशेषग्रहः कारणम् । प्रतिबन्धाभावस्य कारणताश्रयणाद् । न । शक्त्यपलापे हि प्रतिबन्ध एवासम्भवी । तत्र कुतस्तदभावस्य कारणता ।

Trans. : The pūrvapakṣin says that the contradiction of the view of the intrinsic nature of validity cannot be avoided since the positive and negative concomitance of merit (*guṇa*) cannot be explained otherwise (i.e. as *anyathāsiddha*). (The siddhāntin says :) No, the positive and negative concomitance are obtained differently, that is, they are *anyathāsiddha*. A defect (*doṣa*) does obstruct validity and the merit is its opposite. So, the positive and the negative concomitance of a merit, being *anyathāsiddha*, do not confer causality on it (*guṇa*). But thus the merit would assume causality. To explain, the absence of the cognition of a distinguishing feature hinders the means of a valid cognition and the absence of that, i.e. the cognition of a distinguishing feature assumes the status of a causality (of a valid cognition) by construing the absence of obstructing factors as a cause.

(The siddhāntin says :) No. When the potency (*śakti*) has been denied (the status of a separate category), its obstruction (*pratibandha*) simply is not possible. In that case where is the question of conferring the status of causality on the absence of obstructing factors (as the absence depends on the pratiyogin which has a real status)?

Ann. : The pūrvapakṣin says that the presence of a merit and the absence of defects of the causal factors facilitate the generation of a valid cognition. According to him, this contradicts the intrinsic nature of validity proved by the two syllogistic propositions discussed above as the accompaniment of a merit constitutes an extra factor over and above the causes of a cognition. To buttress his point of view, the pūrvapakṣin invokes the maxim of kulyāpraṇayana (see VV, p. 49) and thus attributes two functions to the merit, that of obstructing an invalid cognition and that of facilitating the valid one (just as the streams dug for irrigation may also be used for bathing). However, according to the siddhāntin, the positive (*anvaya*) and the negative (*vyatireka*) concomitance of a merit do not confer the status causality on it because both the positive and negative concomitance (*anvaya* and *vyatireka*) of a merit are considered to be anyathāsiddha. To explain, a defect obstructs validity. Merit is its opposite. The purpose of merit is fulfilled in doing away with the obstruction caused by the defect. Thus the accompaniment of a merit with the causal conditions of a valid cognition and its non-accompaniment with those of an invalid cognition become available by being opposite to each other. Hence, the positive and negative concomitance of a merit, being anyathāsiddha, do not confer the status of causality on it (see *ananyathāsiddhāvanvayavyatirekau kāraṇakḷptiṁ kurvāte. prakṛtau tu pramāvirodhyapramāpratibandhakaguṇādiviṣayatvenopakṣīṇau na kāraṇatvam āvedayitum īśāte*, ibid., p. 49; also cf. *syādevaṁ yadyananyathāsiddhāvanvayavyatirekau kāraṇatvāvedakau syātām tau tu virodhyapramāpratibandhakatvenopakṣīṇau na kāraṇatvamātratvam āvedayataḥ*, CS, p. 217). Still the pūrvapakṣin insists that, even in this situation, one cannot but attribute the status of causality to the merit in the generation of a valid cognition. Here the mention of the term guṇa also indicates 'the absence of demerit' (*atrāpi guṇagrahaṇaṁ doṣābhāvopalakṣaṇam*, VV, p. 49). To confer the status of being anyathāsiddha on the positive and neagative concomitance of a merit, the siddhāntin construes the nature of a merit as opposed to a defect (i.e. the absence of defects). In other words, following the maxim of ghaṭṭakuṭīprabhāta[1], the pūrvapakṣin ascribes the status of causality to the absence of obstructing factors, which the siddhāntin has been trying to avoid. In this way, the status of being a cause comes to be conferred on 'the absence of obstruction' (*pratibandhakābhāva*). The siddhāntin does not agree with the pūrvapakṣin and avers that an obstruction could be possible only when the potency has been accepted as a separate category. If the potency has been denied the status of a separate category by the pūrvapakṣin, then the assumption of its obstruction cannot be upheld logically (*śaktyapalāpe hi pratibandha evāsambhavī*, NRD, p. 50). Consequently, there is absolutely no significance in the conferral of the status of causality on the absence of obstruction (*pratibandhakābhāva*) when the obstruction itself has ceased to exist after the status of a separate category has been denied to the potency (*prāmāṇyaparatastvavādimate śakterabhāvāttadrahitasya pratibandhakatve'tiprasaṅgāt pratibandhāsiddhestadabhāvasya guṇādervā na kāraṇatā*, VV, pp. 49-50).

ननु दोषभावे तदभावरूपगुणाभावात् सामग्रीवैकल्यमेव प्रतिबन्धः। उक्तं हि—'प्रतिबन्धो विसामग्री'ति। न। अन्योन्याश्रयताप्रसङ्गात्। प्रतिबन्धापेक्षो हि तदभावः कारणं कारणापेक्षश्च तदभावः प्रतिबन्ध इति। यदपि मतं कार्यव्यतिरेकद्वारा हि कार्यप्रतिकूलता मन्त्रादेः कारणनिरपेक्षावसीयते। कारणतापि निरपेक्षैवान्वयव्यतिरेकावसेयेति कथमन्योन्याश्रयता? अपि चेयमुत्पत्तौ ज्ञप्तौ वा स्याद्। नाद्यः असम्भवाद्। मन्त्रतदभावयोरपरस्परहेतुत्वाद्। नापि चरमः अज्ञातयोरेव तयोस्तथात्वादिति। तदसत्। कार्याभावावसेयोऽपि हि प्रतिबन्धः शक्तिनिरपेक्षस्त्वया कारणाभाव इष्यते। कारणं च तदभावरूपं, अतो यद्यपि मन्त्रतदभावयोर्न परस्परहेतुता, तथापि तयोः प्रतिबन्धत्वकारणत्वयोरन्योन्योपाधिकत्वाद् उत्पत्तावन्योन्याश्रयता सुस्थितैव।

अतस्तज्ज्ञप्तावन्योन्याश्रयताऽस्खलितेति न गुणानां कारणता। अतस्तदन्वयव्यतिरेकयोरन्यथासिद्धिरिति सिद्धम्। तस्मान्निष्प्रत्यूहं प्रमोत्पत्तेः स्वतस्त्वम्।

Trans. : (The pūrvapakṣin says :) While a defect exists, the absence of the causal factors alone constitutes an obstruction because there is an absence of merit consisting in the absence of defects as it has been said 'the absence of causal factors is an

1. A cartman with the intention of avoiding a tollbooth takes at night an unfrequented road, but finds himself at day-break near that very tollbooth.

obstruction' (*pratibandho visāmagrīti*). (The siddhāntin replies:) No, because this would incur the fault of mutual dependence. (To explain,) the absence of an obstruction depending on the obstruction (which is its pratiyogin) itself constitutes causality and the absence of the causal apparatus depending on it (the causal apparatus) constitutes an obstruction. (In order to escape the fault of mutual dependence) if it is held that the aspect of a mantra obstructing an effect, etc. is determined on the basis of the effect not coming into existence without any reference to the cause and the causality itself is also established independently on the basis of the positive and negative concomitance (*nirapekṣaivānvayavyatirekāvaseyā*), then how would the fault of mutual dependence be applicable? (The siddhāntin asks :) Does this mutual dependence relate to the productive aspect or the cognitive one? The first alternative is not possible since the mantra and its absence are not mutually causal. The (other) last alternative also is not possible since both, being unknown, remain the same, to wit, they are not mutually causal. (The siddhāntin says:) This is not correct. Without depending on the potency, you intend to construe the absence of a cause as an obstruction, which is determined on the basis of an effect not coming into existence and the absence of an obstruction as a cause. Although there is no mutual causality between a mantra and its absence, their obstructing nature and causality (in a respective manner) are due to their mutual upādhis and hence their mutual dependece with regard to the generation aspect stays well-established.

Therefore their mutual dependence with respect to the cognition aspect does not remain unestablished and so, a merit (accompanying a causal apparatus) is denied causality. Consequently it is established that the positive and the negative concomitance of a merit are anyathāsiddha. Hence, the intrinsic view of the generation of validity is without any fault.

Ann. : According to the pūrvapakṣin, the absence of the causal apparatus (*visāmagrī*) can be understood as an obstruction. Hence, the absence of the absence of the causal apparatus, i.e. the absence of *visāmagrī* would constitute a cause. The siddhāntin does not see eye to eye with the pūrvapakṣin on this point because it suffers from the fault of mutual dependence. The absence of an obstruction, which is an important ingredient of a causal apparatus in accordance with the Nyāya view, depends on the obstruction itself since it is the counter-positive of that absence and it is the absence of the causal apparatus which determines the status of an obstruction. Thus, the knowledge of a cause depends on the knowledge of an obstructing factor consisting in the absence of causality and the knowledge of causality is determined by that of the absence of obstructing factors since it is the absence of an obstruction that constitutes causality. Thus the fault of mutual dependence results. Consequently, the status of an obstruction (*pratibandha*), etc. remains unestablished (*tathā ca kāraṇajñāne tadabhāvarūpapratibandhajñānaṁ tajjñāne pratibandhābhāvarūpakāraṇajñānamiti parasparāśrayatvāt pratibandhāderasiddhirityarthaḥ*, VV, p. 50). When the status of an obstruction remains unestablished, it makes no sense to talk about its absence which is held to be an essential ingredient of a causal apparatus according to Nyāya. If the obstructing nature of a mantra, etc. is established on the basis of the absence of an effect (*kārya*) without any reference to the causal apparatus, then the fault of mutual dependence ceases to exist. In the same manner, causality can also be independently determined according to the positive and negative concomitance (*anvaya* and *vyatireka*). Thus obstruction and causality become independent of each other.

To substantiate the postulation of an obstruction, the pūrvapakṣin continues to argue against the fault of mutual dependence. He says the fault of mutual dependence is not tenable whether it relates to the aspect of generation or to that of cognition. In case the defect of mutual dependence relates to the generation aspect, then this cannot be upheld because the mantra and its absence are not mutually causally related. Should this fault relate to the cognition aspect, then also the defect of mutual dependence does not become applicable as the obstruction and its absence, not being known, remain mutually causally unrelated.

The siddhāntin does not subscribe to the pūrvapakṣin's view and avers that the concept of an obstruction and that of causality are mutually dependent. This may be explained as follows : The status of an obstructing factor independent of (*śakti*), known from the absence of an effect, is construed as the absence of causality and causality is interpreted to be the absence of that obstruction.

Then, although they are not causal for each other, their mutual dependence is well-established with respect to the generation aspect as the status of being of an obstruction and that of being a cause are mutually dependent because these upādhis, that is, *pratibandhatva* and *kāraṇatva* are mutually related. To explain, when causality residing in the absence of mantra, etc. is generated, the status of being an obstruction is produced in mantra, etc. and when the status of being an obstruction is produced in mantra, etc., the state of being a cause is brought about in the absence of mantra, etc.[1] Similarly the cognition of *pratibandhatva* and that of *kāraṇatva* are dependent on each other and, as such, their mutual depedence cannot be avoided (*pratibandhatvakāraṇatvayoritaretarāpekṣatvāt jñaptāvapi durvāramitaretarāśrayatvamiti*, VV, p. 52). Because of this mutual dependence being evident, the absence of obstructions does not constitute causality. Consequently, the merit which is construed as the absence of obstructions also does not constitute the state of being a cause (*parasparāśrayatvāt pratibandhābhāvasya kāraṇatvāsambhave tadrūpatvena guṇāderna pramāhetuteti*, ibid., pp. 52-3). Moreover, the positive and negative concomitance of a merit with respect to the generation of a valid and an invalid cognition respectively are established differently (i.e. they are *anyathāsiddha*) as discussed earlier. Therefore, causality is not to be conferred on the merit and thus there is no hurdle in holding the view that validity is intrinsically conditioned from the generation point of view (*utpattau svatastva*).

ज्ञप्तिस्वतस्त्वे अनुमानप्रयोगाः

तथा तज्ज्ञप्तिस्वतस्त्वेऽपि प्रयोगः — प्रमा स्वतो ज्ञायते परनिरपेक्षोत्पत्तिकत्वात् ज्ञानवत्। तथा प्रामाण्यं स्वतो ज्ञायते अप्रामाण्येतरत्वे सति ज्ञानैकधर्मत्वाद् ज्ञानत्ववत्। हेतोः पक्षधर्मत्वे तावदविवाद एव। विपक्षे च बाधः प्रामाण्यसंशयासम्भवो दर्शितः। अनवस्थाप्रसङ्गश्च ज्ञप्तिपरतस्त्वे स्पष्टः। मानान्तरस्यानवश्यम्भावित्वान्नानवस्थेति चेन्न। स्फुरदेव हि मानं विषयातिशयहेतुः। अन्यथा स्थाणुवद् ज्ञानेऽप्यनन्तरमेव सन्देहः स्यात्। तदपि स्फुरणमन्यत इति कथं नानवस्था। अस्मत्पक्षे तु नित्यस्वप्रकाशानुभवत्वाद् ज्ञानस्य, सोपाधेर्मानस्य

1. Cf. *mantrādyabhāvagate kāraṇatve jāte mantrādiniṣṭhaṁ tatkāraṇatvakṛtaṁ pratibandhatvaṁ jāyeta. jāte ca tadgate pratibandhatve pratibandhābhāvatvakṛtaṁ mantradyabhāvaniṣṭhaṁ kāraṇatvaṁ jāyeteti vyaktamutpattāvanyo'nyāśrayatvamityarthaḥ*, VV, p. 52).

च सिद्धेर्नानवस्थाज्ञप्तिपरतस्त्वतयोः प्रसङ्गः। प्रामाण्यसंशयोपपत्तिश्च दर्शिता। नापि सत्प्रतिपक्षता। प्रतिप्रयोगस्य निरस्तत्वाद्। दूषणान्तरासम्भवोऽपि यथायोगमूहनीयः। प्रमा, ज्ञानज्ञप्तेर्व्यवह्रियते परनिरपेक्षज्ञप्तित्वाद् ज्ञानवत्। यद्वा प्रामाण्यं परनिरपेक्षव्यवहारास्पदम्, अप्रामाण्येतरत्वे सति ज्ञानैकधर्मत्वाद् ज्ञानत्ववत्। दोषनिरासस्तूक्तदिशा द्रष्टव्यः। तस्मात् प्रामाण्यमुत्पत्तौ ज्ञप्तौ व्यवहृतौ चान्यनिरपेक्षं वेदादय एव स्वशक्तिवशाज्जनयन्तीति सिद्धम्।

Trans. : In the same way, there is also a syllogistic proposition to prove the intrinsic nature of the cognition of validity : A valid cognition is intrinsically known like a cognition since its production does not need any other factor (over and above the causal factors of a cognition). In the same manner, the validity of a cognition is also known intrinsically like the state of being a cognition since it (validity), being different from invalidity, is a property of a cognition alone. There is no dispute at all about the residence of the hetu in the minor term (*pakṣa*). The contradiction of the contrary instance, consisting in the impossibility of doubt about the validity of a cognition, has (already) been demonstrated. And the fault of infinite regress has been made clear in the context of the extrinsic nature of the cognition (of validity). (The pūrvapakṣin says :) Since another means of cognition (for the validity of a cognition to be made known) is not necessarily needed, there would be no fault of infinite regress. No, this is not so. A means of cognition manifesting by itself brings about a distinguishing feature in a content (i.e. makes it known). Otherwise, later on a doubt may arise about the cognition as in the case of a stump. If the manifestation of the means of a cognition is due to another factor, then how can the defect of infinite regress not apply? As per our view, knowledge consists in the experience which is eternally self-luminous and the means of knowledge has been interpreted as having an upādhi (in the form of an unknown content). So, there is no infinite regress, nor is there any contingency of the validity becoming extrinsic. And the explanation for the possibility of doubt about validity has been shown. There is no fallacy of the reason known as *satpratipakṣa* as the countersyllogism has been discarded. The absence of other faults is to be considered according to the requirement of the situation. A valid cognition is put to use by cognising the cognition itself since it does not need any other cognition (for the cognition of validity) like a cognition. Or validity becomes an object of practical conduct without requiring anything else like the state of being a cognition since it, being other than invalidity, is a property of a cognition alone. The faults can be dispensed with in the manner already explained. Therefore, by virtue of their potency (*śakti*), the Veda, etc. do produce a valid cognition (*prāmāṇyaśabdena tadādhārabhūtā pramā gṛhyate*, VV, p. 55) independently from the points of view of generation, cognition and practical use.

Syllogisms to prove the intrinsic nature of validity

Ann. : The following syllogistic propositions are used by the siddhāntin to prove the intrinsic nature of the cognition of validity: (1) A valid cognition is intrinsically known as it is generated only by the causal factors of a cognition. (2) Validity is intrinsically known since, being different from invalidity, it is the property only of a cognition, like the state of being a cognition (*jñānatva*). The reason consists in being the property of a cognition alone and at the same time being different from invalidity. There is no dispute about its residence in the *pakṣa*. The contradiction of the contrary view and the possibility of doubt about the nature of validity have already been explained (see NRD, p. 40). If a valid cognition is known intrinsically, then there is no place for any doubt with respect to its validity. It is also to be taken into consideration that the use of a syllogistic proposition is justified only when there is some doubt about the major term (*sādhya*). It is also true that a doubt is preceded by certainty and vice versa. Thus there is mutual dependence between doubt and certainty. Hence, the doubt being untenable, there is no ground for the use of a syllogistic proposition to prove the extrinsic nautre of validity. The fault of infinite regress is another stumbling block. If, to cognise the validity of a cognition, another means of a valid cognition is required, then another means of cognition is required to know the validity of that means of a cognition and so on ad infinitum. So, it has to be conceded that a means of cognition being manifest by itself introduces a distinguishing feature in the object, that is, it makes the object known. The reason to take such a stance is that there is no doubt about the cognition (*na ca jñāne kadācidapi saṁśayaḥ. tena tadarthaprakāśa-kāle prakāśamānameṣitavyamiti,* VV, p. 54). Now the question arises: How does the defect of infinite regress apply, when the means of cognition is manifest by itself when the object is being apprehended (*bhavatu mānaṁ meyabhānasamaye bhāsamānam tathāpi kathama-navasthā*? Ibid., p. 54). However, the defect of infinite regress could become applicable when the manifestation of the means of cognition is attributed to some other factor (*tadapi sphuraṇamanyata iti kathaṁ nānavasthā,* NRD, p. 54). The siddhạntin on the other hand says that there is no such defect applicable in respect of his standpoint. As per his view, a cognition is an experience which is always self-luminous. The specific characteristic of a self-luminous and valid perceptual cognition owes itself to the presence of an unknown content in it. The cognition being self-luminous, neither the fault of infinite regress nor the contingency of a valid cognition and its validity being extrinsic is incurred. The possibility of the countersyllogism (*pramā parato jñāyate jñānaviśeṣatvāt apramāvad,* VV, p. 54) on the basis of the reason (*hetu*) consisting in the state of being a specific cognition has already been discarded by interpreting the specific nature in terms of an unknown content. The incurrence of other faults such as the contingency of an invalid cognition becoming intrinsic and the like has already been taken care of. The intrinsic nature of the practical application of a valid cognition also is proved just as the intrinsic nature of a valid cognition and its validity has been proved by the syllogisms discussed above. Thus, after adducing adequate proof in favour of the intrinsic nature of the validity of a cognition from generation, cognition and practical use points of view and rejecting all the objections raised against the intrinsic view of validity, Ānandānubhava concludes the siddhānta view saying that the Vedas, by virtue of their own potency, independently generate a valid cognition (*prāmāṇyaśabdena tadādhārabhūtā pramā gṛhyate. anyathā janayantīti vākyaśeṣānupapattiḥ,* ibid., p. 55) from the points of view of generation, cognition and practical use.

अतिरिक्तशक्तौ पूर्वपक्षनिरूपणम्

ननु शक्तौ किं कृत्यम् ? कार्यं तावत् कारणेभ्य एवोदेतीति । तिलेभ्य एव तैलं, दधि दुग्धेभ्य एवेत्यादिनियमः, तया विना नोपपद्यते । तिला हि तैलं प्रति दध्यादि प्रत्यपीत्यनियमः स्यात् । अतः कार्यकारणनियमसिद्धेः शक्तिरास्थेयेति

चेन्न । शक्तिपक्षेऽप्यस्यानियमस्य तुल्यत्वात् । न हि शक्तेः शृङ्गमस्ति । यत्रैकमेव कार्यं निबद्धं स्यात् । अथ तस्यास्स्वभाव एव नियामकः । तथा तिलादेरेव स्वभावः स्यात् । तर्हि प्रतिबन्धसिद्धये शक्तिराश्रीयताम् । न ह्यग्निः प्रतिबद्ध्यते ।

Pūrvapakṣa view on potency as a separate category

Trans. : What is the purpose of (postulating) the potency (*śakti*)? (If it is the production of an effect,) then an effect emerges only from its own causes. The rule that oil comes only from the sesamum seeds and curd, only from milk, etc. lacks justification without (the postulation of) the potency. The sesamum seeds which produce oil could also produce even curd, etc. (in the absence of the potency and thus inconsistency in the principle of causality would result). Consequently, potency (*śakti*) should be taken recourse to since there is an invariable relation between cause and effect. (The pūrvapakṣin says :) No, the invariable relation between the cause and the effect would equally be absent even when the potency has been postulated. The potency does not have another potency by which only a single effect (to be produced by a particular cause) can be determined. Let then the nature of potency be accepted as a determining factor (for the production of a particular effect). In the same way, the nature of the sesamum seeds, etc. may (for the sake of brevity) be assumed to produce oil, etc. Then to account for the incidence of an obstruction, let us take resort to (the assumption of) the potency. It is not the fire that is stopped from burning (but it is the potency of the fire to burn which is withheld from the act of burning).

Ann. : Ānandajñāna points out that there are three possible grounds to justify the postulation of potency (*śakti*) : 1. the production of a particular effect from a specific cause, 2. establishment of an invariable relation between the cause and the effect, or 3. the possibility of an obstruction (*śakterhi prayojanaṁ kāryotpattirvā kāryakāraṇaniyamasiddhirvā pratibandhasiddhirvā*, VV, p. 55). The Naiyāyika does not subscribe to this view and holds that it is the causal factors alone which bring about a particular effect when they are accompanied by the absence of obstructing factors. It is important to notice that the use of the particle *eva* (*evakāraḥ śaktinirapekṣatādyotanārthaḥ*, VV, p. 56) is to show that the production of an effect does not at all need the potency (*śakti*). On the other hand, the siddhāntin says that it is for the sake of consistency in the law of causality that the postulation of potency is necessitated (cf. *śaktivaśān niyāmakatvasambhavān nāniyamaḥ śaktivāde'sti*, ibid., p. 56). However, the pūrvapakṣin points out saying that the inconsistency could result even on the assumption of the potency unless it is restricted to produce a particular effect by virtue of its own nature. In the light of Vedāntaviveka, this may be understood as follows : The word *śṛṅga* in NRD is used figuratively to signify 'potency' (see *śṛṅgaśabdena śaktiruktā*, ibid., p. 56). There are two possibilities in this respect. Firstly, either the potency is its own effect or secondly, it is its own nature. The first alternative is not acceptable since it suffers from the defect of ad infinitum (*tasyā hi kāryabhūtā vā śaktiḥ svabhāvabhūtā vā? nādyaḥ anavasthiterityarthaḥ*, ibid., p. 56). If the potency (*śakti*) is understood in terms of the nature of the potency of the cause, then why is it not accepted that the very nature of a particular cause can account for the consistency in the cause-effect relationship (cf. *śaktim aṅgīkṛtyāpi svabhāvasya niyāmakatve tiladereva svabhāvo niyāmako'stu*, ibid., p. 56). After these two grounds have been proved untenable, the third ground is now being examined by the author. The postulation of the potency may be purported to explain why an effect is not brought about when a cause is accompanied by certain obstructing factors. In the case of fire, it is not the fire which is precluded from the act of burning but its capacity to burn. The fire, even being present, does not burn something when a moon-stone is placed near it. When it is removed, it burns. This means that it is not the fire which is being stopped from the act of burning but its capacity to burn is withheld when the moon-stone is placed in its vicinity. Therefore, to explain the phenomenon that the act of burning does not take place even when the fire is present, the postulation of the potency as a separate category is necessitated.

न च विसामग्र्यचेव प्रतिबन्धः। तस्यान्योऽन्याश्रयताया उक्तत्वाद्। अतः शक्तौ प्रतिबन्धोऽर्थवानिति चेद्, न। तत्रापि प्रतिबन्धासम्भवात्। तथा हि — शक्तौ कः प्रतिबन्धः? शक्तिनाशकश्चेत्। प्रतिबन्धकापाये कार्यं न स्याद्। न च शक्त्यन्तरं जातम्। कारणाभावात्। प्रतिबन्धकसामीप्यं चेद्, उत्तम्भके सत्यपि

कार्यं न स्यात्। तस्मान्न शक्तेरपि प्रतिबन्धसम्भवः। उभयपक्षानुपपत्तौ च मान-दृष्टकारणपक्ष एवाश्रयणीयः। न शक्तिकल्पितपक्षः। न चात्र मानं समस्ति। अर्थापत्तिस्तावदनुपपत्त्यसम्भवादेव परास्ता। उक्तो हि कार्याद्यनुपपत्त्यसम्भवः। यदपि मानम् अयमग्निरद्विष्ठातीन्द्रियाधारः कारणत्वाद् गुरुत्वाधारवदिति। तद-प्यसद्। विपक्षे बाधकाभावात्। परमाण्वाधारत्वसिद्धेः सिद्धसाधनत्वाच्च। असंयोग-वृत्त्याऽऽधेयत्वविवक्षायामप्ययमेव दोषः। परमाण्वभावस्यापि तथात्वाद्। भाव-त्वविशेषणत्वेऽपि स एव दोषः। तदभावविशेषितत्वस्यापि तथात्वाद्। एतेनाधे-यशक्तिरपि व्याख्याता। न हि प्रोक्षणादिनाऽचेतनेषु व्रीह्यादिषु पुण्यं जन्यते, अन्यो वातिशयो मानाभावात्। किन्तु पुंस्येव। यदाहोदयनः — 'संस्कारः पुंस एवेष्टः प्रोक्षणाभ्युक्षणादिभिरि'ति। अथवैकैवावभृथान्ता यागादिक्रिया; तया च पुंस्येव पुण्यं जन्यते। सेतुगमनक्रिययेवेति युक्तम्। तस्मान्नातीन्द्रियशक्तौ मानं किञ्चिदपीति प्रत्यक्षादिसिद्धप्रतिबन्धाभावादि कारणमिति सिद्धम्।

Trans. : And the absence of causal factors alone should not be construed as an obstruction (*pratibandha*) since the fault of mutual dependence regarding this has already been demonstrated (see supra pp. 84-85). Therefore, the obstruction would be meaningful only when the potency has been admitted (as a separate category). No, the obstruction will not be possible even on the admission of the potency. To explain, what is an obstruction in relation to the potency? If the destroyer of the potency constitutes an obstruction, then the effect should not come into existence when the obstructor (*pratibandhaka*) has been removed (as the potency has already been destroyed by the obstructor). (It cannot be held that) another potency has been born because there was no cause to produce it. Then does the nearness of an obstructor constitute an obstruction? (Then the effect should not come into existence even when a stimulating agent (such as the sun-stone in the context of fire) is present. Consequently, the obstruction (*pratibandha*) is not possible even when the potency has been taken recourse to. When both the alternatives (the views regarding the potency and the cause) are not possible, the view of causality, which is based on evidence, should be adopted, and not the view of the potency which is (merely) imagined. And there is no evidence in support of the view of potency; for the assumption evidence has been discarded only because there is no impossibility of the production of an effect (even without taking recourse to the potency, see *kāryaṁ tāvat kāraṇebhya evodetīti*, NRD, p. 55). For it has already been explained that there is no impossibility of the production of an effect, etc. Also the (following) syllogism (to prove the potency) is untenable : This fire is the locus of that which does not reside in two and which is beyond the reach of the senses because it is a cause like the locus of gravitation (*gurutva*). The reason is that there is no evidence that would falsify the contention that fire is the vipakṣa (contrary evidence, that is the fire is not the locus of *śakti*). There is also a fault of proving that which has already been proved as the fire can become a locus of atoms. The same fault becomes applicable if the locatedness is intended by any other relation than the conjunction. That the reciprocal non-existence of atoms (which does not reside in two and which is beyond the reach of senses) exists in fire by a relation other than the conjunction is well-established (hence the same fault, i.e. *siddhasādhyatva*, is applicable). If beingness (*bhāvatva*) is made to qualify (the mutual absence of atoms, i.e if *bhāvatva* is inserted in the body of the sādhya), then also the same fault remains applicable. If *bhāvatva* is qualified by the reciprocal non-existence of atoms (if the sādhya be *paramāṇvanyo'nyābhāvaviśeṣitabhāvatva*, cf. VV, p. 58), then also the same situation prevails (i.e. the same defect is applicable as a positive entity of the described kind exists in the fire as explained in the Vedāntaviveka). The (untenability of the) potency residing in the located (*ādheya*) gets explained thereby (for lack of evidence as in the case of sahajā śakti, see ibid., p. 58). For there is no evidence to the effect that the act of sprinkling, etc. produces a merit or some excellence in the inert rice-grains, etc. but, of course, only in man (who performs the act of sprinkling, etc.) as Udayana says, "The acts of sprinking (*prokṣaṇa*), wetting in a particular manner (*abhyukṣaṇa*), etc. are intended to generate saṁskāra (*adṛṣṭa*) only in man." Or properly speaking, there is only one sacrificial act up to the sacrificial ablution at the conclusion of a principal sacrifice and it is this act which brings about puṇya only in man as the atoning act of going to the Setu (Rāmeśvaram) does. (This may include begging alms, other expiating acts, etc. which together constitute the atonement (*prāyaścitta*) by which man is absolved of the sins such as the killing of a brāhmaṇa (*brahmahatyā*)). (The pūrvapakṣin concludes that), therefore, there is absolutely no evidence for the supersensible potency. Hence it is established that the absence of obstructions, etc., established by the perceptual evidence, etc. constitute a cause.

Ann. : The pūrvapakṣin discusses the status of the potency as a separate category in the present passage and arrives at the conclusion that there is no evidence in support of the postulation of the potency as a separate category. The argumentation begins as follows : The siddhāntin presents his view that the postulation of the potency over and above the assemblage of causal factors is required to explain why the fire does not burn when an incantation is recited or a moon-stone is placed near it. The pūrvapakṣin replies that this can be explained in terms of the insufficiency or absence of the causal conditions. When the assemblage of causal factors is not sufficient or complete, the act of burning does not take place. However, the siddhāntin does not subscribe to this view as this suffers from the fault of mutual dependence : It is the absence of obstructing factors that constitutes causality and the absence of causal factors constitutes an obstruction (*pratibandha*). Thus, the knowledge of a cause depends on the knowledge of an obstructing factor constituted by the absence of causal factors and the knowledge of causality is determined by that of the absence of obstructing factors. Thus the fault of mutual dependence results, because of which the status of an obstruction, etc. remains unestablished (cf. *tathā ca kāraṇajñāne tadabhāvarūpapratibandhajñānaṁ tajjñāne pratibandhābhāvarūpakāraṇajñānamiti parasparāśrayatvāt pratibandhāderasiddhirityarthaḥ*, VV, p. 50). In the absence of a definite status of an obstruction, the Naiyāyika is not justified in holding the view that the absence of obstructing factors constitutes an essential ingredient of a causal apparatus.

The siddhāntin now makes out a case for the assumption of the potency as a separate category by saying that the fire stops burning because the potency existing in the fire is withheld by the recital of an incantation or by the moon-stone placed near it. The pūrvapakṣin rejects this saying that, even on the acceptance of potency as a separate category, the fire may not stop burning even in the presence of an obstructing factor whether the obstruction is construed as the destroyer of the potency or as the nearness of an obstructing factor (*śaktau pratibandhaḥ śaktināśako vā pratibandha-sāmīpyaṁ vā*, VV, p. 56). In the former case, the act of burning may not result even when the obstructing element has been removed since the fire's capacity to burn has already been annihilated by the obstructor. If, at the removal of the obstructing factor, the production of another power is accepted to explain the act of burning, then this remains inexplicable as there was no cause that would generate another potency to justify the act of burning at the removal of the obstructing element. In the latter case, i.e. when the obstruction is construed as the nearness of an obstructing factor, the act of burning again remains inexplicable when the moon-stone is in the vicinity of the fire while there is a sun-stone placed near the fire. The pūrvapakṣin replies that, in a simialr situation, the obstruction of fire's capacity to burn may not result in the vicinity of a moon-stone. So, in both the cases, the act of burning remains inexplicable. When the views regarding the potency and the cause, discussed above, are not possible, the view on causality, which is based on evidence, should be adopted, and not the view of potency which is merely imagined. So far as the assumption evidence put forward by the siddhāntin to endorse the postulation of the potency is concerned, the pūrvapakṣin says that this has already been refuted as the production of an effect is possible even in the absence of the potency. The pūrvapakṣin also does not accept the syllogism put forward by the siddhāntin : This fire is the locus of that which does not rest in two and which is beyond the reach of the senses since it is a cause like the locus of gravitation (earth or water). To show that this syllogism is not tenable, the pūrvapakṣin lists the following reasons : 1. There is no argument against the contrary view (*vipakṣa*) that the fire is not the locus of that which does not rest in two and which is beyond the reach of the senses. 2. The fire, however, can become the locus of atoms and thus the syllogism suffers from the fault of proving that which has already been proved. 3. The same fault is applicable when the locatedness is intended by any relation other than the conjunction as the supersensible form (*rūpa*) inheres in a diad (*dvyaṇuka*) of fire. 4. The mutual difference of an atom from the fire is beyond the reach of the senses and resides in the fire by a relation other than the conjunction, that is, by the self-linking (*svarūpa*) relation. Thus the fault of proving the already proven is still applicable. To avoid this defect, if bhāvatva as a qualifier is inserted in the body of the sādhya, the same fault is applicable. Or, if 'bhāva qualified by the reciprocal absence of atoms' is made the sādhya, then also the fault of siddhasādhyatva persists as a positive entity qualified by the reciprocal absence of an atom rests in the fire (see *paramāṇvanyo'nyābhāvaviśeṣitasyādviṣṭhātīndriyabhāvasyāgnau bhāvāditi*, VV, p. 58). For these reasons, the syllogism presented above is not capable of establishing the potency as a separate category. The pūrvapakṣin further says that even the postulation of the potency residing in the located (*ādheyaśakti*) lacks justification for the same reasons, as according to Udayana, the acts of sprinkling, wetting in a particular manner, etc. generate neither merit nor excellence in the inert substances like rice-grains, etc. but produce merit only in man. The pūrvapakṣin buttresses this view-point saying that one sacrificial act up to the ablution (*avabhṛtha*), which takes place at the conclusion of the principal sacrifice, creates merit (*puṇya*) only in man as the act of going to the bridge (Rāmeśvaram) absolves the person who has committed a heinous sin. The act of going to Rāmeśvaram may include the act of begging alms and other such expiatory acts which absolve the man of the sins such as the killing of a brāhmaṇa. In this way, after having rejected the arguments put forth by the siddhāntin to prove the existence of the potency as a separate category, the pūrvapakṣin concludes saying that there is no need of such a postulation because the causal apparatus, accompanied by the absence of obstructing factors and established by perceptual evidence, is capable enough to bring an effect into existence.

अतिरिक्तशक्तिसमर्थनम्

उच्यते, न तावच्छक्तौ प्रमाणासम्भवः। तथा हि — अग्निरतीन्द्रियसामान्यवन्निष्क्रियाश्रयः कारणत्वाद् गुरुत्वाश्रयवत्। तेजोद्व्यणुकमतीन्द्रियरूपस्य वायोश्चाधिकरणं सिद्धमित्यतीन्द्रियसामान्यवन्निष्क्रियेत्युक्तम्। परस्य सर्वं योगीन्द्रियगम्यम् अतोऽतीन्द्रियासिद्धेरप्रसिद्धविशेषणः पक्षः। दृष्टान्तश्च साध्यविकल इति चेद्। न। विमतं न गुरुत्वजातिविषयम् इन्द्रियत्वाद् अस्मच्चक्षुर्वदित्यतीन्द्रियसिद्धेः। तर्हि तेजसि स्थितस्थापकत्वसिद्धेः सिद्धसाधनतेति चेन्न। अग्नौ तत्सत्त्वे मानाभावाद्। विमतं स्थितस्थापकवत् तेजोवयवित्वात् सुवर्णवदिति

मानमिति चेन्न। विपक्षे बाधकाभावाद् दृष्टान्ते साध्यसन्देहाद् गुरुत्ववत्तस्यान्यधर्मत्वसम्भवात् प्रभायामनैकान्त्याच्च। अथ विमतं स्थितस्थापकवद् रूपस्पर्शवत्त्वात् कटवदिति मानं, न। विपक्षे बाधाभावात् स्थितस्थापककार्यवत्त्वोपाधिभावाच्च। न च साधनव्याप्तिः। चक्षुरादौ साधनवति उपाध्यनुपलब्धेः।

न च मानं विना ते किञ्चित् सिध्यति, असिद्ध्याद्यभावस्तु स्पष्ट एव। पक्षवृत्त्यादेः स्पष्टत्वात्। नापि सत्प्रतिपक्षता। प्रतियोगे दृष्टान्ताभावात्। विपक्षे च प्रतिबन्धासम्भवो बाधः। यथा च विसामग्र्येव न प्रतिबन्धः तथा स्वतःप्रामाण्यवादे दर्शितम्। नन्वितरत्रापि कः प्रतिबन्धः? शक्तेरभिभव एव। उत्तम्भके च सति पुनरुद्भवः यथा रूपस्यानुद्भूतत्वमुद्भूतत्वं च। ननु रूपस्योद्भूतत्वादिजातिद्वयं भिन्नव्यक्त्युपपद्यते। न चैकस्याः शक्तेः विरुद्धजातिद्वयं घटते। न। अनयोर्जातित्वानुपपत्तेः। रूपत्वादिना हि परापरभावोऽनयोरशक्यः सम्पादयितुम्। रूपे स्पर्शे च क्वचिदेवानयोर्भावात्। विरुद्धातिशयद्वयवत्त्वञ्च एकत्र कालभेदादविरुद्धं भावाभाववत्। अथवा प्रतिबन्धकोत्तम्भकसामीप्यमेव तत्कृतोऽतिशयः भ्रामकमणेरिव। अतः शक्तिपक्ष एव प्रतिबन्धसिद्धिः। एवं च प्रतिबन्धान्यथानुपपत्तिरूपार्थापत्तिरपि शक्या शक्तौ प्रमाणयितुम्। अतीन्द्रियातिशयसिद्धौ प्रोक्षणादिभिरपि व्रीह्यादिष्वेवातिशयो जन्यत इति सिद्धयति। 'व्रीहीन् प्रोक्षती' ति द्वितीयाश्रुतेः प्रोक्षणस्य व्रीहिगुणभावप्रतीतेः।

In support of the Potency as a separate category

Trans. : (The author now undertakes the siddhānta view :) It is not that there is no evidence for (the existence of) the potency. To explain, the fire is the locus of that which, having a universal, is supersensible (or which has a supersensible universal) and which is actionless because it is a cause like the locus of gravitation (the earth or water). The qualifying expressions 'supersensible and having a universal or having a supersensible universal' and 'actionless' have been mentioned in the syllogism since it is already established that the diad of fire (*tejodvyaṇuka*) is the locus of the supersensible rūpa (colour or form) and air (which is supersensible according to the view which holds that air is inferable, and not perceptible). According to the pūrvapakṣin, everything is within the reach of the senses of a yogin. So nothing being established as supersensible, the qualification 'supersensible' in the *pakṣa* remains unestablished (in other words, the *sādhya* qualified by the term 'supersensible' is not established, see *yogisvīkāravādinaṁ prati atīndriyaviśeṣaṇāsiddherviśiṣṭasādhyāprasiddheraprasiddhaviśeṣaṇatā*, VV, p. 60). And (if it is objected that) the illustration does not have the *sādhya* in it, then this is not so (because the supersensible gravitation is established by the following syllogism:) The sense of a yogin (*vimatam*) does not apprehend the gravitation universal (*gurutvatva*) because it is a sense like our eyes and, thus 'the supersensible gravitation' is established. (The objector further raises an objection :) then there is a fault called *siddhasādhanatā* (in the syllogistic proposition put forward by the siddhāntin) since the property of elasticity (*sthitisthāpakatva*) exists in the fire. (The siddhāntin dismisses this objection saying that) this is not so since there is no evidence that the property of elasticity exists in fire. (The objector puts forward the following syllogism to prove his contention :) The fire has the property of elasticity, being fire and a whole (*tejo'vayavitvāt*)[1] just as gold has (elasticity). (The siddhāntin says :) No, this is not acceptable as there is no contradictory argument against the contrary instance;[2] (secondly, the presence of) the sādhya in the illustration is subject to doubt; (thirdly) the property of elasticity could belong to something else (e.g. the earthy portion existing in gold) like gravitation and (fourthly) it suffers from the anaikāntika fallacy in respect of prabhā (since prabhā has the state of being fire (*hetu*) but does not possess elasticity(*sādhya*). (The objector presents another syllogistic proposition to prove the existence of elasticity (*sthitisthāpakatva*) in the fire by saying :) Or let there be another syllogism : The fire (*vimataṁ*) has the property of elasticity since it has the qualities of colour and touch like a mat. The siddhāntin does not accept this because there is nothing which can contradict the contrary instance[3] and there is an upādhi

1. Actually the word *tejo'vayavitvāt* contains two hetus. Consequently, two syllogisms are intended to be adduced here as VV (pp. 60-1) states : *hetāvavayavipadaṁ vimatam uktavidham avayavitvād ityanumānāntaraṁ darśayitum ityavadheyam.*

2. The contrary instance is : Let fire not possess elasticity even though it is both tejas and a whole.

3. The contrary instance in this context is : Let fire not possess elasticity even though it has the properties of colour and touch.

consisting in 'being the effect of elasticity'. And there is no concomitance (of the upādhi) with the probans (*sādhana*) since the upādhi (the effect of elasticity) is not cognisable in the eyes, etc. which have the probans (the unmanifest qualities of colour and touch) in them.

(The siddhāntin says :) Nothing is proved without an evidence in your case (that is, the presence of elasticity in the fire cannot be proved by the objector without providing an unimpeachable evidence). (The siddhāntin now takes care of other faults of the *kāraṇatva* hetu in *agniratīndriyasāmānyavanniṣkriyāśrayaḥ kāraṇatvāt gurutvāśrayavat* by saying that :) The absence of the fallacies of asiddhi, etc. is obvious because of the existence of the hetu in the pakṣa, etc. And the (*kāraṇatva*) syllogism does not have the state of having a countersyllogism for want of any (acceptable) illustration (see VV, p. 60). With respect to the contrary instance, i.e. 'the fire does not have the potency', the impossible incidence of an obstruction constitutes the contradiction (*bādha* of the contrary instance). The manner in which the absence of the causal factors (*visāmagrī*) does not constitute an obstruction (*pratibandha*) has been demonstrated while expounding the theory of self-validity. What constitutes an obstruction on the other view, i.e. the view of potency? The overpowering of the potency itself constitutes an obstruction. When the sun-stone is placed near, the capacity or potency again becomes manifest just as the colour has the state of being manifest or unmanifest. It is proper that the two universals *udbhūtatva*, etc. of colour should rest in two different individuals. And a single potency cannot have two opposing universals in it. No, this is not so since both these properties cannot appropriately be called universals because the state of being para and apara (*vyāpaka* and *vyāpya* respectively) cannot be conceived in respect of these two dharmas (*udbhūtatva* and *anudbhūtatva*) when juxtaposed with the state of being a colour (*rūpatva*), etc. These two properties exist only in some cases of colour and touch. The state of having two opposing excellences may exist in one locus due to difference in time like existence and non-existence. Or, the nearness of the moon-stone (*pratibandhaka*) or the sun-stone (*uttambhaka*) imparts a distinguishing feature (to the potency) just as a loadstone (does to the things made of iron, see VV, p. 63). Consequently, an obstruction gets established only when the potency (*śakti-pakṣe*) has been admitted. In this way, the assumption evidence (*arthāpatti*) : 'otherwise the obstruction would be impossible' also can be put forward to establish the potency (as a separate category). The supersensible excellence (potency) having been established (in substances, etc.), it is proved that some excellence (potency) is generated only in the rice-grains, etc. by the act of sprinkling, etc. By virtue of the accusative case-ending in *vrīhīn* in the scriptural injunction '*vrīhīn prokṣati* ', the act of sprinkling is understood to be imparting some excellence (*atiśaya*) to the rice-grains (i.e. the act of sprinkling imparts excellence to the rice-grains).

Ann. : Putting an end to the impression that there is no evidence to establish the potency (*śakti*) as a separate entity in its own right, the siddhāntin presents a syllogistic proposition to prove the same. It reads as follows : The fire is the locus of that which has a supersensible universal (or which, having a universal, is supersensible) and which is actionless because it is a cause like the locus of gravitation (earth or water). This means that the earth and water, being causal to many effects, have the property of gravitation which, being actionless, has a supersensible universal. In the same way, the fire, also being the cause of burning, should have some entity which, having no action, has a supersensible universal. And that entity can be designated as potency (*śakti*) according to the siddhāntin.

Had the fire been said to be the locus of something actionless, then being the locus of *tejastva* which is an actionless universal, the fault of proving that which has already been proved (*siddha-sādhyatva*) would have been applicable. To avoid this fault, the term 'having a universal' has been inserted in the body of the sādhya. Again the fault of proving the already proven is still applicable since the fire has the quality of colour (*rūpa*) which is actionless and which has the *rūpatva* universal. To escape this fault, the qualifying term 'supersensible' has been added in the body of the sādhya. Even then air can exist in the fire by conjunction and hence the defect of proving the proven would continue to persist since air is also considered to be supersensible according to the view which holds that air is inferable by virtue of the property of touch in it. To escape this fault, the qualifying term 'actionless' (*niṣkriya*) has been inserted in the body of the sādhya as air is not actionless. So the statement of the proposition is that the fire is the locus of something actionless which has a supersensible universal (*atīndriyasāmānyādhāratve sati yanniṣkriyaṁ tadāśrayo'gniriti pratijñārthaḥ*, VV, p. 60). The siddhāntin further explains how the fault of an unestablished qualifying term (*aprasiddhaviśeṣaṇa*) can be avoided. He says that, although there is nothing supersensible according to the pūrvapakṣin since a yogin can perceive everything, still gravitation, dharma, adharma and bhāvanā have been recognized as the supersensible entities by Praśastapāda ('*gurutvadharmādharmabhāvanā atīndriyā*' *iti hi praśastapādaḥ. ato'tīndriyaṁ vastu parasyāpi sammatam*, ibid., p. 60). To further prove that there is no fault of *aprasiddhaviśeṣaṇatā*, the siddhāntin also uses the following syllogistic proposition: 'The sense of a yogin', being a sense organ, does not comprehend the gravitation universal like our eyes and hence the qualifying term 'the supersensible' ceases to remain unestablished (*vimataṁ na gurutvajātiviṣayam indriyatvāt asmaccakṣurvadityatīndriyasiddheḥ*, NRD, p. 60). Again the pūrvapakṣin comes up with another objection saying that there is a property of elasticity in the fire. That is why the objector says that the siddhāntin is going to prove that which has already been established. The latter does not accept this and points out that the property of elasticity does not exist in the fire since there is no evidence to this effect. Upon this the objector presents another syllogistic proposition to prove the presence of elasticity in the fire : The fire has the property of elasticity, being *tejas* and a whole (*tejo'vayavitvāt*) like gold. The siddhāntin says that this is not acceptable because there is no convincing argument against the contrary view (*vipakṣa*) that the fire does not have elasticity. Moreover, the presence of the sādhya in the illustration is doubtful. The reason is that the presence of the property of elasticity in gold is not definite as the presence of elasticity in gold may be taken as existing in the earthen portion of gold (cf. *kiṁ ca suvarṇe 'pratīyamānagurutvavad-atrāpratīyamānasthitasthāpakasyopaṣṭambhakapārthivabhāganiṣṭhatvasambhavānna suvarṇadṛṣṭānte sādhyaṁ niścitam*, VV, p. 61). It also suffers from the fallacy known as *sādhāraṇa anaikāntika* in respect of light (*prabhā*) which has the *tejastva* universal in it but not the property of elasticity. Thus the probans (*hetu*) occurs where the *sādhya* does not exist.

The pūrvapakṣin puts forward yet another syllogistic proposition in support his contention that the fire has the property of elasticity and thus, according to him, the syllogism adduced by the siddhāntin suffers from the fault of siddhasādhanatā. The syllogism reads as follows : The fire has the property of elasticity in it since it has the qualities of colour (or form) and touch like a mat. According to the siddhāntin, this syllogism is not well-equipped to prove the probandum because there is no convincing argument against the contrary instance that the fire does not have the elasticity and also because there is an upādhi in the form 'the state of having an effect of the property of elasticity'. To explain, if the absence of elasticity in the fire was sought to be proved, then there would be no substantial argument to contradict it. Secondly, there is also an upādhi in the form 'the state of having an effect of the property of elasticity' as it does not exist in the eyes which possess the probans (the qualities of colour and touch in an unmanifest form). So, there is no concomitance of the upādhi with the probans, which is its defining characteristic. Thus, the pūrvapakṣin fails to give an unimpeachable evidence to prove that the fire does not have that which is actionless and which has a supersensible universal.

That an obstruction would not take place at all constitutes a contradiction of the contrary instance that there is no potency. The siddhāntin further says that the manner in which the incomplete causal apparatus (*visāmagrī*) does not constitute an obstruction (*pratibandha*) has been shown in the exposition of the theory of self-validity. It is easier to explain the absence of the effect of fire by the potency residing in it as it can be assumed to be hindered by incantations, moon-stones, etc. This capacity becomes manifest either in the vicinity of a sun-stone or when the moon-stone is removed. This is illustrated by taking the example of a loadstone. When a loadstone is placed near a thing made of iron, its stationary state is disturbed by it and it is attracted towards it (loadstone) and when it is removed, the thing made of iron again attains the stationary state. In the same manner, the unmanifestation and manifestation of fire's act of burning can be explained in a satisfactory manner by the postulation of the potency. However, the pūrvapakṣin raises an objection in this context. He says that the two opposing universals 'the state being manifest' (*udbhūtatva*) and 'the state of being unmanifest' (*anudbhūtatva*) cannot rest in the same potency. The siddhāntin replies that these are not universals since universals existing in the same entity enjoy the states of being para (*vyāpaka*) and apara (*vyāpya*) as pṛthivītva and ghaṭatva do in a pot (*ghaṭa*). Such is not the case in respect of *udbhūtatva* and *anudbhūtatva*. In this way they are not universals. However, these dharmas can be held to exist in the same locus at different points of time.

The siddhāntin now introduces the assumption evidence in support of the postulation of the potency as follows : If potency is not accepted to be existent, then the obstruction of the act of burning of fire cannot be explained satisfactorily (cf. *pratibandhānyathānupapattirūpārthāpattirapi śakyā śaktau pramāṇayitum*, NRD, p. 63).. Here Ānandagiri remarks that the natural or inborn potency has thus been proved by the inference and assumption evidences and thereby it is also proved that the supersensible excellence (*ādheyaśakti*) is induced in the rice-grains, etc. by the acts of sprinkling, etc. He clarifies this by saying that the accusative case-ending in *vrīhīn* in the scriptural injunction '*vrīhīn prokṣati*' means that the act of sprinkling imparts excellence (*atiśaya*) to the rice-grains (i.e. the act of sprinkling induces excellence in the rice-grains). This establishes the (induced) potency of the located (*ādheyaśakti*).

यत्तु 'संस्कारः पुंस एवेष्ट' इत्यभिधानं तदश्रुतमीमांसावृत्तान्तस्येत्युपेक्षणीयम्। न हि पुंसो व्रीहिप्रोक्षणजन्यातिशयवत्त्वे किञ्चिन्मानमस्तीति। क्रियैकत्वञ्च प्रोक्षणादिविधिभेदविरुद्धं न शक्यं कल्पयितुम्। क्रत्वर्थपुरुषार्थभेदविरुद्धञ्च। अतोऽग्न्यादेः शक्तिः सिद्धा। यच्च वार्तिककृद्भिरुक्तं 'आत्माविद्यैव नः शक्तिः सर्वशक्यस्य सर्जन' इति तच्छ्रुतिसिद्धमायामयं जगदाश्रित्य न तु व्यावहारिक-प्रमाणसिद्धमित्यविरुद्धम्। तस्माच्छक्तिमदेव कारणं न प्रतिबन्धाभाववद्। अपि च प्रतिबन्धप्रागभावादिविशेषः कारणं किं वा अभावमात्रम्। आद्ये तत्प्रध्वंसादौ कार्यं न स्याद्। द्वितीये तु प्रतिबन्धभावेऽपि कार्यं स्यात्। तदन्योऽन्याभावस्य भावात्। तदन्ये अभावाः कारणमिति चेन्न। ततोऽन्यत्वासम्भवाद्। अन्यो हि प्रतियोगी अन्यश्चान्योऽन्याभाववान्। न चान्योऽन्याभावोऽप्यन्योऽन्याभाववान्। अनवस्थाप्रसङ्गाद्। अभावान्तरस्यानवश्यम्भावित्वान्नानवस्थेति चेन्न। अभावो हि विशेषणादिभावेन प्रतीयते। विशेषणादिभावश्चान्योऽन्याभावप्रतीतौ प्रतीयते। तदप्रतीतौ दूरस्थयोर्विशेषणादिभावादृष्टेः। एवमनन्ताभावदृष्टिसापेक्षाऽभावदृष्टिर्न क्वापि भवेदित्यनर्थफलेयमनवस्थाऽऽपद्यत एव।

अपि च प्रतिकारणं बहवः प्रतिबन्धाः । तेषां च प्रत्येकं बहवोऽभावाः कारणमिति कल्पनागौरवाद्युक्तं प्रतिकारणमेका शक्तिरिति कल्पयितुम् । तस्मात् स्वशक्तिसम्बन्धावष्टम्भेनैव कारणानि नियतं कार्यं जनयन्ति । एवं वेदा अपि धर्मब्रह्मविषयं ज्ञानं जनयन्तीत्यास्थेयं श्रेयोऽर्थिभिः ।

Trans. : The statement that 'a merit (*saṁskāra*) is intended to be generated only in man' is not worth paying attention to as it is the statement of a man who is not acquainted with the discipline of Mīmāṁsā. For there is no evidence that it is man who comes to possess the merit (*puṇya*) produced by the acts of sprinkling the rice-grains, etc. The unity of the sacrificial acts also cannot be conceived because this goes against the difference obtaining in the injunctions of sprinkling, etc. and against the difference in the injunctions contributing to the sacrifice (*kratvartha*) from those contributing to human ends (*puruṣārtha*). Therefore, the potency of the fire, etc. is established. And Sureśvarācārya, the vārttikakāra has said : According to us, only the nescience (*avidyā*) of Ātman is the power which creates everything fit to be created. This (statement of the vārttikakāra) is based on the illusory world established by the śruti, and not on that which is proved by the empirical means of knowing. Hence there is no contradiction between the two. Consequently, that which has the potency constitutes a cause, not that which has the absence of obstructions. (The pūrvapakṣin's stand is further examined as follows :) Does a particular kind of absence, e.g. prior absence, etc. constitute a cause or does merely absence (constitute a cause)? So far as the first alternative (that the prior absence is the cause) is concerned, the effect should not ensue when the prior absence has been destroyed. In case mere absence is taken as a cause, then the effect should come into existence even when the obstruction is present since the reciprocal absence (difference) of the obstruction exists (even then). Let then the absence different from the reciprocal absence be accepted as a cause. This cannot be so since the absence different from the latter is not possible. For the 'other' is the counter-positive and the 'other' has the reciprocal absence. And the reciprocal absence also does not have another reciprocal absence for fear of the fault of infinite regress. If it is held that there would not be any fault of infinite regress since another reciprocal absence does not necessarily follow. No, this is not so. For the reciprocal absence appears as a qualifier, etc. and its being a qualifier, etc. is cognised after it has already been cognised. When that (reciprocal absence) is not cognised, then the state of its being a qualifier, etc. of the two distant objects is not apprehended. Thus, the cognition of the reciprocal absence, which is dependent on the cognition of infinite instances of the reciprocal absence would not at all be possible; in this way, the fault of infinite regress resulting in meaninglessness definitely becomes applicable.

Moreover, there are many obstructions of each and every cause. And (so) many instances of the absence of each obstruction would constitute a cause. Thus this assumption suffers from the fault of laxity. So, it is proper to assume a single potency for a single cause. Then the causes invested with (lit. supported by the relation of) their own potencies only will produce the stipulated effects. In the same manner, it should be held by those seeking their own emancipation that the Vedas (invested with their own potency) also produce knowledge about dharma and Brahman.

Ann. : It is the contention of the pūrvapakṣin that the performance of the subsidiary sacrificial acts such sprinkling, irrigating, and so on produces merit, excellence, etc. only in man. This is not accepted by the siddhāntin who says that this view does not find its place in the Mīmāṁsāśāstra. Moreover, there is no evidence to the effect that puṇya is produced only in man by the act of sprinkling the rice-grains, etc. Also the unity of different sacrificial acts cannot be considered to be the import of the scriptures as the pūrvapakṣin holds as there are different injunctions prescribing different sacrificial acts. Similarly difference between the injunctions contributing to the nature of the sacrificial act (*kratvartha*) and those contributing to human ends (*puruṣārtha*) should be construed as an additional argument against the unity of sacrificial acts. So, the argument put forward by the pūrvapakṣin to endorse his own point of view that it is only man in whom some kind of excellence (*puṇya*) is generated by the acts of sprinkling the rice-grains, etc. does not hold good. In conclusion, the different subsidiary sacrificial acts do produce excellence in the rice-grains, etc. Thus, the potency of the located (*ādheyaśakti*) such as excellence in the rice-grains is also established.

The statement of Sureśvarācārya 'for us the nescience of Ātman is the power which is responsible for the creation of everything worth producing' relates to the world which is the creation of avidyā as stated by the śruti. So far as the potency existing in the fire, etc. is concerned, it is established through the empirical means of knowing. Thus, there is no contradiction between these two kinds of power. When the status of power has been established, the absence of obstructions construed to be an essential defining feature of a cause may be discarded. Instead, that which is invested with the power may be accepted as a cause. The siddhāntin strengthens his stand-point in the following manner : In case, the absence of obstructions accompanying the causal factors is also accorded the status of a cause, then the question arises what kind of absence would constitute a cause. Is it a particular absence, e.g. prior absence of obstructing elements that constitutes a cause or just mere absence in general. If the former alternative is taken cognisance of, then an effect should not come into existence when the prior absence of an obstruction has been destroyed because then there is an absence of the prior absence (*pratibandhaprāgabhāvasya kāraṇatve taddhvaṁsādau kāryaṁ na syāt. tadā tatprāgabhāvābhāvāt*, VV, p. 65). If the latter alternative is given credence to, then an effect must ensue even in the presence of an obstruction since then the reciprocal absence, i.e. difference (*anyo'nyābhāva*) from the obstruction does exist. If, to avoid this undesirable contingency, other instances of the absence of obstructions are to be construed as causes, then this is untenable because the 'other' than the reciprocal absence is not possible (*tato'nyatvāsambhavāt*, NRD, p. 65). The 'other' than the dharmin is the counter-positive (*pratiyogin*) and the 'other' has the reciprocal absence. Let the reciprocal absence being other than the dharmin be the counter-positive. Then, the absence of an obstruction, which is other than the reciprocal absence itself, can be construed as a cause (cf. *bhavatvanyo'nyābhāvasyāpi dharmiṇo'nyatvena pratiyogitvaṁ tathā ca tato'nyasya pratibandhābhāvasya kāraṇatvopapattiriti*, VV, p. 66). The reciprocal absence does not have another reciprocal absence in it as this would incur the fault of infinite regress. To avoid the fault of infinite regress, if it is said that another reciprocal absence would not necessarily be existing in the reciprocal absence, then this is hard to maintain. The reason is that the absence always appears as a qualifier, etc. and its being a qualifier, etc. is apprehended only after the cognition of the reciprocal absence. That (the reciprocal absence) is not cognised between two distant objects and hence there is no apprehension of the state of being a qualifier, etc. relating to them. So, it is necessary for the cognition of the absence either as a qualifier or as a qualificand that the reciprocal absence and its counter-positive should have already been cognised. Hence, to account for the state of being a qualifier or a qualificand, the prior apprehension of the reciprocal absence is essential. Like the first reciprocal absence, the second reciprocal absence also requires another reciprocal absence to explain its cognition as a qualifier, etc. So without the succeeding requisite reciprocal absence, the preceding one would not be apprehended as a qualifier, etc. Consequently, it is untenable to hold that the absence of an obstruction which is other than the reciprocal absence of an obstruction is a cause. If the absence of an obstruction is not a cause, then how can the fire qualified by the absence of an obstruction be construed as a cause? It is at this stage that the siddhāntin introduces his stand-point saying that there is no such anomaly when something having a potency is held to be the cause of a product. Moreover, there are many obstructions with regard to each and every cause and many will be the instances of the absence with respect to those obstructions. This leads to conceptual laxity. It is, therefore, prudent and economical to postulate a single power for a single cause. After the potency has been established as a separate entity, it may safely be held that a cause invested with it will give rise to the effect stipulated to be produced by that cause. Similarly, the Vedas invested with the potency also will confer on man the self-valid knowledge of dharma and Brahman.

वेदानां सिद्धार्थबोधकत्वे कार्यशक्तिवादिनां पूर्वपक्षोद्भावनम्

नन्वेतन्न सहामहे यद्वेदोऽकार्यमपि बोधयतीति । तात्पर्याधीनं हि शब्दस्य प्रामाण्यम् । उक्तं हि 'यत्परश्शब्दः स शब्दार्थ' इति । तात्पर्यं च कार्य एवावधार्यते, सर्वशब्दानां तत्परतयैव प्रयोगदर्शनात् । अतत्पराणां च निष्प्रयोजनत्वात् ।

तथा च 'आम्नायस्य क्रियार्थत्वादानर्थक्यमतदर्थानामि'त्यक्रियार्थानां निष्फलत्वमाशङ्क्य, 'स्तुत्यर्थेन विधीनां स्युरि'ति कार्यपरत्वेनार्थपरत्वं सूत्रितम्। तथा च भाष्यमपि 'दृष्टो हि तस्यार्थः कर्मावबोधनमि'ति। किञ्च शक्तिज्ञानाधीनं हि शब्दस्य बोधकत्वम्। शक्तिश्च कार्यान्वित एवावसीयते। व्यवहाराधीनत्वाच्छक्त्यवगमस्य। व्यवहारो हि गवानयनादिलक्षणकार्यताज्ञानजन्यचिकीर्षासाध्यः। अतो व्यवहारद्वारा शब्दशक्तिः कार्य एवावधार्यते।

नन्विष्टसाधनताबोधाच्चिकीर्षाजनिः। ततः प्रवृत्तिरिति सिद्धे व्युत्पत्तिः किं न स्याद्? अतीतेष्टसाधनताबोधेन व्यभिचारादिति ब्रूमः। अथ कार्यैतकार्थसमवायित्वेनेष्टसाधनता विशेष्येत। तदापि कार्यतानुप्रवेशान्न केवले सिद्धे शब्दशक्तिः सिध्येत्। किञ्च इष्टसाधनताज्ञानाच्चिकीर्षा कार्ये अज्ञाते जायते किं वा ज्ञाते? नाद्यः, अज्ञाते कार्ये चिकीर्षायाः असम्भवात्। विषयज्ञानं हीच्छायाः कारणम्। अतस्तदभावे सा न सम्भवेत्। द्वितीये तु कार्यज्ञानं तदनन्तरभाविचिकीर्षाकारणम्। एतेनैतत्परास्तम्। यदाहुः 'ममेदं कार्यमिति चिकीर्षैवैषा न कार्यताज्ञानमि'ति।

ननु यथा तव गवानयनादिकार्यविशेषव्यवहारावसेयापि शक्तिर्न तं विषयीकरोति, किन्तु कार्यान्वितमात्रं, तथैव कार्यान्वितमपि त्यक्त्वा योग्यान्वितमनन्वितं वा विषयीकरोति। युक्तं चैतल्लाघवादिति। न। यतोऽस्ति विशेषत्यागे हेतुः, विशेषाणामानन्त्याच्छक्तिग्रहासम्भवः। नानुगतकार्यत्यागे हेतुरस्ति। न च लाघवादेव परिग्रहो युक्तः। अतिप्रसङ्गाद्। नापि कल्पनागौरवादेव त्यागः। यत आहुः — 'प्रमाणवन्त्यदृष्टानि कल्प्यानि सुबहून्यपी'ति। स्यान् मतम् — 'पुत्रस्ते जात' इति वाक्यश्रवणानन्तरमुखविकासलिङ्गं हर्षमुन्नीय तत्कारणं च ज्ञानमनन्तरभाविशब्दजन्यं कल्पयतीति सिद्धे व्युत्पत्तिरुपपन्ना। न च हर्षहेतुबाहुल्यादनिर्णयः। प्रकृतेन निर्णयोपपत्तेः। अन्यथातिप्रसङ्गादिति। न। प्राप्तप्रियामरणाभावस्यापि हर्षहेतोः प्रकृतत्वात्।

किञ्च प्रयासबहुलेयं व्युत्पत्तिकल्पना। तथा हि — प्रथमं मुखविकासदर्शनं। ततो हर्षोन्नयनं, पश्चात्तत्कारणज्ञानावधारणं तदनन्तरं च तस्य प्रकृतत्वेन पुत्रजन्मविषयतानिर्णय इति मन्थरेयं व्युत्पत्तिकल्पना अनायाससिद्धकार्यव्युत्पत्तौ सत्यां न युज्यते।

नन्विह 'प्रभिन्नकमलोदरे मधूनि मधुकरः पिबती' ति प्रसिद्धपदसमभिव्याहारादप्रसिद्धे मधुकरपदार्थे व्युत्पत्तिर्लीलालभ्येति। न, विकल्पासहत्वात्। तथा हि — इतरपदार्थेषु किं व्युत्पत्तिः कार्यनिरपेक्षा, तत्सापेक्षा वा? नाद्यः — आद्यव्युत्पत्तेः कार्यनैरपेक्ष्यासम्भवस्य प्रपञ्चितत्वाद्। नेतरः इतरपदार्थवद्, मधुकरपदार्थेऽपि कार्यान्वयस्यावश्यकल्पनीयत्वाद्। अन्यथा व्युत्पत्तिद्वैरूप्यप्रसङ्गात्। कार्यान्विते व्युत्पन्नानामितरपदानां कार्याभावे अबोधकत्वप्रसङ्गाच्च। एतेनोपदेशद्वारापि सिद्धार्थव्युत्पत्तिर्व्याख्याता।

Exposition of the pūrvapakṣa view that action is the import of word

Trans. : (Mīmāṁsaka :) We cannot subscribe to the view that the Veda also produces the knowledge of that which is other than action. The validity of verbal testimony depends on that which is intended to be conveyed by it, for it has been said that the meaning of a word is that for which it is used and the intended meaning (i.e. purport) is determined with respect to action only since all words are used to convey only action and the words which are not used to denote action are purposeless. That is why apprehending the purposelessness of the Vedic sentences not signifying action in deference to the aphorism 'the Veda has action as its purport and the Vedic sentences which do not enjoin action carry no significance', another sūtra 'being syntactically connected with the injunction, they are parts of the injunctive sentences having the object of praise' (Jaiminisūtra, 1. 2. 7) has been enunciated to render the eulogistic sentences (*arthavādavākyas*) meaningful by assigning to them the function of signifying action. Likewise the commentary by Śabara on Jaimini Sūtra, 1. 1. 1 also says that the evident purport of the Vedas is to produce the knowledge of karma (*niyoga*). Moreover, the generation of knowledge by words depends on the knowledge of the faculty of denotation and that is known only through that which is connected with action. The knowledge of the denotative function is dependent on an empirical activity (*vyavahāra*). This activity is brought about by 'the desire to do' produced by the knowledge of the act of bringing a cow, etc. Therefore, the denotative faculty of word is ascertained to signify only action by virtue of the empirical activity.

The 'desire to do' arises out of the knowledge of the means of achieving a desired end. Then the activity takes place. Why should then the denotative faculty of word not be determined to denote an existent entity (as it is ascertained with regard to action)? Because then there would be deviation (*vyabhicāra*) regarding the knowledge of the means of achieving a desired end of the past. Then (to avoid this fault) let the state of being the means of a desired end be qualified by the state of being a producible effect, which exists in the same entity (that is, that which is the means of a desired end can also be brought about by an effort). Even then because of the insertion of 'the state of being a producible effect', the denotative function does not get established to only denote an existent entity. Moreover, does the 'desire to do' owing to the knowledge of the means of a desired end arise in respect of an unknown act or a known one? The former alternative is not feasible since it is not possible that the 'desire to do' can arise in respect of an unknown act since it is the knowledge of an object, which causes the desire to arise. Hence, the desire is not possible when that (the knowledge of an object) does not exist. Regarding the latter alternative, (it may be said that) the knowledge of an act is the cause of the 'desire to do' that arises immediately after it (the knowledge of the act). By this, the view of those is set aside, who say that the cognition 'it is to be done by me' itself constitutes the 'desire to do', and not the knowledge of kāryatā (construed as the cause of the 'desire to do').

(The siddhāntin says :) As the denotative faculty which is determined by a specific empirical activity of bringing a cow, etc. does not denote that specific activity but only that which is connected with action. In the same manner leaving aside also that which has a connection with action, it may denote either that which is connected with a compatible (entity), or that not connected in that manner. And being economical, this is appropriate. (The Mīmāṁsaka says :) No, there is a ground to give up the specific activity (to be the basis for the comprehension of the denotative power) because it is not possible to comprehend the faculty of denotation on account of innumerable specific conditions. (But) there is no reason to give up the common factor (*anugata*), that is action (*kārya*). And it is not proper to adhere to a (particular) view only on the basis of economy (*lāghava*) as this would lead to the fault of over-extension (see VV, p. 71). Also (a certain view) should not be given up only because of prolixity as Kumārilabhaṭṭa has said that a great many unseen (*adṛṣṭa*) entities can be postulated if they are supported by evidence. It could be that the comprehension of the denotative faculty to denote existent entities is justified as the happiness of the person is inferred from the blooming face immediately after he has heard the sentence 'a son is born to you'. (The learner gathers that) the cause of the happiness is the knowledge (of the birth of his son) generated immediately after (hearing) the (above) sentence. This justifies the knowledge of the faculty of denotation to denote an existent entity (i.e. son's birth). And there is no indecision on account of the fact that there are many causes of happiness as what is given in the present context (e.g. the cloth bearing the child's footprint) can decide the point at issue. Otherwise, overextension could result. (Here the cause of happiness is definite, but its comprehension takes place later than that connected with action. So, the denotative function is not comprehended in the birth of the son but may overextend to that which is connected with action).[1] This is not so since the absence of the death of the beloved also exists as a (possible) cause of happiness in consonance with the context.

Moreover in this way, the comprehension of the faculty of denotation requires much effort. As for instance, firstly, the sight of the blooming face, from that the inference of happiness, afterwards follows the knoweldge of the cause of happiness, and immediately follows the confirmation of the birth of a son, as the context is consonant with it (the birth of the son). It is not proper to accept such a view involving tardiness in comprehending (the faculty of denotation) when the effortless comprehension of the denotative power on the basis of action is available.

(The siddhāntin refers to another means of comprehending the denotative function in existent things :) Being stated along with the well-known word (*pibati* in this particular case, etc.), it is very easy to comprehend the faculty of denotation in the

1. See : *atra janmapratipatter harṣahetutvaniścaye'pi na tatra harṣahetau śaktiḥ sidhyati. tasya kāryāpekṣayā vilambitapratipattitvāt. atastaṁ paśyediti vaktur-abhiprāyikakāryānvite padasāmarthyamāstheyam*. VV, p. 72.

word 'bee' in the (following) sentence 'the bee drinks honey from the interior of the blooming lotus' (here the word *madhukara* in association with the verb *pibati* gives the meaning 'one who drinks honey' cf. VV, p. 72). (The pūrvapakṣin says:) No. This view fails to satisfy the alternative viewpoints (raised with regard to it). To explain, is the comprehension of the denotative function with regard to other word meanings independent of action or dependent on it? The first alternative is not possible since it has already been elaborated that the first comprehension of the denotative function is not possible without a reference to action. The other alternative view is also not tenable since like the other word meaning, the connection of action with that of the word 'bee' also has to be postulated. Otherwise, two kinds of approach concerning the comprehension of the denotative faculty would become liable to be conceived. And also the words whose denotative function has been comprehended to denote that which is connected with action would not denote any meaning in the absence of (their connection with) action. By this (the view about) the comprehension of the denotative function to denote the existent things by virtue of a statement gets explained (this means that even the statement 'this is a cow' needs the association of 'action' for the comprehension of the denotative function in deference to the very first comprehension of the faculty of denotation, see ibid., p. 73).

Ann. : The Mīmāṁsaka accepts that the Veda is a means of knowing the nature of dharma but he does not subscribe to the view that it is also a means to know Brahman (*vedasya dharmabodhakatvamaṅgīkṛtya brahmabodhakatvamasahamāno mīmāṁsakaḥ śaṅkate*, ibid., p. 67). In other words, he just does not accept the view that the Veda conveys that which is not connected with action because the meaning of a word is accepted to be that for which it has been used and the intended meaning is always determined in connection with action only since all words are used to denote action or that which is connected with it. The words which are not used to denote action are purposeless. (cf. *āmnāyasya kriyārthatvād ānarthakyamatadarthānām*, MS, 1. 2. 1). Accordingly, the purport of the Veda is to enjoin sacrificial acts and if a Vedic sentence does not enjoin any act, then it is to be interpreted in such a manner that the apparent meaningless expression is rendered meaningful by being associated with an injunction. Thus the Vedic expressions conveying eulogy or censure assume significance only when they enter into a syntactic relation with, or become subsidiary to, injunctive sentences. Śaṅkara quotes Śabara in his commentary on the fourth aphorism saying that the evident purport of the Veda is to produce the knowledge of niyoga (cf. *tasya vedasya; dṛṣṭo'rthaḥ dṛṣṭaṁ prayojanaṁ, yat karmāvabodhanaṁ niyogajñānam*, VV, p. 68). This is corroborated by the fact that the meaning of a word is conveyed through the denotative faculty and that denotative faculty is comprehended in a situation in which a prompted activity is the guiding factor. For instance, the denotative faculty to denote a cow is comprehended for the first time by the learner when he observes a young man bringing a cow after hearing the command of his elder since the act of bringing the cow depends on the desire which is generated by the knowledge of the command to act conveyed by the elder's sentence 'bring the cow'. It is given to understand that a desire to act in us arises when we come to know that a particular act will help achieve our desired end. If merely the knowledge of a means to achieve a desired end is admitted to prompt one to act, then there is violation in the case of the knowledge of the means of obtaining the past desired end since it evidently does not prompt one to act at the present moment. And if the state of being a means to a desired end is qualified by the state of being a producible effect, then also the faculty of denotation to denote purely an existent object is not established as the state of *kāryatā* has already made its way into it (*kāryatānupraveśān na kevale siddhe śabdaśaktiḥ sidhyet*, NRD, p. 69). Now the question arises. Does 'the desire to do', which is due to the knowledge of the means of a desired end, arise in respect of a known act or an unknown one? The latter is not possible as the desire with regard to an unknown objective can never be generated since it is only the knowledge of an object that generates the desire to attain the desired object. This means that the knowledge of an achievable end does give rise to a desire to act in the direction of achieving it. This sets aside the view that the cognition 'this is to be done by me' itself constitutes the desire to undertake an activity and there is no other intervening psychological event of having a desire subsequently other than the above-mentioned cognition. This means that, according to Prabhākara, the knowledge of kāryatā itself may be construed as the 'desire to do' itself and not that the desire is generated by the knowldge of an activity to be undertaken. The Advaitin has a different view that it is the knowledge of an achievable end that generates a desire which in turn motivates one to attain it. The Prābhākara Mīmāṁsaka does not accept that there is an intervening desire between the cognition 'this is my task' and the actual performance of the act. This may, however, be taken note of that, according to him, the desire is secondary even if it is present. Being present, it only indicates the knowledge that this is an activity which ought to be undertaken by 'me'.

The denotative power of a word known from the specific empirical activity of bringing a cow, etc. does not take into consideration that a particular activity of bringing the cow, etc. So, there is a ground to give up the specific instance for two reasons : 1. the comprehension of the faculty of denotation is rendered difficult because of infinite specific conditions and 2. the fault of over-extension. For these two reasons, the denotative faculty to denote a specific entity cannot be accepted. So, the entity which is divested of all specific characteristics but connected with action only can become the pratiyogin (*pratiyogiśabdo viṣayaparaḥ* cf. VV, 75) of the faculty of denotation. Even the connection with action could be relinquished and an object syntactically compatible or otherwise would then become the pratiyogin of the denotative faculty (cf. *kāryajñānajanyacikīrṣākāryavyavahāraliṅgāvagatā'pi padaśaktiś cikīrṣākāraṇībhūtakāryajñānaviṣayagavānayanādiviśeṣaṁ na viṣayīkaroti. ānantyavyabhicārābhyāṁ viśeṣasya śaktiviṣayatvānupapatteḥ. ataḥ sarvaviśeṣānugataṁ kāryānvitamātraṁ śabdaśaktirgocarayati. tathā kāryānvitasyāpi tyāgena sarvatrānugatam anvitam arthamātraṁ vā śabdaśaktiviṣayo bhaviṣyatīti*, VV, p. 70).

According to the Prābhākara Mīmāṁsakas, the assumption to accept a denoting power in bare entities not connected with kārya lacks justification because then the view of abhihitānvaya becomes applicable. Thus, the meaning of a sentence is rendered non-verbal according to the view of the Prābhākara Mīmāṁsakas (see *tathā cābhihitānvayaprasaṅgād vākyārthapratīteraśābdaprasaṅgāt*, ibid., p. 71). The reason is that anvaya (*vākyārtha*) which, not being the denotatum of the faculty of denotation, would cease to be verbal. They subscribe to theory of anvitābhidhāna which holds that the meaning of a sentence is always in relation with action (*kāryānvita*). According to them, the evidence in this regard is the experience of the person who for the first time comes to know the meaning of a word from an empirical situation in which, for example, the activity of bringing a cow has taken place. So the faculty of denotation is comprehended in an object connected with action and not in a bare existent object which is not connected with action. The siddhāntin says that in case kārya is understood as a qualification to prompt, then it is also to be given up from the scope of the faculty of denotation to avoid prolixity. In other words, an entity connected with action is not the pratiyogin of the faculty of denotation (*yadapi kāryeṇa prayojakaviśeṣaṇe gauravāt kāryānvitaṁ na śaktipratiyogīti*, VV, p. 71). After that the denotative power can be understood in an existent entity in the following way : When one hears the birth of a son, one becomes happy. This is inferred from one's blooming face. The cause of happiness is the knowledge generated by the sentence which conveys the message that one is blessed with a son. In this way, the faculty of denotation is comprehended in 'the birth of a son', which is an existent entity. (*putrajanmavākyaśravaṇānantaraṁ śroturvadanavikasanaliṅgena harṣotpattiranumīyate 'ayaṁ harṣavān vikasitavadanatvāt madvadi'ti. sa ca harṣaḥ priyārthajñānapūrvakaḥ harṣatvān madīyaharṣavat. tasya ca kuto janmeti jijñāsāyāṁ śabdānantarabhāvitvāt tasya tato janma niścīyate. ato harṣahetau putrajanmani siddhe 'pi śabdaśaktiḥ sidhyatītyarthaḥ*, ibid., p. 71). The fact is that the birth of a son is under consideration and hence there is no scope for indecision about the cause of happiness. The opponent says that there are more reasons than one for the happiness of the person. Hence there could be indecision about the cause of happiness. Moreover, the comprehension of the denotative power in a particular object is tardy when we understand the meaning of an existent object without its being associated with action. On the other hand the determination of the power of denotation with regard to the meaning of a word is very simple when the word is in association with action.

The siddhāntin adduces an instance in which the denotative faculty is comprehended in an unknown existent entity when it is used with a well-known word. To illustrate, to understand the meaning of the word 'bee' is easy when it occurs in the sentence 'a bee drinks honey from the interior of a blooming lotus'. The opponent does not accept this since this view fails to explain the following alternative view-points : Is the comprehension of the denotative power with regard to other word meanings independent of action or dependent on it? The first alternative is not possible since it has already been explained that the comprehension for the first time is not possible without the association of some activity. The other alternative view is also not possible as the connection of action with the meaning of the word 'bee' has to be assumed like the other word meaning. Otherwise two kinds of approach of comprehending the denotative power would have to be postulated. In that case the other words whose denotative function has been comprehended in connection with action would not denote any meaning when they are not associated with action. This explains why the comprehension of a denotative function in connection with existent objects by virtue of a statement (such as, this is a cow) is not tenable as this also has to be understood in association with action for fear of incurring the above-mentioned contingency of two approaches regarding the comprehension of the faculty of denotation.

यत्तु मानं विवादाध्यासितः शब्दव्युत्पत्तिगोचरः प्रमेयत्वाद् उभयवादिसिद्ध-प्रमेयवदिति, तदसत्। कार्यत्वोपाधिहतत्वाद्। गवादिव्यक्त्यानैकान्त्याच्च। आकृतिः शब्दार्थ इति हि स्थिताः शब्दार्थविदः। ननु व्यक्तिरपीदमादिशब्दगोचरः। न। तस्य पुरोदेशादिसंसर्गोपाधिकत्वात्। स तटस्थ एवोपाधिरिति चेन्न। सोऽयं देवदत्त इत्यत्र लक्षणाविरहापत्तेः। यदपि विवादपदानि पदानि न कार्यान्वितस्वार्थे नियतसामर्थ्यानि पदत्वात् कार्यपदवदिति मानं, तदप्यसत्। सिद्धसाधनत्वात्। न हि कार्यान्वितमात्रे सामर्थ्यमाश्रयामः। अपि त्वन्विते कार्ये कार्यान्वयान्वयिनि वा। तदभावानुमाने च दृष्टान्ते साध्यविरहः। कार्यपदस्याप्यन्वितकार्यविषयत्वात् कार्यान्वयान्वयिविषयत्वाद्वा।

Trans. : The syllogistic proposition that the existent entity is the denotatum of a word because it is knowable like the one accepted by both the sides, is untenable. The reason is that it is vitiated by an upādhi consisting in the state of being an effect (*kāryatva*) and also from the anaikāntika fallacy in respect of an individual cow, etc. For the semanticists (*śabdārtha-vidaḥ*) hold the view that it is the universal which is signified by a word. The view that the individual is also a denotatum of the pronominal stems like *idam*, etc. is not acceptable since this is due to the association of the adjuncts like the place in front, etc. But that may be taken as an indifferent upādhi (thus it would not form a part of the denotatum of a word). In that case it would lead to the inapplicability of the faculty of indication (*lakṣaṇā*) in the sentence 'This is that Devadatta (whom we saw in Mumbai)'. Also the syllogism 'the words (other than those denoting action) do not invariably denote their own meanings connected with action since they are words like an action word' is untenable as it suffers from the fault of proving that which is already established. For we do not settle down to accept that the denotative faculty signifies only that which is connected with action but we accept the power of word to denote the syntactically connected action or the one connected with that having a connection with action. When the absence of the probandum is sought to be inferred, the illustration (*kāryapada*) will cease to have the sādhya in it. The reason is that an action word also has as its domain either the syntactically connected action or a denotatum connected with that having a connection with action.

Ann. : The pūrvapakṣin would not accept the syllogism put forward by the siddhāntin to prove that an existent entity is the denotatum of a word since it happens to be vitiated by the *kāryatva* upādhi. Although there is no concomitance of the reason with *kāryatva*, still the upādhi is not concomitant with the sādhya. To explain, the state of being a denotatum exists in *kāryatva* but *kāryatva* does not exist in itself (*nanu sādhanavyāpterabhāve'pi na sādhyavyāptiḥ. vyutpattigocare'pi kāryatve kāryatābhāvād ityāśaṅkya doṣāntaramāha*, VV, p. 74). This is the reason why the fallacy known as *sādhāraṇa anaikāntika* is being pointed out in the above syllogism. An individual is a knowable (*prameya*) but it is not the pratiyogin of the denotative faculty. The reason is that the semanticists (*śabdārthavidaḥ*) hold that a universal is the pratiyogin of the denotative faculty of a word, and not the individual. This means that the state of being a denotatum does not exist in the individual as per the theory of the semanticists, whereas the reason consisting in the state of being a knowable exists in it. To escape the fallacy of *sādhāraṇa anaikāntika*, if it is held that an individual is also the denotatum of the pronominal words *idam*, etc. as, for example, in the expression *so'yaṁ devadattaḥ*, then it may be attributed to the individual's association with the space in front, etc. In case the space in front is construed as an indifferent upādhi, then the individual would cease to be within the domain of the denotative faculty and, hence, the feasibility of invoking the faculty of indication in the sentence 'This is that Devadatta' would just vanish. To explain, the pronominal words *saḥ* and *ayam* being *upalakṣaṇas* would keep out of the domain of the denotative faculty and the term devadatta having been divested of the upādhis would cease to be a fit case for the application of the faculty of indication as there would not be any incompatibility in the absence of the terms *saḥ* and *ayam* (cf. *upādherupalakṣaṇatve so'yam ityatra tadetaddeśakālayoraśabdārthatvād devadattasvarūpamātrasya vidhūtopādhikasya śabdābhyāṁ pratipādyatve sati lakṣaṇābhāvāpattiriti* VV, p. 74).

The power to signify an existent connected with action is sought to be disproved by the following syllogism just as the power to denote an existent has been rejected by the pūrvapakṣin (*siddhe'-rthe padasāmarthyanirāsavatkāryānvite'pyarthe tatsāmarthyam anumānabalānnirasituṁ śakyamityāśaṅkyāha*, ibid., p. 74) : The words other than the kāryapadas (*kāryapadavyatiriktāni padanītyarthaḥ*, ibid., p. 74) do not invariably denote their own meaning connected with action since they are padas like a kāryapada. In other words, that which is connected with action is not invariably the denotatum of the non-action words. This can be other than that which is connected with action. The upholders of the view that action is the denotatum of a Vedic word do welcome the view that words other than action words do not invariably denote an existent connected with action (*kāryānvitaṁ na niyamena śaktipratiyogīti kāryavādināmiṣṭameva*, ibid., p. 74). Thus the syllogism seeks to prove that which has already been proved. Hence it is untenable. It is also not admissible that a non-action word denotes only that which is connected with action. On the other hand a non-action word signifies either a syntactically connected action or that which is the locus of the connection described by action (*kāryānvayānvayinī = kāryānvayaḥ kāryarūpo'nvayaḥ tadanvayi tadādhāraḥ, sa ca kāryamitaracca sambandhasya dvyādhāratvāt*, NP on CS, p. 150). If it is sought to infer the absence of the probandum, then the illustration (*kāryapada*) will cease to have the sādhya in it as either the syntactically connected action or that which is the locus of the connection described by action is the domain of the action word (*kāryapada*).

अथ मानं कार्यं न समस्तपदसामर्थ्यप्रतियोगि अन्वयातिरेकित्वात् पदार्थान्तरवदिति । न । अन्वितेन व्यभिचाराद् । योग्यान्विते हि सर्वपदानां भवता शक्तिरिष्यते । अतः स्फुटो व्यभिचारः । एवं निष्प्रत्यनीका कार्य एव शक्तिराश्रयणीया । प्रयोगस्तु — विवादाध्यासिता (शब्दशक्ति) अन्वितकार्यगोचरा कार्यान्वयान्वयवद्गोचरा वा व्यवहारबोध्यत्वाद् यथा परकीयगवानयनज्ञानमिति । विपक्षे चोक्तनीत्या व्युत्पत्तिविरहाच्छब्दप्रामाण्यविरहो बाधः । दूषणान्तरविरहस्त्वतिरोहित एव । तस्माच्छब्दशक्तितात्पर्यान्यथानुपपत्त्या कार्ये वेदः प्रमाणम् । न सिद्ध इति निश्चीयते । यदपि वेदः सिद्ध एवार्थे प्रमाणं प्रमाणत्वाद् अक्षवदित्यनुमानं, तत्राग्निर्हिमस्य भेषजमिति भागे बाधोऽसिद्धिश्च । विवादगोचरो धर्मीति चेत्, तदापि मन्त्रभागे असिद्धिः । मन्त्रोऽपि हि कोऽपि धर्मी । स हि भवतां देवताधिकरणन्यायेन प्रमाणम् । अस्माकं चाप्रमाणम् । अतो विवादगोचरत्वाद् मन्त्रोऽपि धर्मी तत्रासिद्धिश्च हेतोः । न चात्र विपक्षे बाधः कश्चिद् । अतो यत्किञ्चिदेतदिति ।

Trans. : Also the (following) syllogism is not tenable as it suffers from the defect of deviation in respect of that which is syntactically connected : Action is not the pratiyogin (*viṣaya*) of the denotative power of all words because it is different from the syntactic connection[1] like any other denotatum. For, as per your view, all words denote that which is connected with a compatible denotatum. Hence, the defect is evident. That is why an unimpeded denotative power residing only in action should be taken recourse to. The syllogism to this effect is as follows : The denotative power (which is the subject of dispute) has as its domain either the syntactically connected action or that which is connected with the locus of the connection described by the action since this is known from the empirical activity (of bringing a cow, etc.) like the knowledge of the other person's act of bringing a cow. That the absence of the comprehension of the faculty of denotation leads to that of the authenticity of the verbal testimony in consonance with the method mentioned above (see VV, p. 75) is a deterrent to the contrary instance (*vipakṣa*). The absence of other defects, too, is obvious. Hence, it is ascertained that the Veda is a valid means of producing the knowledge of action, and not that of an existent entity. Otherwise, the purport and the denotative

1. *yogyetarānvayādanyatvāditi hetvarthaḥ*, VV, p. 75.

power would become impossible (this assumption evidence proves that the Veda denotes only action, *kāryaparyavasāyitve śaktitātparyayoḥ siddhayoranyathānupapattiḥ āmnāyasya kāryaika-niṣṭhatvaṁ pratiṣṭhāpayatīti*, VV, p. 75). The syllogism that the Veda is an evidence only for an existent entity because it is a valid means of knowledge like a sense organ suffers from the bādha fallacy in respect of the Vedic statement 'the fire is the remedy of cold' (which is a restatement of what is experienced in our day-to-day life and hence does not enjoy the status of a *pramāṇa*). The reason (also) suffers from the fallacy of svarūpā-siddhi as the state of being a valid means of knowledge does not exist in the said portion of the Veda. If (to escape this eventuality) the rest of the Veda is made the minor term (*pakṣa*), then also the fallacy of svarūpāsiddhi is applicable in the mantra portion (which is not considered to be the means of a valid cognition (*pramāṇa*)). If a mantra, which is accepted by you to be a valid means as per the principle laid down in the Devatādhikaraṇa, is made the dharmin, then the reason suffers from the defect of svarūpāsiddhi (i.e. the state of being a means of valid cognition does not exist in the mantra). For we do not accept it as a valid means of knowledge. And in this syllogism, there is no contradictory argument against the contrary instance (*vipakṣa*). (The reason is thus bereft of an argument conducive to prove the probandum, i.e. rendered *aprayojaka*). (And) so, the syllogism does not serve any purpose.

Ann. : The syllogism of the siddhārthavādin is : Action is not the pratiyogin (domain) of the denotative power of all words since it is different from the syntactic connection of a compatible entity like another denotatum, e.g. a pot which is other than the syntactic connection and which is also not the pratiyogin of the denotative power of all words. The kāryavādin says that this syllogism is untenable since it suffers from the defect of deviation in respect of that which is syntactically connected. To explain, the reason consists in being different from the syntactic connection with another compatible member. It exists in that which is syntactically connected with another compatible denotatum but the absence of being the domain of the denotative power of all words, that is the sādhya does not exist in it. Thus the fault of deviation is quite evident (*yogyetarānvayādanyatvāditi hetvarthaḥ. tadanyatvaṁ yogyetarānvite'pi vidyate. na ca tatra samastapadasāmarthyaviṣayatvābhāva iti vyabhicāraḥ*, VV, p. 75). That is why the pūrvapakṣin proposes that an unimpeded denotative power to signify action alone should be taken recourse to. Lest this should be taken as a proposal without any proof, he adduces the following syllogism as an evidence: The denotative power of word has as its domain either the syntactically connected action or that which has the connection with the locus of the connection described by the action since this is known from the empirical activity (of bringing a cow, etc.) like the knowledge of the other person's act of bringing a cow. The illustration relates to the prompting knowledge of the madhyamavṛddha, which is inferred from his act of bringing the cow (*madhyamavṛddhapravṛttyanumitapravartakapratyayaṁ dṛṣṭāntayati*, ibid., p. 75). The person, who sees this event, comes to know that the young man, who brings the cow, knows the meaning of the sentence uttered by the elder. So, it is known from the empirical behaviour of the young person that the syntactically connected action or that which has the connection with the locus of the connection described by the action is the domain of the faculty of denotation like the knowledge of the young person which prompts him to undertake the act of bringing the cow. This requires some elaboration so that various components of the syllogistic proposition may be comprehended in the right perspective. Had it been said that action is the denotatum of a word, then this would have been contradicted as the action can be a denotatum only of an action word, and not that of a word which means an existent entity. To avoid such a contingency, the qualifiction 'all' has been added in the major term (sādhya). Another point that requires mention is that Ānandajñāna has interpreted the reason used in the syllogism as 'being different from the syntactic relation of another compatible entity'. The reason exists in that which is connected with the compatible entity in which the absence of the domain of the faculty of denotation of all words does not exist. Thus, the defect of deviation is applicable as that which is syntactically connected is the pratiyogin of the denotative faculty of all words according to the view of the siddhāntin. Since the syllogism of the siddhāntin suffers from these defects, the pūrvapakṣin proposes that an unimpeded denotative power to signify only action should be taken recourse to. In order to escape the charge of putting forward a view without any proof, he adduces the syllogism, referred to above, as an evidence.

The pūrvapakṣin proceeds further and continues to fortify his position against the siddhāntin. He says that if action was not accepted as the domain of the power of denotation, then in accordance with the principle indicated by the statement 'there is no ground to relinquish the common element in the form of 'action', the existent entity too would not be the pratiyogin of the faculty of denotation. In this way, the faculty of denotation itself would cease to exist. Consequently, the contingency of the absence of the authenticity of verbal testimony would be incurred, which will act as a deterrent to the contrary view that the connected action is not the domain of the denotative faculty (*nānugatakāryatyāge heturastītyādinoktanyāyena siddhamapi sā na gocarayettataḥ śaktyagrahādagṛhītaśaktikasya śabdasyābodhakatvādaprāmāṇyaṁ prasaredityarthaḥ*, VV, p. 75). The absence of other defects is obvious. Now the pūrvapakṣin invokes the assumption evidence and says that, if the Veda was not admitted to be a valid means of producing the knowledge only of action, then both the purport of the Veda and the denotative faculty would be divested of the feasibility. Moreover, the pūrvapakṣin endorses his standpoint by rejecting the following syllogistic proposition of the siddhāntin : The Veda is a valid means of generating the knowledge only of an established existent entity since it is the means of a valid cognition like the sense organs such as eyes, etc. He points out that this syllogistic proposition suffers from the faults such as contradiction (*bādha*) and svarūpāsiddhi (the instance of the probans not existing in the the dharmin (*pakṣa*). The Vedic sentence 'the fire is the remedy of cold' is not a valid means of knowledge as it is a restatement of what is already known from our day-to-day experience. This is the fallacy known as *bādha*. Also the reason suffers from the fault of svarūpāsiddhi since the state of being a valid means of knowledge does not exist in *agnirhimasya bheṣajam*. To escape this problem, if the remaining part of the Veda is made the dharmin (*pakṣa*), then also the fallacy of svarūpāsiddhi is applicable in respect of the mantra portion of the Veda since the mantra does not constitute a valid means of knowledge according to the pūrvapakṣin. Invoking the principle of devatādhikaraṇa, the siddhāntin accepts the authenticity of the mantra as a valid means of proof and makes it the dharmin. The pūrvapakṣin points out the defect of svarūpāsiddhi as, according to him, the state of being a valid means of cognition does not reside in it. Moreover, there is no contradictary argument against the contrary view that the Veda is not a means of producing the knowledge of an existent entity. Thus the absence of a conducive argument against the contrary instance divests the siddhāntin's syllogistic proposition of it's effectiveness to prove the sādhya. Hence, the syllogism adduced by the siddhāntin is not at all capable of proving his own view-point and hence does not deserve consideration, concludes the pūrvapakṣin.

कार्यशक्तिवाद्युक्तयुक्तिनिराकरणपूर्वकम् उत्तरपक्षारम्भः

अत्रोच्यते — न तावत्तात्पर्यं कार्य एवेति शब्दस्य निश्चयः सम्भवी । तद्धेत्वसम्भवाद् । नन्वित्थंभावः प्रयोजनबलात् कल्प्यते । दृश्यते हि 'कटस्त्वया कर्तव्यः' 'ग्रामो गन्तव्यः' इत्यादेरेव वाक्यस्य प्रयोजनवत्त्वं, न । 'पुत्रस्ते जातः' 'दिष्ट्या वर्धसे' 'चिरं जीव', 'उरुकल्याण हतास्ते परिपन्थिनः' इत्यादेः प्रियाख्यानस्यापि प्रयोजनवत्त्वदर्शनाद् । अकार्येऽपि च भोजनाभावे परं 'विषं भङ्क्ष्वे' ति तात्पर्यमाप्तवाक्यस्य प्रसिद्धम् । कर्ममीमांसासूत्रभाष्यवशात् कार्य एव तात्पर्यं, वेदस्य तत्परस्यैवार्थवत्त्वं च निश्चीयते इति चेन् मैवम् । ब्रह्ममीमांसासूत्रभाष्यविरोधाद् । ब्रह्मण्येवोपनिषत्समन्वयं 'तत्तु समन्वयादि' ति सूत्रयामास भगवान् वेदव्यासः । तदनुसारि च श्रीमच्छारीरकभाष्यं प्रसिद्धम् । तस्मात् कर्मप्रकरणगतानामेव 'सोऽरोदीदि' त्यादिवाक्यानां कर्मपरतामसूसुचज्जैमिनिराचार्यः । इत्थमेव भाष्यकारोऽपि बभाषे । अन्यथा कथमात्मविचारे ज्योतिर्ब्राह्मणं मैत्रेयीब्राह्मणं चात्र प्रमाणमित्याह स्म । तस्मान्न युक्तं सर्वो वेदः कार्यपर्यवसायीति ।

The presentation of the siddhānta view after refuting the arguments of the exponent holding the action view

Trans. : Now the siddhānta view is being explained : It is not possible to have a definite view that a word is purported to denote action only since there is no ground to have such a view. Let it be held that such a view is postulated on the basis of a purport. For the following sentences are seen to have such a purport 'you should make a mat', 'you should go to the village', etc. No. Such endearing expressions as 'a son is born to you', 'fortunately you prosper', 'may you live long, 'your enemies have been vanquished, O! Fortunate one.', etc. are also seen to have a purpose. The sentence 'consume poison' spoken by a trustworthy person is well-known for its having a purpose in the prohibition of eating. The ascertainment that the Veda is meaningful when it is purported to denote action only on the basis of the commentary on the Mīmāṁsāsūtras, is not acceptable as it goes against the commentary on the Brahmamīmāṁsāsūtras. Bhagavān Vedavyāsa (Bādarāyaṇa) has enunciated the aphorism '*tattu samanvayāt*' to show that only Brahman is the import of the Upaniṣads. And it is well known that the commentary on it by Śrī Śaṅkara is consonant with that. Therefore, only the sentences 'he wept', etc. that occur in the chapter on karma are construed by Jaimini as having the action as their signification. Śabara too spoke in exactly the same strain. Otherwise, why would he have quoted Jyotirbrāhmaṇa and Maitreyībrāhmaṇa as evidence in the context of deliberation on the (nature of) soul? Consequently, it is not proper to determine action alone as the import of the whole of the Veda.

Ann. : Now begins the presentation of the view of the siddhāntin after the view of the pūrvapakṣin has been refuted with reasoned arguments. He says that it is not possible to definitely say that a word signifies only action as there is no substantial argument in the favour of this view. If it is argued by the kāryavādin that such a view is postulated on the force of the state of having a purport as is clear from the following sentences: 'you should make a mat', 'you should go to the village', etc., then the equally forceful statements such as 'a son is born to you', 'fortunately you prosper', 'may you live long!', 'your enemies have been vanquished, O! Fortunate one', etc. also have a purpose. Even when an elderly trustworthy person says to his son 'consume poison', it does not at all mean that he should consume poison and die. Rather, it is purported to convey the sense that he should desist from eating at an enemy's place. Moreover, the argument that the Veda has the action alone as its import on the basis of the commentary on the Karmamīmāṁsāsūtras does not carry conviction since it goes against what the commentary on the Brahmamīmāṁsāsūtras has got to say. Bādarāyaṇa, the author of the Brahmasūtras enunciated the aphorism '*tattu samanayāt*' in order to show that only Brahman is the import of the Upaniṣads and in consonance with that, the commentary on Brahmasūtras was written by the illustrious Śaṅkara. That only action is not the import of the Veda becomes clear when Jaimini indicates that the sentences 'he wept', etc. occurring in the section on karma only are purported to denote action. It means that elsewhere the denotative faculty signifies existent entities also. The commentator Śabara also spoke in the same strain. Otherwise it would become difficult to explain why he quoted from the Jyotirbrāhmaṇa and the Maitreyībrāhmaṇa of the Bṛhadāraṇyaka while deliberating on the nature of the soul which is undoubtedly an existent entity. Hence the siddhāntin concludes that it is not proper to view that the whole of Veda is purported to signify action only.

ननु विवादपदं कार्यपरं वेदत्वात्, संप्रतिपन्नवदित्यनुमानात्तथात्वमध्यवसीयते। न, भाष्यवचनविरोधाद्। उक्तं हि तद्वचनं 'ज्योतिर्ब्राह्मणमि'त्यादि। ब्रह्मपरतालिङ्गविरोधाच्च। तथा हि — 'सदेव सौम्येदमि'ति ब्रह्मणा उपक्रम्य 'तद्धास्य विजज्ञा' विति ब्रह्मणैवोपसंहरति। तथा च 'तत्त्वमसी'ति नवधाऽभ्यासादिकं लिङ्गान्तरं वेदान्तस्य ब्रह्मपरत्वे स्पष्टम्। 'ब्राह्मणो न हन्तव्य' इत्यनेन व्यभिचाराच्च। इदमपि वाक्यं संकल्पकार्यतापरं यथा 'नेक्षेतोद्यन्तमादित्यमि'ति चेन्न। युक्तं ह्यनीक्षणवाक्यस्य कर्तव्यतापरत्वं प्रजापतिव्रतप्रकरणाद् न तथेह किंचिद्गमकमस्ति। न च तथात्वं कल्पयितुं युक्तम्। हननस्य प्राप्तेष्टसाधनताविपर्ययबोधेन वाक्यस्य चरितार्थत्वाद्। अस्तु तर्हि तदन्यत्वे सतीति विशेषणमिति चेन्न त्वत्पक्षे व्यर्थत्वाद्। न चात्र विपक्षे बाधः कश्चित्। तस्मान्न कार्यपरता सर्ववेदस्येति स्थितम्।

Trans. : The pūrvapakṣin says that the same view (that action alone is the import of the Veda) is acsertained from the following syllogism : The Upaniṣadic sentence denotes action since it is the Veda like the well-known sentence 'bring the cow'. The siddhāntin does not accept this since this goes against the statement of Śabara in his commentary (on the Mīmāṁsāsūtras). His statement '*Jyotirbrāhmaṇam*', etc. has (already) been quoted. And this (also) goes against the indications which help determine that Brahman is the import of the Upaniṣadic statements. To explain, beginning with Brahman in the sentence 'In the beginning (i.e. before creation), my dear, this was Being alone', the Upaniṣad concludes with Brahman only stating that 'then did he know (that he is Being itself)'. Likewise, another indication consisting in the repetition of the sentence 'thou art that' nine times clearly demonstrates that the import of the Vedānta is Brahman. Also (the view that the

Veda denotes only action) suffers from the defect of deviation in the sentence 'The brāhmaṇa should not be killed'. If it is said that this sentence also denotes an activity in the form of a resolve as is seen in the sentence 'Do not see the rising sun', then this is not correct. It is proper to construe the sentence 'prohibiting the seeing of the rising sun' as meaning a mental activity in the form of making a resolve since it occurs in the section on Prajāpativratas beginning with the sentence '*tasya vratam*'. There is no such indication in the present context. So, it is not proper to construe the sentence 'The brāhmaṇa should not be killed' in that way. The sentence 'The brāhmaṇa should not be killed' serves its purpose by conveying the knowledge that killing is the opposite of the state of being a means to a desired end (the siddhāntin construes a prohibitive sentence as the absence of activity leading to indifference, which is obviously not an activity, see BSS on 1. 1. 4). (To do away with this defect, the pūrvapakṣin proposes to insert the qualification 'being different from a negative sentence' in the body of the minor term :) Then let the minor term (*pakṣa*) be qualified by the phrase 'being other than a prohibitive sentence'. (The siddhantin says :) It is of no use in your case (since you hold that the import of a negative sentence is action (*kārya*) like that of an injunctive sentence). And also there is no contradictory evidence against the contrary instance (that the Upaniṣadic sentence does not denote action). Therefore, it is concluded that the action alone is not the import of the entire Veda.

Ann. : To determine the purport of the Veda, Ānandajñāna referred to three conditions : 1. purpose, 2. the statement of a trustworthy person and 3. a syllogistic proposition (*prayojanabalādarthaniścayaḥ āptavākyasāmarthyādvā anumānavaśādvā*, VV, p. 77). The first two conditions were discussed in the foregoing paragraph. The third condition, namely, the syllogistic proposition is going to be discussed in this section.

The term *vivādapadam* stands for an Upaniṣadic sentence (*vivādapadamityupaniṣadvākyamucyate*, ibid., p. 78). The pūrvapakṣin attempts to prove the injunctive nature of an Upaniṣadic sentence saying that it is a part of the Veda and the whole Veda is purported to signify action alone. But the siddhāntin does not accept the view of the pūrvapakṣin as it goes against that of Śabara, who has quoted from the Jyotirbrāhmaṇa and the Maitreyībrāhmaṇa of the Bṛhadāraṇyaka during his deliberation on the nature of the soul, which is decidedly an existent entity. The second argument that the whole Veda is purported to denote action belies the fact that the Upaniṣads contain so many statements which touch upon the nature of Brahman. To exemplify, Chāndogya Upaniṣad, at one place, starts with the mention of Brahman, the Ultimate Reality and concludes with Brahman saying that Śvetaketu understood what his father had instructed him about Brahman, that is, he understood that he was the Being itself. This shows that the Upaniṣads mainly dwell on the nature of Brahman and the ways to realize It. The famous Mahāvākya '*tat tvam asi*' which has been repeated nine times corroborates the same fact.

The negative sentences that occur in the Veda cannot signify action since the negation of some act at most can mean indifference rather than an action. The prohibitive sentence 'The brāhmaṇa should not be killed' is not on a par with the negative sentence 'He should not see the rising sun', which signifies 'making up one's mind', which is a mental activity as the sentence occurs in the section on the Prajāpati observances (*prajāpativratas*), which begins with the sentence *tasya vratam* but no such indication occurs in the context of the prohibitive sentence 'The brāhmaṇa should not be killed'. The purpose of this sentence is fulfilled if an absence of 'the state of being a means to a desired end' is conveyed by it. The siddhāntin does not approve of a revision in the form of adding a qualification to the minor term 'being different from a negative sentence' in the syllogism to avoid this defect as this revision does not wield any significance so far as the Mīmāṁsaka's view is concerned. The reason is that the Mīmāṁsaka considers a negative sentence to be on a par with an injunctive sentence. Thus revising the syllogism as *niṣedhavākyānyatve sati upaniṣadvākyaṁ kāryaparaṁ vedatvāt* is a futile exercise. Moreover, the siddhāntin points out that there is no contradictory argument against the contrary instance that the Upaniṣadic sentence does not (always) signify an act. In the absence of such an argument, the reason is disrobed of its capacity to prove the probandum that the import of the Veda is action alone. On the basis of this analysis it can be fairly concluded that action alone is not the import of the whole Veda.

पदानां कार्यबोधकत्वनिराकरणम्

नापि शब्दशक्तिरपि कार्य एव सम्भविनी। तथा हि — यद्यपि व्यवहारः शक्तिग्रहहेतुः, तथापि योग्यान्वितेऽनन्विते वा शक्तिर्निश्चीयते। गवानयनादि-विशेषान्वयवत् कार्यान्वयस्यापि त्याज्यत्वात्।

ननु कार्यज्ञानजन्यचिकीर्षासाध्यप्रवृत्तिनिमित्ता व्युत्पत्तिः कथं कार्यं जह्यात्। इत्थं — यद्यपि कार्यविषयिणी इच्छा चिकीर्षा, तथापि नासौ कार्यज्ञानजन्या। कार्यस्य दुःखहेतुत्वात्। कार्यं हि जनयन्ति श्राम्यन्ति करणानीति तद्दुःखोपजनकारणं प्रसिद्धम्। अत एवेदं भगवताप्यनूद्यते 'दुःखमित्येव यत्कर्म कायक्लेशभयात्त्य-जेदि'ति। किञ्च हितं हितसाधनं चेच्छागोचर इति प्रसिद्धम्, अनुभवसिद्धञ्च। तथा च न्यायवार्तिकं 'फलस्य प्रयोजकत्वादि'ति। तत इष्टसाधनत्वमेव प्रवर्तकम्। कृतिसाध्यतैकार्थसमवायित्वं तूपलक्षणमिति नातीतेष्टसाधनत्वादिना व्यभिचारः। नापि कृतिसाध्यतायाः प्रवर्तकता। अस्तु वा कार्यमेव प्रवर्तकम्। तथापि न कार्यान्विते सर्वपदानां व्युत्पत्तिस्सम्भविनी। कार्यपदस्य तदसम्भवात्। कार्ये कार्यान्वयस्यासम्भवाद्। अन्विते कार्ये सर्वपदानां व्युत्पत्तिरिति चेन्न सर्वपदानां पर्यायत्वप्रसङ्गाद्। यथा तेऽन्यान्वितस्वार्थस्य सर्वपदशक्तिविषयत्वेप्यपर्यायता एवमितरान्वितकार्यशक्तिपक्षेऽपीति चेन्न। वैषम्याद्। इतरत्र हि स्वार्थानां भेदादपर्यायता। न चैवं ते कार्यस्य भेदोऽस्ति। कार्यस्यैकत्वेऽपि गवाद्यर्थभेदाद-पर्यायतेति चेन्न। तस्यापदार्थत्वाद्। अथ तस्योपसर्जनत्वेन पदार्थता। न कार्य-पदस्यानन्तार्थत्वप्रसङ्गात्।

Refutation of the view that word denotes action

Trans. : Also the denotative power of a word having only action as its domain is not possible. To explain, although an empirical activity is the cause of comprehending the power of denotation, still the denotative power is ascertained to signify either that which is compatibly connected or the one not connected (in such a way). For the connection of action is to be relinquished just as the specific connection of the act of bringing a cow, etc. is given up (in the process of comprehending the denotative power).

(The pūrvapakṣin asks :) How can the process of comprehending the denotative faculty exclude 'action' when the very comprehension of the faculty of denotation depends on the empirical behaviour brought about by the 'desire to do', produced by the knowledge of the act (of bringing a cow, etc.)? In the following way : although cikīrṣā means a desire having an act as its domain, still it (*cikīrṣā*) is not produced by the knowledge of the act (of bringing a cow, etc.) because doing an act causes pain. The instruments of action bring about an act and tire. Therefore it is well-known that doing an act is the cause of increase in pain or suffering. That is why it has also been reiterated by Lord Kṛṣṇa in the Bhagavadgītā, 18. 8 "Thinking 'this is merely painful' if one relinquishes actions because of physical suffering" (then such a renunciation is termed rājasic). Moreover, it is well-known and empirically verified that one's own welfare and a means to it are the objects of desire. The Nyāyavārttika corroborates the same view when it says that it is the (desired) result that induces activity. It, therefore, means that the state of being a means to a desired end alone prompts one to act. If 'the state of being achievable by effort existing in the same entity' is an upalakṣaṇa of the state of being a means to a desired end, then the latter would not suffer from any deviation in respect of the state of being the means of a desired end of the past. Nor does the state of being achievable by effort become the prompter of an act. Or let the kārya itself be the prompter of an act. (If the kārya is accepted as the prompter of an act, then it should also be accepted as the domain of the faculty of denotation : *tasya śaktiviṣayatvamapi svīkartavyam*, VV, p. 81). Even then it is not possible to accept the comprehension of the denotative faculty of all words to denote that which is connected with action because this is not possible in respect of an action word because the connection of action cannot exist in action. Then let the denotative power of all words be accepted to signify the syntactically connected action. No, (if this view is accepted, then) all words would become synonymous. (The pūrvapakṣin says that the contingency of synonymity would not be incurred) even when the action syntactically connected with the other compatible entities is accepted as the domain of the denotative function of all words just as, in your case, there is no synonymity even though a denotatum connected with another compatible is viewed as the domain of the denotative faculty of all words. This is not so since the two instances do not have any similarity. (In accordance with the siddhāntin's view, that which is connected with the other compatible is the domain of the faculty of denotation). So, there is no synonymity because the individual denotata are different. But in your view there is no such difference in respect of the action. If you hold that there would be no synonymity because of the difference in meanings such as a cow, etc. inspite of the unity of action, then this is not so since a cow, etc. do not enjoy the status of being the primary denotatum. The pūrvapakṣin makes a proposal : Let then the cow, etc. (even) being secondary be meant (by the action word). (The siddhāntin says that if this view is accepted), then the contingency of an action word meaning infinite number of things would be incurred (see VV, p. 82).

Ann. : After concluding that action is not the import of the entire Veda, the siddhāntin further adds that only action is also not the pratiyogin of the denotative power of a word. To explain, although the comprehension of the faculty of denotation depends on the empirical activity brought about by 'the desire to do' produced by the knowledge of the act after hearing the sentence of the elder 'bring the cow', still the denotative power is comprehended only to signify that which is compatibly connected or not connected at all, after relinquishing the connection of action like the specific connection of a cow, etc. (*gavānayanādiviśeṣānvayavat kāryānvayasyāpi tyājyatvāt*, NRD, p. 80). The pūrvapakṣin asks : How can justifiably the action be kept out of the purview of the faculty of denotation while its comprehension takes place because of the empirical behaviour of bringing the cow and so on, which is brought about by 'the desire to do' generated by the knowledge of the act of bringing the cow, etc. Upon this the siddhāntin makes an observation saying that the desire having the action as its object is construed as cikīrṣā, but that does not mean that it is generated by the knowledge of the act of bringing a cow, etc. since it is well-known that undertaking an activity is a source of suffering (*kāryasya duḥkhahetutvāt*, ibid., p. 80). In support of this, the Bhagavadgītā, 18. 8 has been quoted. The whole verse means : In case one gives up actions for fear of physical suffering, thinking 'this is only painful', then his renunciation of actions is due to rajas and, hence, he will not obtain the fruit of renunciation. The siddhāntin continues to argue further saying that it is well-known and empirically verified that it is one's own welfare and a means to attain it, which are the objects of desire. He also quotes from Udyotakara's Nyāyavārttika to endorse his standpoint that it is actually the desired fruit which prompts one to undertake an act to attain it. This is how the siddhāntin arrives at the conclusion that it is only the state of being a means to a desired end that actually prompts one to undertake an act (*tata iṣṭasādhanatvameva pravartakam*, NRD, p. 81). Though the desired end should be achievable in order that one may be prompted to act, yet the state of being a means to a desired fruit inhering in the same entity as is within the reach of our effort does not in any way encroach upon the view that it is only iṣṭasādhanátā which prompts one to act since the residence of 'the state of being achievable by effort' in the desired fruit is an upalakṣaṇa and, thus, the state of being achievable by effort can be kept out of the scope of that which induces an activity directed towards the attainment of the desired fruit (see ibid., p. 81). Then the pūrvapakṣin comes up with another proposal 'Or, let then only niyoga (*kārya*) be the prompter of an act'. The pūrvapakṣin's view that kārya or niyoga is the prompter of niyojya to undertake the act is also not without trouble. The siddhāntin says that if the pūrvapakṣin views that it is the kārya that prompts one to act, then it should also be the pratiyogin of the denotative power of a word (*tarhi tasya śaktiviṣayatvamapi svīkartavyam*, VV, p. 81). According to the Vedāntaviveka, there could be three possible alternative interpretations in respect of the kārya view : Is that which is connected with action the denotatum? Or is the connected action itself the denotatum? Or is the locus of the connection of action (*kāryānvayānvayin*) denotatum? The siddhāntin says that the first alternative is not possible since all words cannot denote that which is connected with action because the connection of action cannot reside in action. So far as the second alternative that the connected action can be the denotatum is concerned, it would render all words synonymous. Consequently, this also is not a tenable proposal. The pūrvapakṣin tries to defend his position. He says that his view is like that of the siddhāntin. The siddhāntin holds that there is no synonymity even when all words denote their meanings which are compatibly connected with others. In the same manner, the pūrvapakṣin says, there would be no synonymity according to the view that action which is compatibly connected with another denotatum is the pratiyogin of the power of denotation of a word. The siddhāntin does not see eye to eye with the pūrvapakṣin on this and says that the two instances do not have any similarity. According, to the siddhāntin's view, the absence of synonymity among words is due to difference in the individual meanings of the words themselves. However, the action is a single unit and, so it does not differ. Hence, the synonymity of all words can not be avoided when the connected action is accepted as the signification of all words. The pūrvapakṣin again comes up with a solution saying that, though action is one, yet there can be difference due to its relation with another compatible pratiyogin such a cow and the like. (*itarapadārthapratiyogibhedāt*). But such a component is secondary and hence cannot be included within the domain of the denotative faculty. However, the pūrvapakṣin clarifies saying that even the secondary component could also be taken as the denotatum of a word. But the siddhāntin points out saying that, if this view is accepted, then the contingency of an action word meaning infinite number of things would be incurred (see VV, p. 82).

स्यान्मतम्— कार्यान्वयान्विते पदानां शक्तिर्निश्चीयते। न च कार्ये तदसम्भवः। कार्यतदितरान्वयस्योभयनिष्ठत्वादिति चेद्, न। कार्यान्वयस्य कार्ये असम्भवात्। तथा हि — किं कार्यं विशेषणमन्वयस्य, किं वोपलक्षणम्। नाद्यः — अन्वयस्य कार्यविशिष्टस्य कार्यान्वये सति कार्यस्य सम्बन्धद्वयप्रसङ्गाद्। युगपच्च कार्यान्वययोर्विशेषणता विशेष्यता चाऽऽपद्येत। न चैतत्सर्वमुपपन्नम्। अलौकिकत्वात्। तत्कल्पने चातिप्रसङ्गात्। तदेवं न कार्यं विशेषणमन्वयस्य। नापि द्वितीयः कल्पः, अकार्यस्य शक्तिगोचरत्वप्रसङ्गात्। तस्माद्व्यवहारावसेया नामपदानां शक्तिः न कार्यमङ्घ्रिकनीनिकयापि स्पृशति। सति चैवं कार्यव्युत्पत्त्यनुमानं कार्यपदस्य व्युत्पत्त्यसम्भवप्रसङ्गबाधाद्, विपक्षे बाधकतर्काभावाच्च शङ्किताप्रयोजकम्। मुखविकासादिव्यवहारगम्यहर्षादिना चानैकान्तम्। अतो न सर्वपदानां कार्यशक्तिर्न्याय्या। प्रयोगस्तु — विवादपदानि पदानि नान्विते कार्ये शक्तिमन्ति विधिपदेतरत्वाद् मन्त्रवत्। तथा न कार्यान्वयान्वयिनि शक्तिमन्ति पदत्वात् कार्यपदवदिति। विपक्षे सर्वपदानां पर्यायत्वप्रसङ्गः। उक्तनीत्या कार्यपदस्य व्युत्पत्त्यसम्भवप्रसङ्गश्च बाधः। दूषणान्तरविरहे त्वविवाद एव। एवं च सति 'पुत्रस्ते जात' इत्यत्र सिद्धार्थव्युत्पत्तौ नानुपपत्तिः। न च हर्षहेतुबाहुल्यादनिर्णयः। प्रकृतेन निर्णयोपपत्तेः। अन्यथातिप्रसङ्गात्। प्राप्तप्रियामरणाभावोक्तिसम्भवेऽप्यसौ 'पुत्रस्ते गच्छती'ति साङ्गुलिप्रसारणव्यपदेशात् पश्चान्निर्णयः। अन्यथा प्रवृत्त्या कार्येऽपि व्युत्पत्तिर्न स्यात्। कार्याविवेकाग्रहादपि प्रवृत्तिसम्भवात्। न च शिशुजन्मवत्प्राप्त-

प्रियाम्मरणाभावोऽस्य निरपेक्षोऽवसीयते । प्राप्तप्रतीतिसापेक्षत्वात् । सा च प्रसवान्तरस्य मरणहेतुत्वान्वयापेक्षेत्यतः शिशुजन्मैव झटिति बुद्धिस्थम् । उपजीव्यत्वाच्च पुरःस्फूर्तिकं हर्षकारणं कल्पयितुं युक्तम् । एवं चोपदेशप्रसिद्धपदसमभिव्याहाराभ्यामपि सिद्धे शक्तिर्लीलालभ्यैव । तदयं प्रयोगः — विवादाध्यासिता आकृतिः कार्यनिरपेक्षा शब्दशक्तिगोचरः आकृतित्वाद् यथा कार्यत्वमिति । न तावत् कार्यत्वमुपाधिः । साध्याव्यापकत्वात् । शब्दशक्तिगोचरेऽपि कार्यत्वे कार्यत्वाभावाद् । विपक्षे शब्दप्रामाण्यासम्भवो बाधः । एवं निरवद्या सिद्धे व्युत्पत्तिः । अतस्सिद्धं सिद्धे वेदः प्रमाणमिति ।

Trans. : This is a pūrvapakṣa view : The power of words is ascertained to signify that which has the connection with the locus of the connection described by action and it is not impossible for action to be the domain of that denotative power. For the connection of action and of other than the action exists in both. No, because it is not possible that the connection of action exists in the action (*kāryānvayasya kārye asambhavāt*, NRD, p. 82). To explain, does action qualify the connection or does the action (merely) indicate it? The first alternative is not tenable as it would occasion two connections of the action when the connection qualified by the action gets connected with the action. And, hence, both the state of being a qualifier (*viśeṣaṇatā*) and that of being a qualificand (*viśeṣyatā*) would occur simultaneously in the action as well as in the connection.[1] Being empirically unverifiable, all this is not logically viable. And, if such a postulation is taken recourse to, then it would lead to the fault of overextension (e.g. *adharma*, like *dharma*, could then be construed as a means to *abhyudaya*, VV, p. 82). So, in this way

1. The compound word *kāryānvayānvayini* (= *kāryānvayānvite*), which has relevance in the present context, requires explanation to clarify the point at issue. Its component *kāryānvaya* means the connection of kārya. It is a genitive tatpuruṣa. In this the term *kārya* qualifies the term *anvaya*. When we take into consideration the term *anvayin* (that which has *anvaya*), it is the term *kārya* which is understood to be *anvayin* and, therefore, it becomes the qualificand. In this way the term *kārya* is made to act both as viśeṣaṇa and viśeṣya. Cf. *kāryānvayetyatraikaḥ sambandhastadanvayītyatrāpara ityarthaḥ. kiṁ ca kāryānvayetyatra kāryasya viśeṣaṇatvamanvayasya ca viśeṣyatvam anvayītyatra cānvayasya viśeṣaṇatvaṁ kāryasya viśeṣyatvamiti yugpadeva viśeṣaṇatvaviśeṣyatve pratyekamanayoranyonyāpekṣayā syātām*, NP on CS, p.150. For a different interpretational nuance, see supra, p. 119.

the action cannot qualify the connection. The second alternative (*upalakṣaṇapakṣa*) is also not acceptable since this would make that, which is other than the action, the domain of the faculty of denotation (because only the syntactically connected would become the pratiyogin of the faculty of denotation, and not the action as it has ceased to be the qualifier and the *upalakṣaṇa* does not constitute the domain of the denotative faculty, cf. *viśeṣaṇasyaiva kriyāsambandhitvaniyamāt kāryasya ca viśeṣaṇatvābhāvāt anvayavata eva śaktigocaratvaṁ na tu kāryasyetyarthaḥ*, VV, p. 83). Therefore, the denotative power of the name words ascertained from the empirical activity does not at all include action in its scope. Such being the case, the syllogism to infer action as the domain of the faculty of denotation would be rendered ineffective (*aprayojaka*) for two reasons : one, the impossibility of an action word being invested with the denotative function and two, because of the absence of the contradictory argument against the contrary view (that word has the capacity to denote an entity other than the action). And the fault of deviation exists in respect of happiness, etc. which are inferred from the empirical situations like the blooming face, etc. (whether happiness or the birth of the son is signified by the term *harṣādinā*. In both the cases, the fallacy known as *anaikāntika* is applicable as both happen to be existent entities and are known from the empirical situations but neither has *kāryatā*). Hence, the capacity of all words to signify action is not at all supported by reason. In this context, the syllogism, too, reads : The words (a pot, etc. which are other than the injunctive ones) do not have the power to denote the (syntactically) connected action since they are other than the injunctive words like a mantra. In the same way, they are not invested with the power to denote that which has the connection with the locus of the connection described by action (*kāryānvayānvayi*) since they are words like an action word (*kāryapada*). In the contrary instance (when the denotative power of word denotes the connected action) all words would be rendered synonymous. Because of the defect of laxity (*gauravaprasaṅgeneti yāvat*, ibid., p. 84) as referred to above, the impossibility of an action word (*kāryapada*) having the denotative function constitutes the bādha fallacy. There is no controversy so far as the absence of other faults is concerned. This being the case (i.e. when action is not the domain of all words), it is not improper to assume the power of words to denote an existent entity in the illustration 'a son is born to you'. And there is no question of any indecision because of the mutiplicity of causes of happiness since a decision can duly be arrived at by virtue of the context (like a cloth bearing the footprint of the son). Otherwise, it would give rise to overextension (e.g. the absence of the death of the beloved could be thought of like the son's birth, etc. see VV, p. 84). Even if there is a possibility of the statement of the absence of the demise of the beloved, still a decision can be taken on account of the statement with a pointing finger: Here goes your son (this event might happen later on. Still it can lead to the comprehension of the denotative function of a word to denote an existent entity like the son's birth). Otherwise there would not be any comprehension of word's power to signify even action from the empirical activity (of the madhyamavṛddha) since the non-comprehension of the distinction among many (impending) activities may also occasion an empirical activity (cf. ibid., p. 84). The absence of the death of the beloved is not independently understood like the birth of the son as the knowledge of the absence of something depends on the cognition of its counterpositive (*pratiyogin*), which requires another childbirth as the cause of death. Therefore, the birth of a son comes to the mind instantaneously (after the delivery rather than the absence of the death of the beloved). And since the birth of the son is the source (of happiness), it is proper to assume it as the cause of happiness coming to the mind first of all. In this way, the faculty of denotation is easily comprehended in a word to signify an existent entity by virtue of the statement (of an authentic person) and the proximity of a well-known word (in a sentence). Here is a syllogism to this effect: The universal (*ākṛti*), independent of kārya, is the domain of the denotative faculty because of the state of being a universal like the state of being an effect (*kāryatva*). The state of being an effect is not an upādhi as it is not concomitant with the sādhya as the state of being an effect does not exist in itself although it is the domain of the faculty of denotation (*śabdaśaktigocare'pi kāryatve kāryatvābhāvāt*, NRD, p. 86). That the verbal testimony would be rendered impossible is a deterrent to the contrary instance (that ākṛti is not the domain of the faculty of denotation). In this way, there is no hurdle in postulating the capacity of a word to signify an existent entity. Consequently, it is established that the Veda is a valid means of knowing the existent entity (*siddha*).

Ann. : According to the pūrvapakṣin, the denotative function of a word is determined to denote that which has connection with the locus of the connection described by the action and, as such, it would not be impossible for the action to be the pratiyogin of that denotative power. For the connection of action and of that which is other than the action exists in both. However, this view is not accepted because the connection of action cannot exist in the action (*kāryānvayasya kārye asambhavāt*, ibid., p. 82). To clarify the point at issue, two questions have been raised: 1. Is kārya the qualifier (*viśeṣaṇa*) of the connection or 2. Is it merely an indicator (*upalakṣaṇa*)? If the first question is replied in the positive, then the following problem would crop up : When the connection qualified by the kārya enters into relation with the kārya, this comes to mean that the kārya is first related to the connection as a qualifier and then the connection will be related to the kārya as a qualifier. This results in an anomalous situation of having both the action and the connection as the qualifier and the qualificand at the same time. This is not plausible as this instance cannot be empirically verified (cf. *kāryeṇa viśeṣitasyānvayasya punaḥ kāryeṇānvaye prathamato viśeṣaṇatayā kāryasyānvayena sambandhaḥ paścād viśeṣyatayā tasya tena sambandha iti sambandhadvayaprasakterviśeṣaṇapakṣānupapattirityarthaḥ*, VV, p. 82). Insistence upon this empirically unverifiable instance would lead to the undesirable contingency of adharma becoming the cause of *abhyudaya* like dharma, which defies logic and compromises the scriptural authority on ethical principles (*alaukikakalpane kalpanāyā niraṅkuśatvād adharmasyāpi dharmavadabhyudayahetutvaprasaktiḥ*, ibid., p. 82). So, it is preferable to discard the view that kārya qualifies the connection. The second alternative which proposes that the kārya could be construed as an indicator. According to this view, as interpreted by Ānandānubhava, kārya would be kept outside the domain of the denotative function of a word. Hence, that which comes within the domain of the denotative power would be other than the kārya. The reason is that it is the qualifier which can have relation with the action and, according to this view, kārya ceases to be a qualifier. So, only that which is connected can become the domain of the denotative faculty, and not kārya (*viśeṣaṇasyaiva kriyāsambandhitvaniyamāt kāryasya ca viśeṣaṇatvābhāvāt anvayavata eva śaktigocaratvaṁ na tu kāryasyetyarthaḥ*, VV, pp. 82-83). Even when the action is construed as only differentiating the connection (*vyāvartakatvamātra*), which is a common feature of both the *viśeṣaṇa* and the *upalakṣaṇa*, that which is the locus of the connection of action (*kāryānvayānvayī*) cannot be the domain of the denotative faculty (*kāryasyaviśeṣaṇopalakṣaṇānugatānvayavyāvartakatvamātrāṅgīkāre'pi na kāryānvayānvayini śaktisiddhiḥ*, ibid., p. 83). When only that which is syntactically connected is construed as the prayojaka of the domain of the denotative faculty, the circuitous statement (*kāryānvayānvayini*) does not serve any meaningful purpose (*anvitamātrasya prayojakatvasambhave kāryānvayānvayinīti vakrimokterakiñcitkaratvāt*, ibid., p. 83). With this in the background, it can be fairly concluded that the faculty of denotation which is determined on the basis of an empirical activity does not at all cover kārya in its ambit as it has been kept outside its scope as discussed above, although the knowledge of action can be taken as the prompter of the empirical acitivity (*kāryasya pravartakatve'pi śaktyaviṣayatvamupapāditam upasaṁharati*, ibid., p. 83). To endorse this position, two grounds have been adduced by Ānandajñāna : 1. The impossibility of the comprehension of the denotative function of either an injunctive term or other than it to denote the locus of the connection of action because of the defect of laxity and 2. If it is admitted that the connected action is the domain of the faculty of denotation, then the contingency of all words becoming synonymous would be incurred (*kāryānvayānvayigocarā śaktiriti sādhane liṅādipadasya padāntarasya ca vyutpattyasambhavaḥ gauravaprasaṅgāt. anvitakāryaviṣayaśaktisādhane paryāyatvāpatterna śakterupapattiḥ*, ibid., p. 83). Given such a situation, the syllogistic proposition to infer the faculty of import in a word to signify action is rendered ineffective because of the following reasons : 1. The bādha fallacy : the denotative faculty of a word to denote action is contradicted in view of the explication presented above, 2. There is no contradictory argument against the contrary view that an entity which is other than kārya can be the import of words, and 3. The sādhāraṇa anaikāntika fallacy : the state of being knowable from an empirical activity (*vyavahāra-bodhyatva*)[1] exists in happiness, whereas the state of being kārya does not exist in it. Consequently, the fallacy known as sādhāraṇa anaikāntika exists in the 'happiness'. Consequently, it is not at all plausible to postulate the denotative faculty in words to signify action alone. The following syllogistic propositions are put forward to furhter endorse the view that action is not the domain of the denotative faculty of all words : The words (under dispute, i.e. the words other than the injunctive ones) are not invested with the denotative faculty to denote a connected kārya as they are different from the injunctive words like a mantra. The upholder of the view of anvitābhidhāna does not accept the faculty of import to signify an unconnected kārya. Hence, to avoid the fault of proving that which is already proved, the term *anvita* as a qualifier of kārya has been inserted in the syllogistic proposition. The connected action is not the domain of the denotative power existing in the word mantra. Thus, the illustration has the sādhya in it. For the mantrapadas are invested with the capacity to generate the cognition of that which is other than action in accordance with the principle discussed in the devatādhikaraṇa (cf. VV, p. 83). In a similar way, the words (the subject of dispute) do not denote that which is the locus of the connection of action since they are padas like an action word. In case the contrary view that word has the faculty of import to denote the connected kārya is accepted, then all words would be rendered synonymous since the import of all words would then be 'the connected action'. Thus, the impossibility of an action word having the power of denotation constitutes the bādha fallacy.

Since kārya cannot become the pratiyogin of the denotative faculty of all words, it is not improper to hold the view that a word also can denote an entity which is already existent as, for example, in the sentence 'a son is born to you' and the like. In this regard, the objection that it is difficult to decide which is the cause of the happiness that is known from the blooming face of the father who has received the news of the birth of his son, is not viable as that can easily be decided from the contextual situation. Although

1. For *vyavahārabodhyatva* (the state of being knowable from an empirical activity) as hetu see NRD, p. 75.

there is a possibility of the information of his beloved having not died during delivery, still other indications such as the cloth bearing a saffron foot-mark of the son, etc. are enough to dispel the confusion as to which is the cause of happiness. In case this is not admitted, then it would be difficult to decide as to which of several things such as a cow, a stick, etc. brought by the madhyamavṛddha is to be understood as the import of the sentence uttered by the elder. This indecision would then lead to the absence of comprehension of the faculty of denotation by virtue of the empirical activity of the madhyamavṛddha, which is considered by the pūrvapakṣin to be the cause of understanding the denotative capacity of words to signify action. The argument of indecision would do away with the possibility of kārya becoming the domain of the denotative faculty. The psychological aspect of the argument of the pūrvapakṣin is also difficult to substantiate. The absence of the death of the wife during delivery cannot be understood without any reference to its pratiyogin, that is the death of the beloved and its cause. So, this requires the knowledge of the counter-postive. But after the delivery, first of all the birth of the son comes to the mind instantaneously rather than the death of the wife. The birth of the son is the cause of happiness. So, naturally it should come first. It is cumbersome to assume first death and its cause and then its absence. So, being a natural cause of happiness, the birth of the son is naturally understood as the import of the utterance of the messenger, which is obviously and undoubtedly a siddhārtha (cf. *yā pratiyogipriyāmaraṇaprāptiḥ sāpi prathamaṁ na pratheta. prasavāntarasya maraṇahetutāparāmarśādhīnatvādityarthaḥ. kiṁ ca putrajanmanā priyāmaraṇe prāpte tadabhāvo vācyaḥ. atastasya putrajanmopajīvitvādupajīvyaputraprasavasya puraḥsphūrtikatvād vākyārthanirdhāraṇasiddhiḥ*, VV, p. 85). In this way it is very easy to comprehend the power of words to signify existent entities also with the help of the statement of an authentic person and the proximity of a well-known word in a sentence. Thus the possibility of comprehending the denotative function of words in situations other than the imperative ones being there, now the siddhāntin presents a syllogistic proposition in support of the siddhārtha view: ākṛti is the domain of the denotative faculty of words without any reference to kārya since it has the state of being ākṛti like the state of being an effect. Although the individual is also indicated in the process and thus becomes the domain of the indicative function of a word but it does not lead to any fault as the individual also is an existent entity. The denotation of an individual by the pronominal stems like *idam*, etc. with the help of the adjuncts in the form of space in front, etc. cannot be avoided. Even being comprehended by lakṣaṇā, the pūrvapakṣin has to accept the individual as the domain of the denotative faculty of another word. As such, the denotative function to signify an individual should be taken recourse to, although it is comprehended by lakṣaṇā (*ākṛteḥ śabdārthatve'pi vyaktyāliṅgitāyāstathātvena vyakterapi śabdānubhavānna vyabhicāraḥ. idamādiśabdavācyatā ca vyakterupādhidvārā vārayituṁ na śakyate. lakṣyatve'pi tasyā vācyatvasya padāntareṇa tvayāṅgīkāryatvāditi bhāvaḥ*, VV, pp. 85-86). In this context, it may be presented that the state of being an effect is not an upādhi as pointed out by the pūrvapakṣin since it is not concomitant with the sādhya. The reason is that the state of being an effect does not reside in itself although the state of being an effect is the domain of the faculty of import (*śabdaśaktigocare'pi kāryatve kāryatvābhāvāt*, NRD, p. 86). That the verbal testimony itself would become impossible would contradict the contrary instance. The syllogistic propostion adduced above does not suffer from any other fallacy and, thus it may be fairly concluded that there is no deterrent to the postulation of the capacity of words to signify existent entities. As such, this establishes that the Veda is a valid means of knowing the existent entities.

वेदानां सिद्धवस्तुबोधकत्वे प्रयोगः

प्रयोगस्तु — विवादपदं सिद्ध एव प्रमाणम्, अबाधितानवगतसिद्धनिश्चयकारणत्वात् प्रत्यक्षवदिति । नन्वेवपदं व्यर्थं, तत्त्यागे च साध्याविशिष्टता । न । ब्रह्मज्ञानविधौ शाब्दे, ब्रह्मणोऽपि शब्दमानत्वाद् । अतः सिद्धसाधनतानिवृत्त्यर्थमेवपदं निरवद्यम् । विपक्षे च सिद्धे शाब्दव्यवहारहानिप्रसङ्गो बाधः । उक्तनीत्या प्रकारान्तरेणापि तदसम्भवाद् । असिद्ध्यादिविरहस्त्वतिरोहित एव । तस्मात् कार्य एव शब्दव्युत्पत्तिः तत्रैव वेदः प्रमाणमिति मतिमोक्षादेवायमाग्रहो दुर्विनीतानामित्युपेक्ष्यते । सिद्धे च सिद्धेऽर्थे वेदस्य प्रामाण्ये सर्वज्ञे जगदन्तरात्मनि निखिलप्रपञ्चोपादानकारणे ब्रह्मणि वेदान्ताः प्रमाणमित्यास्थेयम् । न तु प्रधानादौ । तस्यानात्मनोऽचेतनस्य श्रूयमाणेक्षणपुरस्सरस्रष्टृत्वानुपपत्तेः । चेतनस्य श्रुतिसिद्धतत्तादात्म्यापरोक्ष्यान्मोक्षासम्भवाच्च । न च गरुडोऽहमितिवत्तत्तादात्म्यम् अवास्तवम् । तप्तपरशुग्रहणदृष्टान्तेन तस्य वास्तवत्वोपदेशात् ।

A syllogism to prove that the Veda is a means of producing the knowledge of existent entities

Trans. : The syllogistic proposition reads as follows : The sentence (*satyaṁ jñānam anantam,* etc.) is a valid means to know an existent entity alone since it is the cause of ascertaining an unsublated and unknown existent entity like perception. The pūrvapakṣin says that the particle *eva* is of no use and without its use the probans and the probandum would become non-different. The siddhāntin says that this is not the case. In an injunctive sentence which enjoins the knowledge of Brahman, the verbal testimony becomes the means of knowing Brahman also. Therefore to avoid the state of proving that which has already been proved, the insertion of the particle *eva* is without any fault. The incurrence of the absence of verbal usage in respect of existent entities constitutes a contradictory argument against the contrary instance. Even differently in consonance with the jñānavidhi, the verbal usage regarding Brahman is not possible. The absence of fallacies such as asiddhi, etc. too is quite evident. So, the thoughtless insistence of the ill-educated on the view that the denotative faculty is comprehended in a word to denote kārya alone and that the Veda is a valid means of knowing only that (kārya) is worth disregarding.

When the Veda as a valid means to know the existent has been established, it should be held that the Upaniṣads are a valid means of knowing Brahman, the Omniscient Inner Self of the universe, which is the material cause of the whole phenomenon and not the pradhāna, etc. because it would not be proper to hold the view that the inanimate pradhāna, etc. are the cause of creation as this would go against the Upaniṣadic statement that the Creator did reflect before the creation. Also for the reason that the liberation of the conscious self would not be possible by realising its identity with the pradhāna, etc. as propounded by śruti. And (it is not proper to interpret) this identity as metaphoric (unreal) like that in the statement 'I am Garuda'. The veracity of the identity (of the conscious self with Brahman) has been ratified by the illustration of 'catching hold of a heated axe' (for details, see VV, p. 89).

Ann. : Making the sentence containing the words *satyam, jñānam,* etc. as the minor term, the siddhāntin puts forward a syllogism to prove the siddhārtha view : Like perception, the sentence (*satyaṁ jñānam anantam,* etc.) is a valid means of knowing the existent entities since it is the cause of ascertaining an unsublated and an unknown existent entity. These words make known an existent entitiy just as perception makes known an entity which is neither sublatable nor previously cognised. The pūrvapakṣin objects to the use of the particle *eva* because, according to his view, its inclusion in the syllogistic propostion does not serve any purpose as he holds the view that a Vedic word is a valid means of knowing only an injunction about contemplation (*pratipatti*). Hence, he does not subscribe to the view that a Vedic word is a valid means of knowing an existent entity. So, even when the siddhāntin says *siddhe pramāṇam,* there is no defect of siddhasādhyatva as an existent entity, being a remnant of an injunctive sentence, can become an object of another means of knowledge and so, the use of the particle *eva* is redundant (*vivādapadaṁ siddhe pramāṇam-ityukte siddhasādhyatvādyabhāvāt pratipattikartavyatāprāmāṇyavādinā ca siddhe prāmāṇyānabhyupagamāttasya vidhiśeṣatvenānuvādāt siddhatvādeva mānāntarayogyatvāditi bhāvaḥ,* VV, p. 87). The pūrvapakṣin continues to argue that, if the particle *eva* is removed, then the sādhya and hetu would be rendered non-different. The siddhāntin does not agree with the pūrvapakṣin and explains the reason for the use of the particle *eva*. He says that in the injunctive sentence prescribing the contemplation of Brahman, the Vedic word becomes a means of having the knowledge of Brahman also. In this way, the defect of *sidhasādhyatā* applies. That is why the siddhāntin says that the purpose of the use of the term *eva* is to do away with the fault of *sidhasādhyatva* (*vijñāya prajñāṁ kurvīta ityādiśabdāt brahmajñānasya vidheyatvapakṣe tadviśeṣaṇatayā brahmāpi śābdamiti siddhasādhyatvaṁ tannirasitumevapadam,* ibid., p. 87). Besides, there is a substantial argument against the contrary instance. To explain, the contingency of the absence of the verbal usage in respect of the existent entities on the acceptance of the opposite view constitutes a contradictory argument against the contrary instance. Moreover, the syllogism does not suffer from any other fallacies like *asiddhi*, etc. Despite this, if the pūrvapakṣin continues to adhere to the view that the Vedic word is purported to signify action alone, then this deserves to be disregarded as a thoughtless figment of imagination.

Thus the siddhāntin succeeds in maintaining that words are invested with the denotative function to signify existent entities also. Therefore, the Upaniṣads are a valid means of knowing the Omniscient Brahman who is the material cause of the creation. The Sāṅkhya view that pradhāna is the cause of creation is not acceptable since it is mentioned in the Upaniṣads that the Ultimate Reality did contemplate before it created the world and the inanimate pradhāna is not capable of performing the act of contemplation. Moreover, as mentioned in the scriptures, the cause of liberation is the realisation of one's identity with the Ultimate Consciousness. If the unconscious prakṛti were postulated as the Ultimate Reality and the cause of the creation, then the Upaniṣadic statements regarding the state of liberation of the conscious self by realising the identity with Brahman would become untenable. In case it is replied by the pūrvapakṣin that this identity which has been propounded as the cause of liberation is metaphoric, then this is not true as, by the illustration of catching hold of a heated axe, it has been clearly demonstrated that the identity of the individual self and Brahman is real, and not metaphoric (*satye tu pratīci brahmaṇi sākṣātpratibaddho mucyata iti bruvatī chandoga-śrutirjīvātmanaḥ sattādātmyaṁ vāstavaṁ manyate,* VV, p. 89).

मायाशबलितं ब्रह्मैवोपादानं, माया तु तत्सहकारिमात्रमिति निरूपणम्

ननु तवापि मायावादिनो मायैवोपादानं, न तु अविक्रियं ब्रह्म । अतस्तवाप्युक्तानुपपत्तिस्तुल्येति । न । तस्येन्द्रजालकुशलस्येव माययोपादानत्वोपपत्तेः । तथा च शास्त्रम् — 'इन्द्रो मायाभिः पुरुरूप ईयत' इति मायां तु प्रकृतिं विद्यान् मायिनं तु महेश्वरम् इति चामुमर्थं बोधयति ।

Brahman qualified (lit. variegated) by māyā is the material cause, māyā is merely an associate

Trans. : The pūrvapakṣin says that, according to you, who subscribe to the theory of māyā, only māyā is the material cause (of creation), and not the unchangeable Brahman. Therefore the aforesaid unintelligibility is equally applicable in your case. The siddhāntin rejects this saying that Brahman can be understood as the material cause by virtue of Its māyā like a deft magician. And also the scriptural references 'The Lord appears in many forms on account of his magical powers' and 'Know prakṛti as His māyā and Maheśvara as its Lord' convey this very import.

Ann. : In accordance with the siddhānta view, the meaning of the term sat is not the pradhāna as the act of contemplation cannot be performed by it since it is unconscious. The pūrvapakṣin says that the same charge can be levelled against the siddhāntin that it is not intelligible how the act of contemplation can be performed by the immutable Brahman. The siddhāntin refutes this and says that the unchangeable Brahman can perform such an act by virtue of māyā and, thus, It can assume the state of being both the material as well as the efficient cause of the whole phenomenon. The siddhāntin quotes from the scriptures to substantiate this very view. In the first quote from the Bṛhadāraṇyaka Upaniṣad, 2. 5. 19, the Lord has been described as assuming a great many forms by virtue of the māyā with His nature remaining intact. The second quote is from the Śvetāśvatara Upaniṣad, 4. 10 which describes prakṛti as the māyā of the Lord. From these quotes it becomes crystal clear that Brahman in association with the māyā appears as the varied phenomenon. As if corroborating this, Śaṅkara in his commentary on Brahmasūtra 2. 1. 28 refers to gods and magicians who appear as diverse objects without undergoing any change in their own nature (cf. *loke'pi devādiṣu māyāvyādiṣu ca svarūpānupamardanenaiva vicitrā hastyaśvādisṛṣṭayo dṛśyante. tathaikasminnapi brahmaṇi svarūpānupamardanenaivānekākārā sṛṣṭir-bhaviṣyatīti*, BSS 2. 1. 28).

मायाशब्दस्य ज्ञानार्थकत्ववर्णनम्

नन्वत्र मायेति ज्ञानं कस्मान्नोच्यते। प्रज्ञानामत्वेनापि क्वचिदभिधानग्रन्थे मायाशब्दः पठ्यते। तथा सति 'मायाभि'रिति बहुवचनमप्युपपद्यते। उपासनज्ञानैः परमात्मा बहुरूपोऽवगम्यत इत्यर्थः। 'मायां तु प्रकृतिमि'त्यत्र ब्रह्मणो गुणो ज्ञानं मायेत्युच्यते। प्रकृतिता च तस्य निमित्तकारणता। प्रक्रियतेऽनयेति व्युत्पत्तेः। ब्रह्मणो निर्गुणत्वान्न ज्ञानं तद्गुण इति चेद्, न। 'तदैक्षत' 'यः सर्वज्ञः' इत्यादि-श्रुतिविरोधाद्। अपि च ब्रह्मैव मूलप्रकृतिः। न माया, 'येनाश्रुतं श्रुतमि'त्यादेः एकविज्ञानेन सर्वविज्ञानं प्रतिज्ञायैतत्सिद्धये 'सदेव सोम्येदमग्र आसीद्' 'यथा सोम्यैकेन मृत्पिण्डेन सर्वं मृन्मयं विज्ञातम्' 'ऐतदात्म्य'मिति सद्दृष्टान्तं सर्वस्य सल्लक्षणब्रह्मात्मत्वाभिधानात्। तथा च ब्रह्मवित्पूज्यचरणप्रणीतं प्रमाणोपेतं सूत्रम्

— 'प्रकृतिश्च प्रतिज्ञादृष्टान्तानुपरोधा'दिति । कूटस्थता तु ब्रह्मणोऽविनाशिता । नापरिणामिता । न च परिणामिनो नाशपुरस्सरः परिणाम इति नियमः । हेम-परिणामेऽदर्शनाद् । न चैवं मायायाः प्रपञ्चोपादानत्वे मानमस्ति । तस्माद् ब्रह्मैव जगद्रूपेण परिणमत इति प्रधानकारणपक्षवन्मायाकारणपक्षोऽप्युपेक्ष्यत इति ।

Exposition of the view that 'māyā' means 'knowledge'

Trans. : (The pūrvapakṣin raises a query) : Why does the word 'māyā' not signify knowledge? In some lexicons it has been given as a synonym of intelligence (*prajñā*). Thus, the use of plural in 'māyābhiḥ' also becomes possible (justified). It would then mean that the Lord is known in many forms by meditations having the form of knowledge (*upāsanajñānaiḥ*). In the mantra '*māyāṁ tu prakṛtiṁ vidyāt*', it is Brahman's property of knowledge which is called māyā and being prakṛti it means the instrumental cause in consonance with its grammatical derivation 'that by which a thing is produced'. Being attribute-less, Brahman does not have the attribute of knowledge. No, this (that Brahman does not possess the attribute of knowledge) will contradict the scriptural statements 'he reflected', 'he who is all-knowing', etc. And also it is Brahman who is the original cause (both the efficient and material casue), and not māyā. To endorse the assertion of the knowledge of all by the know-ledge of one by the scriptural statements 'by whom unheard becomes heard', etc., the whole is stated with illustrations to be of the nature of Brahman having the essence as existence in the passages: 'My son! prior to creation only Existence was there', 'Just as by knowing one lump of clay, the whole which is made of clay is known', 'All this has the self as its essence', etc. And to that effect, this is the authoritative aphorism composed by the venerable knower of Brahman, namely, Bādarāyaṇa : *prakṛtiśca pratijñādṛṣṭāntānuparodhāt*, Brahma-sūtra, 1. 4. 23 'Brahman is to be considered the material cause as well in order to be in harmony with the proposition and the example.' The unchangeable nature of Brahman means 'the state of not being destructible' and not 'the state of not being transformable'. It is not a rule that something transformable undergoes transformantion preceded by its destruction; for this is not seen in the transformation of gold. And in this way there is no proof that māyā is the material cause of the universe. Therefore, it is only Brahman who transforms Itself into the world and, hence, the view that māyā is the material cause of the universe should also be disregarded like the one that pradhāna is the material casue.

Ann. : The word *māyā* may be taken as a derivative of the root *maya gatau*. The verbal roots meaning movement (*gati*) also denote attainment (*prāpti*) and knowledge (*jñāna*). Sāyaṇa commenting on *adhārayat pṛthivīṁ viśvadhāyasamastabhnānmāyayā dyāmavasrasaḥ*, Ṛgveda, 2. 17. 5 cd has interpreted the term *māyayā* as *prajñayopāyena*. This has been hinted at in the translation of this passage. So, the signification of the root *maya* as proposed here sounds plausible and so appears to be the point of view of the ekadeśisiddhāntin. He continues to hold that if the meaning of the word *māyā* is taken to be intelligence or prajñā, then the word *māyā* occurring in the scriptural passage *indro māyābhiḥ pururūpa īyate* can mean meditation-knowledge : The Lord is known in many forms by virtue of the instances of meditation-knowledge. The objection that the word *māyā* has not been used by the elders in this sense is not tenable. Ānandajñāna (VV, p. 90) quotes a verse in which māyā has been given as a synonym of the intellect (*prajñā*):

mano mahān matirbrahmā pūrbuddhiḥ khyātirīśvaraḥ,
māyā prajñā tathā medhā smṛtiśca paripaṭhyate.

The ekadeśin says that if one takes māyā in the sense of intelligence, then it may be postulated as an attribute of Brahman. This will serve two purposes : One, the scriptural passages in which Brahman is mentioned to think, to meditate, to reflect before the creation would be cogently explained and two, Brahman can be understood as creating the world through knowledge. In this way Brahman can rightly be assumed to be the original cause, and not māyā. He quotes the scriptural passages in support of his view that if Brahman is the primary cause, then by knowing Him, everything else becomes known just as by knowing a lump of clay all else made of clay is known. In this respect he also quotes the Brahmasūtra, 1. 4. 23 of Bādarāyaṇa : 'Brahman is to be considered the material cause as well, in order to be in harmony with the proposition and the illustration.' He corroborates his stand-point by construing the term *kūṭasthatā* as 'the state of not being liable to destruction' and not as 'the state of not being transformable'. To exemplify this, he says that the transformation of gold is not preceded by its destruction. Hence, like pradhāna, māyā also cannot be taken as the cause of creation. Instead it is Brahman That transforms itself into the world. This is the ekadeśin's view.

मायाशब्दस्य ज्ञानार्थकत्वनिराकरणम्

उच्यते, न तावन्मायेति ब्रह्मणो गुणोऽभिधीयते। तस्य गुणासम्भवाद्। असङ्गाद्वितीयं हि ब्रह्म श्रुतावनेकशः श्रूयते। तत्कथं गुणवत्सम्भवेद्। विज्ञायते च साक्षात् 'साक्षी चेता केवलो निर्गुणश्चे'ति। अत एवेक्षणादि स्वरूपज्ञानावष्टम्भादभ्युपेयम्। न च प्रकृतिशब्दो निमित्तपरः। न ह्यकस्माद्रूढित्यागो योगमाश्रित्य युज्यते।

यत्तूपासनाज्ञानावष्टम्भेन 'मायाभिरि'ति बहुवचनव्याख्यानं, तदसमञ्जसम्। उपासना हि मानसी क्रिया। न ज्ञानम्। यदपि ब्रह्मप्रकृतित्वे मानं तदनुमोदामहे। न माया प्रकृतिरिति तु न क्षम्यते। ब्रह्मणो मायाशबलितस्य मूलप्रकृतिता हि श्रौती। तथा हि — क्वचिदधिष्ठानप्राधान्येन व्यपदेशः। 'सदेव सोम्येद'मित्यादि। तथा मायाप्राधान्येन निर्देशः 'नासदासीन्नो सदासी'दित्युपक्रम्य 'तम आसी'दित्यादिश्रुतौ शतशः प्रसिद्धः। तथा —

आसीदिदं तमोभूतमप्रज्ञातमलक्षणम्।
अप्रतर्क्यमविज्ञेयं प्रसुप्तमिव सर्वतः॥ मनुस्मृतिः 1.5

इत्यादिस्मृतीतिहासपुराणेषु बहुलमुपलभ्यते। न च नैकरूपस्य जगत उपादानविकल्पोऽवकल्पते। अतो मायाशबलितं ब्रह्मैव मूलप्रकृतिः। अपि च कूटस्थासङ्गमिदं ब्रह्म न विना मायां कारणतां यायात्। केवलाद्वैतरूपं च ब्रह्म 'एकमेवाद्वितीयमि'ति सविशेषणश्रुत्या बोध्यते। कूटस्थशब्दश्च कूटवत्तिष्ठतीति निष्क्रियतामाह न त्वविनाशिताम्। तत्र वृत्त्यसम्भवाद्। हेमादिपरिणामोऽप्यविचारितसुन्दरव्यवहारसिद्ध इति वक्ष्यते। एतामेव दृष्टिमाश्रित्य सौत्रं परिणामोदाहरणम्। व्यावहारिको हि परिणाम आचार्येणोपासनार्थमास्थीयते। अन्यथा कथं कार्यमिथ्यात्वबोधकं 'वाचारम्भणं विकारो नामधेयं मृत्तिकेत्येव सत्यमि'ति वाक्यं प्रमाणयति स्म भगवान् सूत्रकारः 'तदनन्यत्वमारम्भणशब्दादिभ्य' इति। कथं वा 'नेह नानास्ति किञ्चने'त्यनात्मजातस्य प्रतिपन्नोपाधौ निषेधकं वाक्यं न पश्येत्।

Refutation of the view that māyā means knowledge

Trans. : The siddhānta view is being presented : 'Māyā' is not at all said to be the attribute of Brahman because of the impossibility of any attribute existing in it; for it has been mentioned in the scriptures many times that Brahman is unattached and non-dual. Then how can it be said that it possesses attributes? It is also directly known that Brahman is 'witness, consciousness, non-dual and attributeless'. Therefore, the act of thinking and so on should be understood by taking recourse to knowledge as Its nature (but, of course, in association with māyā).[1] And the word *prakṛti* does not signify an instrumental cause since to give up the conventional meaning without any reason, by taking recourse to the grammatical derivation, is not proper.

The explanation given to clarify the use of plural in the term '*māyābhiḥ*' by taking recourse to the meditations of the form of knowledge is improper. Meditation is a mental activity. It is not knowledge. We do accept the evidence adduced in support of Brahman as the primary cause but the view that māyā is not prakṛti cannot be accepted. The scriptures declare that Brahman qualified by māyā is the primary cause. To explain, somewhere the cause is stated primarily from the point of the substratum (that is Brahman) as 'My son, prior to creation it was only Existence', etc. Likewise it is declared a hundred times in the śruti 'it was darkness' etc. beginning with 'there was neither non-existence nor existence' that māyā is primarily the cause of the creation. Similarly references like 'it was all darkness, unperceivable, uninferable, unthinkable, beyond what is known or unknown and as if incapable of producing any effect (lit. as if asleep all around)', etc. are available in abundance in the smṛti, itihāsa and purāṇa literature. A composite world cannot originate alternately from mutually independent causes. Therefore, Brahman in association with māyā is the only primary cause (of this composite creation). Moreover, the unchangeable and the unattached Brahman cannot assume causality without māyā. The absolutely non-dual Brahman is made known by the qualified scriptural

1. Consciousness, which is reflected in the modification of māyā having the preponderance of rajas functioning as the cause of universe designed to be created, is construed as the act of thinking. Cf. *sisṛkṣitasamastaprapañcakāraṇarajassamadhikamāyāvṛttipratibimbitacaitanyamīkṣaṇam*, VV, p. 92.

statement 'only one, without a second'. The word *kūṭastha* meaning 'which stays like a peak, i.e. which does not move' signifies 'absence of motion', and not 'the state of being indestructible' as the word *kūṭastha* cannot denote it. It will be stated that the illustration of the transformation of gold, etc. is not a well-considered illustration (in this context) although it appears to be nice at the empirical level. (However,) only from the empirical point of view, the illustrations of transformation have been included in the Brahmasūtra 2. 1. 14. The Ācārya has taken recourse to (the illustration of) transformation on the empirical plane for the purpose of meditation. Otherwise, why did the honourable author of the aphorisms (bhagavān sūtrakāra) regard as an authority the Upaniṣadic passage describing the unreality of transformation, 'The transformation is just a name that exists in word only (i.e. it does not really exist), the reality being only clay' in the context of the Brahmasūtra 2. 1. 14 'That the effect is not different from its cause is understood from the statements consisting of the word *ārambhaṇa* and such others'. Or why should he not take notice of the negative statement, 'None of the infinite number of things exists in this (Brahman), the known substratum'?

Ann. : The siddhāntin does not accept the view that the word *māyā* signifies knowledge. Nor can this knowledge be an attribute of Brahman as nothing can be predicated of Brahman, who, being one without second, always remains unattached. However, it may be accepted that It is knowledge itself and hence, on account of this nature, the act of thinking as regards Brahman before creation can be justified as explained by Ānandajñāna (see supra p. 149 fn. 1). The siddhāntin does not subscribe to the view which sets forth that meditation is knowledge. Śaṅkara discusses this issue in his commentary on the Brahmasūtra 1. 1. 4. He says that meditation (*upāsanā*) is a mental activity. At this point he draws a distinction between knowledge and activity by explaining that knowledge is object-dependent, whereas the activity is agent-dependent. When a particular object is lying in front of us in broad daylight and when our sense organ is in contact with it, cognition just takes place. It does not require any extra effort since it depends on the object. On the other hand this is not the case with activity since it depends on the will of the person whether he wants to meditate or not. In case he does not want to sit for meditation even if he is called upon to do so, he will just not sit for that purpose. Unlike in the case of knowledge, activity entirely depends on the agent whether to execute a particular command or not. So, meditation is not knowledge. Therefore, this view is not correct. So far as the use of plural number in *māyābhiḥ* is concerned, it may be ascribed to the difference existing in the illusory cognition or its kinds (*bahuvacanaṁ tu mithyājñānabhedādekasyāmeva māyāyāṁ prakārabhedādvā draṣṭavyam*, VV, p. 92).

For the sake of argument the siddhāntin accepts the view of the ekadeśin that Brahman is the primary cause but the view that māyā is not prakṛti deserves to be rejected outright. It is māyā accompanied by which Brahman assumes the state of being the primary cause according to the śruti. He clarifies this saying that both kinds of statements are available in the scriptures. At some places it is said that Brahman which is the substratum of māyā is the primary cause. The Upaniṣadic illustration to this effect is 'O! My son before creation it was only Existence'. This is with reference to Brahman which is the substratum of all. This is indicative of other such scriptural examples. At other places there are such passages as state that māyā is primarily the cause as, for example, in the Nāsadīyasūkta of Ṛgveda : 'There was neither non-existence nor existence', it was all darkness, etc. The illustrations which say that before creation only ajnāna existed are found in abundance in the scriptures and it is this ajnāna which is the material cause of the universe (cf. ibid., p. 93). To corroborate his view point, the siddhāntin also quotes from the Manusmṛti 'it was all darkness, unperceivable, uninferable, unthinkable, beyond what is known or unknown and as if incapable of producing any effect (lit. asleep all around)' and says that the smṛti, itihāsa and purāṇa literature teem with such references. This is the reason why he avers that there is no other effective alternative to Brahman in association with māyā to account for this variegated creation. According to the siddhāntin, Brahman in association with the indescribable māyā is both the efficient and the material cause of the manifold phenomenon. The immovable and unchangeable Brahman cannot assume the state of causality without māyā.

The ekadeśin says that the word *kūṭastha* signifies the 'indestructible' nature of Brahman but the siddhāntin does not accept this and says that it denotes the absence of movement. Taking clue from the illustrations of modification, the ekadeśin advocates the view of Brahmapariṇāmavāda and says that the transformation is not necessarily preceded by destruction. To explain his point he gives the example of the transformation of gold into different ornaments which keep on changing, whereas gold remains intact. In the same way Brahman gets transformed into the visible creation without having undergone any change. The siddhāntin rejects this standpoint of the ekadeśin saying that the term *kūṭastha* signifies the absence of movement and not that of destruction or change as the word *kūṭastha* is not invested with the denotative function to signify the state of being indestructible. He further remarks that the illustration of gold and its transformation into ornaments appears to be fine empirically but it does not capture the spirit of the scriptures so far as the nature of Brahman is concerned. The siddhāntin explains the purpose of giving the examples of modification in the aphorisms composed by Bādarāyaṇa. He says that such illustrations are meant for the lower and medium level seekers of Truth (*mandamadhyamādhikāriṇor anugrahārthaṁ vyāvahārikapariṇāmopādānamiti bhāvaḥ*, VV, p. 94). The siddhāntin clarifies his stand saying if this had not been the case why did the author of the aphorisms (sūtrakāra) approve the authority of the Upaniṣadic passage describing the unreality of transformation? The concerning passage means : 'The transformation exists just in word, the reality being only clay' in the context of the Brahmasūtra 2. 1. 14 : 'That the effect is not different from its cause is understood from the statements comprising the word *ārambhaṇa* and such others'. Or how can he not take notice of the negative statement, 'None of the infinite number of things exists in this (Brahman), the known substratum (*pratipannopādhau*)?'

नेह नानास्ति किञ्चनेति वाक्यार्थविचारः

नन्वत्र नानाशब्देन नानात्वमुच्यते गोशब्देनेव गोत्वम् । तेन ब्रह्मणि नानात्वं निषिध्यते । अतो ब्रह्मैकमेवेति वाक्यार्थः संपद्यते । नानात्वस्य नानापदेनोक्तत्वात्त्वशब्दोक्तिस्त्वदीया व्यर्थेति चेत् । न । अस्या गोत्वशब्दोक्तिवदर्थवत्त्वोपपत्तेः । यथा हि गोशब्दस्य गोत्वमर्थ इत्यनेन व्यक्तेर्निष्कृष्य सामान्यमुच्यते । एवं प्रकृतेऽपि निरवद्यमिति ।

उच्यते — नानाशब्दः किं नानात्वमेवाह उत — कथञ्चिद्व्यक्तिमपि । आद्ये त्वशब्दोक्तिर्व्यर्था । नानाशब्देनैव निष्कृष्टस्य सामान्यस्याभिहितत्वाद् । द्वितीये तु नानारूपः प्रपञ्चो निषिद्धः स्याद् । नानाशब्दस्योद्दामत्वाद् यथा नात्र कश्चिद् गौरस्तीति ।

स्यान्मतम्, सामान्यानां साक्षात् परस्परसंसर्गात्मकवाक्यार्थताऽसम्भवादन्यत्र व्यक्तेः कथञ्चिच्छब्दार्थत्वमास्थीयते । ब्रह्मणि तु साक्षन्नानात्वनिषेधसम्भवे कुतो व्यक्तेः शब्दार्थत्वावसरः । व्यक्तिनिषेधे च प्रत्यक्षादिविरोधो दुर्वार इति । मैवम् । 'नेहनानास्ति किञ्चने'ति नानात्वमात्रनिषेधे किञ्चनेतिपदवैयर्थ्यप्रसङ्गाद् । न हि नानात्वमप्यनेकं, येन किञ्चनेत्यर्थवत् स्यात् । प्रत्यक्षादिविरोधोऽपि चन्द्रभेदनिषेध इव नेह प्रभवति । किञ्च प्रपञ्चस्य मिथ्यात्वाद् मायामयत्वमास्थेयम् । मिथ्यात्वे चास्य मानवत्त्वमवोचाम इष्टसिद्धिविवरणे । वक्ष्यामश्चात्रापि द्वितीयाध्याये । तस्मान्माययैव सच्चिदानन्दात्मस्वरूपं ब्रह्म जगदाकारेण शुक्तिरिव रूप्याकारेण विवर्तत इति स्थितम् ।

Deliberation on the meaning of the sentence *neha nānāsti kiñcana*

Trans. : The pūrvapakṣin says that here the word *nānā* denotes the universal inhering in *nānā* (that is *nānātva*) just as the word *go* denotes the universal cowness (*gotva*). Thus, the state of being many is denied in Brahman. Therefore the meaning of the sentence comes to be 'Brahman is only one'. If the state of being many (*nānātva*) is denoted by the word *nānā*, then the affix *tva* mentioned by you is of no use. No, since the mention of the affix *tva* is as meaningful as that of the word *gotva*. To explain, the sentence that the word *go* means *gotva* describes the universal (*gotva*) as disntinguished from the cow-individuals. In the same way, the statement that the term *nānā* means *nānātva* in the present context is without any fault.

The siddhānta view is being presented : Does the word *nānā* denote only the state of being *nānā* (*nānātva)* or somehow (i.e. through *sāmānya* an individual also). If the first alternative is accepted, then the mention of the affix *tva* is of no use since the derived universal *nānātva* has been denoted by the very term *nānā*. On the acceptance of the second alternative, the variegated phenomenon stands negated (this is the siddhānta view) because the word *nānā* is prominent (i.e. it denotes the phenomenon in general through *nānātva*, cf. *uddāmatvāt* = *nānātvadvārā prapañcasāmānyabodhakatvāt*, VV, p. 96) as, for example, the sentence 'there is no cow here' (in this example the go-uninversal cannot be negated as it is not available. So, the negation of an individual cow qualified by the universal cowness should be understood here, cf. *dṛṣṭānte gotvasāmānya-niṣedho na sambhavati. tasyātrāprasakteḥ. evaṁ ca gotvaviśiṣṭa-vyaktiniṣedha evābhyupeya iti bhāvaḥ*, ibid., p. 96).

This could be viewed like this : Since there is no possibility of universals directly entering into a mutual syntactic relation, an individual somehow has to be accepted as the denotatum of a word. When it is possibile to directly negate the state of being many in Brahman too, how can there be any scope of an individual to be denoted by the term *nānā*? If an individual is negated, then its contradiction by perception, etc. cannot be avoided. Such is not the case. If only the state of being *nānā* is sought to be negated by the expression '*neha nānāsti kiñcana*', then the use of *kiñcana* would be rendered redundant since the state of being *nānā*, being a universal, cannot be many because of which the term *kiñcana* could be invested with some sense. As in the case of the negation of the difference of the moon, the contradiction (of the negation of *prapañcavyakti*) by perception, etc. also does not become applicable here. Moreover, being mithyā (indescribable, lit. unreal), the phenomenon should be taken as a product of *māyā* (*māyāmaya*). And to prove the indescribability (*sadasadvilakṣaṇatva*) of the phenomenon, we have adduced evidence in our commentary known as Vivaraṇa on Iṣṭasiddhi (by Vimuktātman) and we will also dwell upon it here in the second chapter of this work (NRD, p. 226 ff). Hence, it is established that, only in association with māyā, Brahman of the nature of Existence, Consciousness and Bliss appears as this creation just as a conch-shell does as silver.

Ann. : In this section the author discusses the meaning of the Upaniṣadic declaration *neha nānāsti kiñcana*. To begin with, he presents the pūrvapakṣa view by suggesting the meaning of the term *nānā* in order to situate the point at issue. The word *nānā* means the state of being infinite, that is, the universal *nānātva* like the word *go* which means *gotva*. If this is accepted, then the word *nānā* in the Upaniṣadic statement would mean 'infinite number of things' and consequently, the Upaniṣadic sentence '*neha nānāsti kiñcana*' would mean 'none of the infinite number of things exists in this (Brahman)'. Thus, the meaning of the sentence would be 'Brahman is one only'. However, he points out saying that if the word *nānā* was accepted to mean the universal *nānātva*, then the addition of the affix *tva* after *nānā* would be rendered meaningless. The reply given to this problem is as follows : The word *go* means *gotva* in accordance with the view 'a word denotes *ākṛti*'. In the same way, the word *nānā* would mean *nānātva* 'the state of being many or infinite' (*prasiddhaṁ hi gośabdasya gotvamabhidheyam. ākṛtiḥ śabdārtha ityabhyupagamāt*, VV, p. 95)*. Or, we can say : we use the word *nānātva* while clarifying the signification of the word *nānā* just as we use the word *gotva* while explaining the word *go* after segregating it from the individual. Therefore, the universal *nānātva* is used in a way as if it were segregated from the word *nānā* (cf. *tathāpi gośabdasya gotvamartha iti vyakterviviktaṁ sāmānyaṁ grāhayituṁ vyākhyātāraḥ śiṣyān prati vyācakṣate. tathā nānāpadasya nānātve vācye siddhe'pi vyakterniṣkṛṣya sāmānya-kathanārthaṁ vyākhyānamarthavadityuktameva samarthayate*, ibid., p. 95). In case the word *nānā* is construed as meaning an individual, then the variegated phenomenon is negated in Brahman. The word *nānā* has been interpreted to signify the phenomenon in general through the word *nānātva* (see *uddāmatvāt = nānātvadvārā prapañca-sāmānyabodhakatvāt*, ibid., p. 96). The illustration given in the text in this context is 'There is no cow here' in which the denial of the universal *gotva* is not possible as it is not availabe here. Hence the negation of the individual cow qualified by the universal cowness should instead be understood in the illustration under consider-ation (*dṛṣṭānte gotvasāmānyaniṣedho na sambhavati tasyātrāpra-sakteḥ, evaṁ ca gotvaviśiṣṭavyaktiniṣedha evābhyupeya iti bhāvaḥ*, ibid., p. 96).

The author further analyses the problem from the opponent's view-point to arrive at tenable conclusion. The denotations in the form of universals cannot directly enter into a syntactic relation. That is why, by invoking the faculty of indication, the individuals are brought into picture in order that the syntactic relation may

---

*The portion of Vedāntaviveka, pp. 96-97 has been added by the editor.

become possible. But there is no such possibility in the context of Brahman as the state of being infinite (*nānātva*) can be directly negated in It (*brahmaṇi tu sākṣānnānātvaniṣedhasambhave kuto vyakteḥ śabdārthatvāvasaraḥ*, NRD, p. 96). Thus, the word *nānā* need not signify an individual. However, if an individual is construed as the signification of the word *nānā*, then the Upaniṣadic sentence *neha nānāsti kiñcana* would mean the negation of the variegated phenomenon in Brahman. But this will be contradicted by perception, etc. This statement makes sense only when the reality of creation is not denied. It is clear from the remark made by the author in respect of the difference of the moon. When we see two moons in place of one, the difference existing in the second moon is denied. In this situation there is no perceptual contradiction as the second moon is not real; it is illusory. So the denial of the second moon is not contradicted by perception. On the other hand, if the phenomenon of creation is held to be real, then the denial of it in Brahman is liable to be contradicted by perception. The pūrvapakṣin says that though there is no perceptual contradiction so far as the illusory moon is concerned since the perceptual cognition of the second moon is brought about because of some defect, still the perception of the phenomenon of creation is not generated by any such defect. So, in the denial of the phenomenon in Brahman, the perceptual contradiction does take place. At this point the siddhāntin clarifies saying that it is the defect in the form of māyā that is responsible for the perception of the phenomenon of creation. Hence, the perceptual cognition in this case is also illusory. Therefore, there is no perceptual contradiction if the phenomenon is denied in Brahman.

It may be given consideration in the present context that it is not possible to deny the state of being infinite in Brahman as it is not available in It. However, Ānandajñāna points out : In such a situation, the use of the word *kiñcana* would be rendered redundant because *nānātva* cannot be many (numerically) (cf. *brahmaṇi nānātvaniṣedho'sambhavītyāha neheti. asambhave kiñcanapada-vaiyarthyaṁ hetumāha nānātveti*, VV, p. 96). In conclusion, the siddhāntin says that the unreality of the phenomenon of creation should be admitted as it is a product of māyā. The author further adds that he has discussed this issue in his commentary entitled Vivaraṇa on Iṣṭasiddhi by Vimuktātman on the same lines and will also discuss it here in the second chapter of the present work (NRD, p. 226 ff.). It is therefore established that, only in association with māyā, Brahman of the nature of Existence, Consciousness and Bliss appears as the universe just a conch-shell appears as silver due to some defect.

ब्रह्मणि सच्चिदानन्दानामभिन्नत्वप्रतिपादनम्

ननु सदनुगतं व्यावृत्तात् कुम्भादेरिव चिदानन्दादेर्भिन्नं कथं तत्स्वरूपं भवेद् । एवं चिदानन्दाद्यपि भिन्नं नान्योऽन्यस्वरूपमभ्युपेयम् , भेदप्रतीतिविरोधाद् । उच्यते, नात्र भेदप्रतीतिविरोधः । चन्द्रस्येव हि सतः प्रातीतिको भेदः इष्यते वास्तवस्तु भेदो नोपेयते । तन्मानाभावाद् । अथ मानम् — सच्चिदानन्दादेः भिन्नं, चाक्षुषत्वात् कुम्भवदिति । तत्र यदि वास्तवो भेदः साध्यः ततोऽप्रसिद्ध-विशेषणता दृष्टान्ते च साध्यविरहः । अवास्तवादिसाधने च सिद्धसाधनता । कुम्भादिभेदेन चानैकान्तम् । न हि भेदः कुतश्चिद्भिन्नः अनवस्थाप्रसङ्गाद् । अस्तु तर्हि तदन्यत्वे सतीति विशेषणम् , न । भेदस्य भेदाभावे ततोऽन्यत्वासिद्धेः । अथ भेदो वास्तवः, अबाधितप्रसिद्धिसिद्धत्वाद् आत्मवदिति मानम् , न । विशेषणासिद्धेः, श्रुत्या बाधाच्च । 'नेह नानास्ति किञ्चने'ति श्रुतिर्भिन्नं वस्तु निषेधतीत्युक्तम् । दृष्टान्ते च साध्यविकलता । अहङ्कार एव हि प्रसिद्ध आत्मा च । स चावास्तव एवास्माकम् । विपक्षे बाधाभावात् पक्षबाधकतर्कसद्भावाच्च शङ्किताप्रयोजकता । तथा हि — यदि सत् कुम्भादिभ्यो भिन्नं भवेद् न भवेत्तदा कुम्भादयः सन्तीति प्रतीतिः । कुम्भादौ सत्प्रतीतिः सत्ताजातिसम्बन्धादिति चेन्न । गोत्वादौ सद्व्यवहाराभावप्रसङ्गाद् । नायं दोषः, गोत्वादौ स्वरूपसत्ताश्रयणादिति चेन्न । तेष्वनुगतसद्व्यवहारविरहापत्तेः । गोत्वादिषु स्वरूपसत्त्वसाधर्म्येण सत्ताध्यारोपात् सत्सदित्यनुगम इति चेन्न । द्रव्यादिष्वपि तथैवानुगमप्रसङ्गाद् । न च मुख्यसत्ताऽभावान्न द्रव्यादिषु सत्तारोपः 'सदेव सोम्येदमि'त्याद्यागमसिद्धस्य सर्वात्मनो मुख्यसत्त्वस्य भावात् । सत्तया सहैकार्थसमवायाद् गोत्वादिषु सद्व्यवहारानुगम इति चेन्न । गोत्वसत्तासमवाययोः सत्प्रत्ययानुगमविगमप्रसङ्गाद् । एतेन गोत्वादिष्वपि सत्त्वस्योपाधेर्वा सम्बन्धोत्प्रेक्षाऽपस्या । सत्त्वेनोपाधिना वा गोत्वादीनां सम्बन्धेष्वपि हि सद्व्यवहारानुगमानुपपत्तिस्तुल्या । तेष्वपि सत्त्वादिसम्बन्धेऽनवस्थापत्तेर्न क्वापि सत्प्रतिभासो भवेत् । सत्त्वेन स्फुरन्नेव हि सम्बन्धोऽन्यत्र सदिति प्रत्ययनिमित्तम् । स्वरूपसत्त्वेनैव ज्ञातः स तथास्त्विति चेत्तर्हि 'सदेव सोम्येदमि'त्यादिवेदोदितसर्वस्वरूपसत्ताश्रयणेन सर्वत्र सद्व्यव-हारोपपत्तावनन्तसत्ताकल्पनावैयर्थ्यम् । ततः सदन्तरकल्पनेऽनवस्थानात् सत्ता-प्रतीतेर्मूलक्षतिरक्षता । अतः श्रुतिन्यायसिद्धे विगलिताखिलभेदे सतत्त्वे जगदध्यस्तं सद्व्यवहारगोचर इत्यास्थेयम् । तदेवं तर्कबाधादिबहुदोषदुष्टत्वात् सद्भेदे नानुमाना-न्तरमपि सम्भवेत् ।

Exposition of the view of the identity of existence, consciousness and bliss in Brahman

Trans. : The pūrvapakṣin asks a question : How does the accompanied existence constitute the nature of Brahman when it is different from consciousness and bliss like that (the existence), which, accompanied in other pots, is different from a pot, etc. In the same way, consciousness and bliss are also distinct, and they should not be taken as mutually identical as it goes against the cognition of difference (existing in them). The siddhāntin says that there is no contradiction of the cognition of difference here. What is intended is an apparent difference like that of the moon, and not a real difference. There is no proof that the difference is real. The pūrvapakṣin presents a syllogistic proposition (to prove that existence is different from consciousness and bliss) : Being visible like a pot, existence is different from consciousness, bliss, etc. (Now the siddhāntin analyses it saying that) if a real difference is going to be proved (*sādhya*), then the fault known as *aprasiddhaviśeṣaṇatā* is incurred (as the real difference is not accepted as per siddhāntin's view) and the sādhya is absent in the illustration. In case the unreal difference is going to be proved, then the fault known as *siddhasādhanatā* becomes applicable (as it is already proven). The fallacy known as *sādhāraṇa anaikāntika* also applies as there is no difference from the difference of a pot but it (the difference of a pot) is visually perceptible. Difference is not different from anything else otherwise it would lead to infinite regress. Then let 'the state of being other than difference' qualify the reason in the syllogism. But this cannot be accepted as there is an absence of difference from difference. Consequently, 'the state of being other than difference' remains unestablished. Let then difference be real because it can be taken as established because of its own unsublated knowledge like the soul. No, since the qualification (*abādhita* in the reason) is not established and it is contradicted by the śruti. It has already been mentioned that the scriptural statement *neha nānāsti kiñcana* denies the existence of any entity other than Brahman. The illustration does not have the sādhya in it as the soul does not have any difference. In case the ego (*ahaṅkāra*) alone is accepted as the soul, then that is only unreal in our system of thought (that is, in Advaita, the ego is not admitted to be a real entity). There is no contradictory argument against the contrary view (that existence is not different from conscioussness and bliss) but there is a contradictory argument against what is to be inferred by the syllogistic proposition (that is, the difference of existence from consciousness and bliss). In this way the capability of the syllogism to prove the sādhya is rendered doubtful (*śaṅkitā-prayojakatā*). To explain, if existence was different from a pot, etc., then a pot, etc. would not be cognised as existing. In case it is proposed that the cognition of existence in a pot, etc. is due to their relation with the sattā universal, then this is not to be accepted because this would lead to the absence of usage of existence in respect of *gotva*, etc. This is not a fault as this would be resolved by taking recourse to the existence-universal consisting in its own form (*svarūpasattā*) in *gotva*, etc. This cannot be resolved in this way as this would lead to the absence of the usage of the generic property of existence regarding them (*teṣvanugatasadvyavahāravirahāpatteḥ*, NRD, p. 99). By superimposing sattā on *gotva*, etc. on account of its similarity with the state of being existent consisting in its own form (*svarūpa-sattva*), the common property of existence can be cognised in *gotva*, etc. Then the same would also become applicable in the case of the substances, etc. And it cannot be held that sattā cannot be superimposed on the substance, etc. because of the absence of the primary sattā in them when there exists the primary existence comprising all as established by the scriptural enunciations 'O my son! Prior to the creation it was only Existence' and the like. The pūrvapakṣin makes a proposal : Let the common property of existence in *gotva*, etc. be cognised as *sattā* inheres in the cow, etc. along with *gotva*, etc. (i.e. by the relation of *ekārthasamavāya*). This is not acceptable because this would lead to the absence of the cognition of existence in the samavāya relation of *gotva* and that of *sattā*. By this, the assumption (*utprekṣā*) of the relation of *sattva* (universal) or *upādhi* in *gotva*, etc. (to account for the usage of existence = *sadvyavahāra*) should be discarded; for the cognition of existence in the relations of *gotva*, etc. because of the *sattva*-universal or *sattva-upādhi* would be equally unintelligible. If the relation of sattva be assumed in the relations (for the cognition of existence in the relations), then the contingency of infinite regress would be incurred and thus there would not be any cognition of existence anywhere (even in the pots, etc.) Then the relation manifesting itself as existing (*sattvena*) can be the cause of the cognition of existence elsewhere. If that (relation) known only as existing in its own form (*svarūpasattvenaiva*) is assumed to be the cause of the cognition of existence, then the usage of 'it exists' everywhere can become possible by taking recourse to the existence comprising the forms of all (*sarvasvarūpasattā*), which has been enunciated in the Vedic expressions 'O my son! Prior to the creation it was Existence only', etc. This being the case, the assumption of innumerable instances of sattā would be rendered redundant (*anantasattākalpanāvaiyarthyam*, NRD, p. 100). Because of the defect of infinite regress by the postulation of another existence (other than Existence) for the cognition of sattā, the very fundamental concept of sattā would be jeopardised. Consequently, it should be held that the world superimposed on the Supreme Existence, bereft of all differences and established by śruti and the rules laid down in the scriptures, is the object of the usage 'it exists'. Hence, in this way, another syllogism to prove the difference of existence (from consciousness and bliss) is not possible as the syllogistic proposition (to prove difference) analysed above is vitiated by many defects in the form of adverse arguments, contradictions and the like.

Ann. : In the present passage the author discusses the problem of the identity of existence, consciousness and bliss, which constitute the essential nature of Brahman. He begins by presenting the pūrvapakṣin's view in the form of a query : How can existence constituting the Ultimate Reality be identical with consciousness and bliss when existence common to pot, etc. is different from them? It means that existence is different from a pot, etc. In the same way existence is also different from consciousness and bliss.

As such, they cannot be mutually identical since this will go against the cognition of difference existing among the three constituents of Brahman. The siddhāntin replies that there is no contradiction of the cognition of difference here. What is intended in the present context is the apparent difference like that of the (second) moon but not the real one since there is no proof to that effect. Upon this the pūrvapakṣin comes up with the following syllogism to prove the status of difference : Existence is different from consciousness, bliss, etc. since it is perceptually visible like a pot. Here existence is the pakṣa where difference is to be inferred on the basis of perceptual cognition. The siddhāntin analyses this syllogistic proposition. He says that if the real difference is the probandum, then it suffers from the fault known as *aprasiddhaviśeṣaṇatā*, that is, the very existence of the probandum is not established since, according to the Advaita system of philosophy, there is nothing which is really different from Brahman and, as such, Brahman does not have any difference in It. If the unreal difference is going to be inferred, then this is the case of proving that which has already been proved as the Advaitin accepts unreal difference. In case real difference is the sādhya, then the illustration, a pot, does not possess it since it is not admitted to be different from Brahman by the Advaitin. Also, the fallacy known as *sādhāraṇa anaikāntika* exists because difference from a pot, etc. is perceptually visible but it does not have another difference in it since difference, having another difference, would incur the fault of infinite regress. The pūrvapakṣin proposes a revision in the form of a qualification of the probans 'being other than difference (*bhedānyatve sati*)' in order to dispense with the fallacy known as *sādhāraṇa anaikāntika*. The siddhāntin replies that this is not tenable since difference does not have another difference in it because of the fault of infinite regress. As such, the qualification of the probans as suggested by the pūrvapakṣin could not help do away with the fallacy known as *sādhāraṇa anaikāntika*.

In order to set aside the fault of *aprasiddhaviśeṣaṇatā* in the syllogism, the pūrvapakṣin now proposes another syllogism to prove the reality of difference. It reads : Difference is real as it is established by its unsublated cognition like the soul. The siddhāntin points out several defects in this syllogistic proposition. The qualification 'uncontradicted' (*abādhita*) of the probans is not established. Besides, the reason also stands sublated (*kālātītaśca*, VV, p. 98) because the Upaniṣadic statement *neha nānāsti kiñcana* denies that any entity other than Brahman exists. The probandum (*sādhya*) also does not exist in the illustration (soul) since, according to the pūrvapakṣin, it is only ego that is construed as the soul but it is not recognised as real by the siddhāntin. As such, how can the real difference reside in the unreal one (cf. *kiṁ cātmaśabdenāhaṅkāro'bhidhīyate,* VV, p. 98). If the witness of the ego is accepted as the soul, then the fault known as *āśrayāsiddhi* is incurred because it is not recognised by the pūrvapakṣin (*na dvitīyaḥ tasya tavāsiddherāśrayāsiddhyāpatteḥ,* ibid., p. 98).

Now coming to the preceding syllogism, the siddhāntin points out another defect in it saying that there is no contradictory argument against the contrary view that existence, consciousness and bliss are identical (cf. *sataścidānandāderbhedasādhane doṣāntaram-āha vipakṣa iti,* ibid., p. 98). However, there is an argument which contradicts what is going to be inferred by the syllogism. To explain, if existence is different from a pot, bliss, etc. (*ādipadena cidānandādi gṛhyate,* ibid., p. 98), then there cannot be any cognition of existence in a pot, etc. If it is said that the cognition of the existence of a pot, etc. can be accounted for by the fact that the sattā universal inheres in them, then it cannot be so as this would lead to the absence of the usage of existence as regards *gotva,* etc. because *gotva,* etc. do not have the sattā universal in them. The pūrvapakṣin replies that that can be explained by taking recourse to the self-same sattā (*svarūpasattā*) in *gotva,* etc. but then there cannot be any cognition of the common attribute of existence in *gotva,* etc. as the self-same *sattā* is exhausted in each locus, which is a deterrent to the cognition of the common attribute of existence in respect of *gotva,* etc. The pūrvapakṣin asserts that the cognition of the common attribute of existence can be explained by superimposing sattā on them as it is similar to the self-same *sattā*. However, then the superimposition of *sattā* can be extended to the substances, etc. in the same way to account for the cognition of existence with respect to them. This would lead to the elimination of the sattā itself. This contingency can somehow be taken care of by holding that the sattā cannot be superimposed on substances, etc. because the primary sattā has ceased to exist in the new dispensation (cf. *āropitasattāyā anāropitasattāpūrvakatvāt anāropitasattvābhāve tadāropāsambhavāt,* ibid., p. 99). Thus substances, etc. would cease to cognised as existent. However, subscribing to the view of the Advaita Vedānta that the primary sattā does exist as is well-known from the statements of the scriptures such as 'O ! My son, prior to the creation it was only Existence', we can say that there can be a usage of 'it exists' also in respect of substances, etc.

However to prove the usage of existence in respect of *gotva*, etc., the pūrvapakṣin invokes the relation of *ekārthasamavāya.* He says that the sattā universal inheres in a cow along with *gotva*, etc. Thus the sattā universal gets connected with *gotva* etc. by being in the same locus. As such, the usage of existence in respect of *gotva* and so on can be accounted for by virtue of the relation of *ekārthasamavāya* (cf. *yeṣu gavāśvādiṣu gotvādisamavāyaḥ teṣu sattāpi samavaiti. tathā caikasminnāśraye samavāyopādhergotvādiṣu sadvyavahārānugatiḥ*, VV, p. 99). Ānandajñāna, however, remarks in the present context that the eternal substance (*nityadravya*) and the relation of inherence, i.e. *samavāya*, do not reside anywhere by the relation of inherence. As the relation of *samavāya* does not reside anywhere by the relation of *samavāya*, it also cannot exist anywhere with sattā by the relation of *ekārthasamavāya.* How can the relation of samavāya, which is admitted not to reside anywhere by the relation of inherence, be assumed to enter into the relation of *ekārthasamavāya* with sattā. As such, there will be no cognition of existence in respect of *gotva* and samavāya (*nityadravyasamavāyayorasamavetatvamiti sthiterasamavetasamavāyasya sattayaikārthāsamavāyāt gotve samavāye ca sadvyavahāranugamo na syāt*, ibid., p. 99). However, this problem can be avoided as regards *gotva* by virtue of the relation of *ekārthasamavāya* as explained above. But the cognition of existence in respect of the relation of samavāya defies explanation by the relation of *ekārthasamavāya* because it is not admitted to reside anywhere by the relation of samavāya (*gotve yathoktaprayojakasattve'pi samavāye'sattvāditi*, ibid., p. 99).

Moreover, the postulation of the relation of *sattva*-universal or *sattva*-upādhi with *gotva*, etc. lacks plausibility since the cognition of existence in the relation of *sattva*-universal or *sattva*-upādhi with *gotva*, etc. remains unacceptable in the following way. If, to account for the cognition of existence in respect of the relations of sattva with *gotva*, etc., the relation of sattva with these relations is postulated, then the defect of infinite regress is incurred as another sattva-relation would be required for the relation existing between the sattva and the assumed relation. Since the relation of sattva with *gotva*, etc. is rendered untenable and infructuous because of the fault of infinite regress, the cognition of existence in *gotva*, etc. and elsewhere would not be possible. If, to avoid the fault of infinite regress, the relation with sattva, being unknown, is admitted to be cause of the cognition of existence, then this is not logical as that which is never known as existing is construed as non-existent. Then how can that which is non-existent like the hare's horn be the cause of the cognition of existence (*yanna kadācidapi sattvena jñāyate tadasadityucyate. ato na tasya sadvyavahārahetutā śaśaviṣāṇavadityāśayaḥ*, VV, p. 100)? If the relation with sattva, etc., being known by its own form, is admitted to be the cause of the cognition of existence elsewhere, then innumerable sattvas consisting in individual forms would have to be postulated. This would lead to the defect of prolixity (gaurava). The siddhāntin proposes a way out by saying that, instead of innumerable sattvas, it would be better to accept the authentic sattā of the form of all as known from the scriptural statement '*sadeva somya*', etc. to account for the cognition of existence in all. To imagine another *sat* would lead to the defect of infinite regress since still another *sat* would have to be postulated for the usage of existence in respect of this *sat* so on and so forth. Because of the defect of infinite regress, the very first *sat* would also cease to be cognised as existent (*yadi vaidikam akhaṇḍaikarasaṁ sat antareṇa sadantaraṁ parikalpyate tadā tatrāpi sadvyavahārāya sadantarakalpanāyāṁ yugapadanantasattāpratītyayogādādyamapi sattvaṁ na pratīyeteti nādye'pi sadvyavahāra iti*, ibid., p. 100). This will strike at the very root of the cognition of existence with respect to everything. On the other hand taking recourse to the Ultimate Existence as referred to above, there would not be any hurdle in cognising the whole world as existent as it would then derive its existence from that Supreme Existence (Brahman) upon which the world is superimposed.

Thus, the Ultimate Existence stands proved to be devoid of difference. This is also established by śruti and the scriptural rules. In view of the above analysis, the siddhāntin does not accept the following syllogisms to prove the difference of existence from consciousness and bliss : *atha sat ānandāderbhidyate ghaṭasamānādhikaraṇatvāt tadgatarūpavat. yadvā sattvaṁ jaḍavṛtti sadvṛttitvāt meyatvavadityādiprayogāt sadbhedam āśaṅkamānaṁ pratyāha*, ibid., pp. 100-01. So, he concludes saying that the syllogism to infer the difference of *sat*, discussed above, is found vitiated by several inconsistencies in the form of adverse arguments, contradictions, etc. Likewise, other syllogistic propositions to prove the difference of existence (from consciousness and bliss) are not possible as they are likely to be vitiated by inconsistencies in a similar manner.

सच्चिदानन्दानां भेदपूर्वपक्षमुपन्यस्य तेषामभेदव्यवस्थापनम्

अथ मानम् — सन्न चिदानन्दाद्यभिन्नं चक्षुर्ग्राह्यत्वात् कुम्भवद् अनेकवृत्तित्वाद्वा कुम्भत्ववदिति। नैवम्। अभेदाभावो हि त्वया भेदो अन्योऽन्याभावो वा आश्रयणीयः। परस्परविरोधिनोरन्यतरनिषेधेऽन्यतरविधानाश्रयणात्। तत्र नाद्यः, भेदसाधनस्य दूषितत्वात्। चरमे विकल्पे आद्यो हेतुरन्योऽन्याभावेनानैकान्तः। न च तदन्यत्वेन हेतुर्विशेषणीयः, तदसम्भवाद्। न ह्यन्योऽन्याभावादन्यत्वं सम्भवतीत्युक्तम्। द्वितीयस्तु हेतुरेवासिद्धः। मया हि सति सर्वः प्रपञ्चो वर्तत इतीष्यते, न तु तत् सर्वत्र वर्तत इति।

ननु यथा ते दृक्दृश्ययोर्भेदाद्यतिरिक्तो अभेदाभावस्तथा सच्चिदानन्दादीनामभेदाभावः साध्यः स्याद्। न। अप्रसिद्धत्वात्। त्वया हि भेदाभेदयोरन्यतरनिषेधेऽन्यतरविधिरिष्यते। यतस्ते भावाभावौ वस्तुनी इति मतम्। अतोऽप्रसिद्धो भेदाद्यतिरिक्तोऽभेदाभावो न साधयितुं शक्यः। आगमविरोधाच्च। 'सदेवेत्यु'पक्रम्य 'तत्त्वमसी'त्यन्तेन सद्रूपस्य ब्रह्मणश्चिदात्मैक्यं सतात्पर्येणागमेन बोध्यते। अतस्तद्विरोधो दुर्वारः सतोऽभेदाभावानुमाने। तस्मान्न सतो भेदोऽनुमेयः। नाप्यभेदाभाव इति स्थितम्।

नन्वेवमप्यनुभवात्मनोर्भेदो मनसावसीयते। अहमनुभवामीत्यनुभवाश्रयतयात्मनो मनोऽवगम्यत्वाद्। ज्ञानं च भिन्नाश्रयविषयं प्रसिद्धम्। प्रयोगस्तु — विवादपदं भिन्नाश्रयविषयं ज्ञानत्वात् कुम्भज्ञानवद्। अनात्मविषयत्वमत्रोपाधिरिति चेन्न। परात्मज्ञाने साध्याव्यापकत्वाद्। नित्यात्मप्रकाशेनात्मनोऽस्फुरणे च 'सुखमहमस्वाप्समि'ति सुषुप्तिकालीनात्मा न परामृश्येतेति बाधकतर्कसद्भावाद् न शङ्कितोपाधितापि। न। आत्मनोऽगम्यताश्रुतेः 'यन्मनसा न मनुते येनाहुर्मनो मतमि'ति हि श्रुतिः। अत आत्मनो मनोऽगम्यत्वाद् न तद्भेदस्तद्गम्यः। स्वप्रकाशत्वाच्चात्मनो न भेदो मानगम्यः। न हि धर्मिप्रतियोगिनावस्पृशन्मानं भेदं संस्पृशेत्। तथात्वे च भेद इत्येवावभासेत। न त्विदमस्माद् भिन्नमिति। स्वरूपभेदपक्षेऽप्ययं दोषतुल्यः। वस्तुनो निरपेक्षत्वाद्। भेदस्य सापेक्षदृष्टिविषयतया प्रसिद्धस्य वस्तुस्वरूपतोच्यते किं वा ततोऽन्यस्य। नाद्यः, सापेक्षनिरपेक्षदृष्ट्योस्तादात्म्यायोगाद्। द्वितीये तु संज्ञाविवादः स्यात्। तस्मान्न वस्तुस्वरूपं भेदः नापि वस्तुसंस्पर्शी भेदग्रहः।

ननु विशिष्टज्ञानं विशेषणज्ञानपुरस्सरं न तु विशेषणगोचरम्। अन्यथा कथं 'सुरभि चन्दनमि'ति विशिष्टज्ञानं भवेद्। अतः स्वप्रकाशस्यापि भेदग्रहो नानुपपन्नः। न। शब्दादिभेदस्य चाक्षुषत्वप्रसङ्गाद्। यत्र सामग्र्यभावेऽप्यापरोक्ष्यं दृश्यते तत्रास्माकं नित्यानुभवादेव तदापरोक्ष्यम्। यथास्मिन्नाकाशदेशे पक्षी प्लवत इत्यापरोक्ष्यम्। तस्मान्न स्वतस्सिद्धस्य भेदो मानगम्य इति सिद्धम्।

Establishment of the identity of Existence, Consciousness, Bliss preceded by the exposition of their difference

Trans. : (Apprehending from the siddhāntin a syllogism to prove non-difference), the pūrvapakṣin presents a syllogism (to prove the absence of non-difference of existence from consciousness and bliss) : Existence is not non-different from consciousness and bliss, etc. since it can be perceived by the eyes like a pot or since it has the property of being existent in many like the state of being a pot. This is not so. You have to take the 'absence of non-difference' either as difference (*bheda*) or mutual non-existence (*tādātmyābhāva* or *anyo'nyābhāva*). On negating either of the two mutually opposite, the other stands accepted. Among the two, the first alternative (that is, when *abhedābhāva* is construed as *bheda*) is not acceptable as the reason used to prove the reality of difference has been proved to be fallacious. If the second alternative is accepted, then the first reason (the state of being perceivable by the eyes) suffers from the fallacy known as *sādhāraṇa anaikāntika* in respect of mutual non-existence. And the reason cannot be qualified by 'the state of being other than mutual non-existence' as it is not possible since it has already been stated that there is nothing which can be other than the mutual non-existence. The second reason itself (*anekavṛttitvāt*, i.e. the state of being existent in many) is *asiddha* as it does not exist in the pakṣa, i.e. *sat*. The siddhāntin intends to say that, according to him, the whole universe exists in Existence (*sat*) and not the other way round (i.e. Existence does not exist anywhere, lit., in all).

The pūrvapakṣin proposes 'As you accept the absence of non-difference to be other than the difference, etc. between the seer and the seen, let that absence of non-difference (*abhedābhāva*) between existence, consciousness and bliss be the probandum'. (The siddhāntin says :) No, this is not well established. (Then how can it be the sādhya when it is not accepted by both the sides?) It is intended by you that, when either bheda or abheda is negated, the other stands accepted because, according to your view, both existence and non-existence are real entities. Therefore, the absence of non-difference other than bheda, etc., being unestablished, cannot be proved (i.e. cannot construed as the *sādhya*). Moreover, this is contradicted by the scriptures : Beginning with 'It was only existence...' and concluding with 'That thou art', the scripture purposefully makes known that Brahman of the nature of existence is one with consciousness. Therefore, the contradiction of the scripture cannot be avoided if the absence of non-difference from existence is to be inferred. As such, the conclusion is that neither difference from existence is inferable nor the absence of non-difference.

Thus also (although the above syllogism has failed to infer the difference from *sat,* still the pūrvapakṣin says that) the difference between the experience (knowledge) and the soul is known by the mind as the soul can be known by the mind as the locus of knowledge in the experience 'I know'. That the locus and the content of knowledge are different is well-known. The syllogism to prove this is as follows : I-knowledge (the subject of dispute) has a different locus and a different content because of the state of being knowledge like the knowledge of a pot. If it is said that the state of being a content other than the soul is an upādhi, then this is not so as in the knowledge of other's soul, the upādhi is not concomitant with the sādhya (as the soul obviously becomes a content in the knowledge of other's soul). In the event of the soul not being made manifest by the eternal light of the soul, the soul of deep sleep would not be remembered as 'I slept happily'. Because of this contradictory argument, even the doubtful upādhi ceases to be available. No, (being self-luminous, the soul is not known by the mind) as there is a scriptural statement about the unknowability of the soul : Which is not known by the mind but by which the latter becomes known. Therefore, not being comprehensible by the mind, its difference (also) cannot be known by it. Also the soul being self-luminous, its difference cannot be known by a means of knowledge; for a means of knowledge which does not manifest the dharmin and the pratiyogin also does not produce the knowledge of their difference. (In case the existence of the dharmin itself is accepted as conducive to the cognition of difference, cf. VV, p. 103), then only bare difference would be known, and not as) 'this is different from that' (cf. ibid., p. 103). The same fault would be applicable if difference is construed as the nature of the thing itself (*svarūpabheda*) as the thing does not require any reference for itself (i.e. it is *nirapekṣa*). Is the difference, which is well-known as being an object of cognition requiring a reference (*sāpekṣa*), called the nature of the thing itself or is some other difference (than the well-known one) the nature of a thing ? The first alternative is not tenable since there cannot be non-difference (*tādātmya*) between that which is relative and that which is indifferent. Regarding the second alternative, it is only a difference of opinion about the nomenclature (which does not carry any significance). Therefore, difference is not the nature of a thing nor does the cognition of difference make the thing its content.

(The pūrvapakṣin continues to attempt to put across his view-point saying that) a qualified cognition is preceded by the cognition of the qualifier but the qualifier does not become the content of the qualified cognition. Otherwise, how would the qualified cognition 'the sandal is fragrant' take place? As such, the cognition of difference of the self-luminous soul is also not impossible. No, since on accepting, this the difference from a sound, etc. would become liable to have the property of being visible. When an immediate cognition takes place even without the causal apparatus being present, that cognition takes place by virtue of the eternal knowledge (in the form of witness perception, *sākṣipratyakṣa*) just as the immediate cognition of a bird flying here in the sky does. (Here the immediate cognition of ākāśa is to be understood as witness perception). Therefore, it is established that the difference of the self-proven soul does not become an object of a means of cognition.

Ann. : The pūrvapakṣin does not subscribe to the Advaitin's view that existence is identical with consciosness and bliss. To prove his point of view, he puts forward the following syllogistic proposition : Existence is not non-different from consciousness and bliss, etc. since it can be perceived by the eyes like a pot, or since it has the property of being existent in many like the state of being a pot. Not accepting the syllogistic proposition presented by the pūrvapakṣin, the siddhāntin asks him what, according to him, the probandum (*sādhya*) means. Does it mean difference (*bheda*) or mutual non-existence (*anyo'nyābhāva*)? The two alternative significations of the 'absence of non-difference' depend on how the term *abheda* is interpreted. Is it taken to mean identity (*tādātmya*) or oneness (*aikya*). If it is taken to denote identity, then the absence of *abheda* means 'mutual non-existence'. If it is taken to mean 'oneness', then its absence is construed as difference (*tādātmye tadabhāvo'nyonyābhāvaḥ aikye tadabhāvo bhedaḥ*, VV, p. 101). Both *bheda* and *abheda* are mutually opposite. If either of the two is rejected, the other stands adopted. Thus if the sādhya is construed as difference (*bheda*), then this is unacceptable as the reality of difference has already been refuted. If the second denotation of the absence of *abheda* is accepted, then the first reason 'the state of being perceivable by the eyes' is rendered *anaikāntika* as *anyo'nyābhāva* does not another *anyo'nyābhāva*, but it is visually perceivable (*cakṣurgrāhya*). It is no use qualifying the sādhya with the qualification 'the state of being other than *bheda*' since there is no difference of difference (*bhedasya bhedābhāve tato'nyatvāsiddheḥ*, ibid., p. 101; also see NRD, p. 101). So far as the second reason is concerned, it suffers from the fallacy known as *svarūpāsiddhi* as 'the state of being existent in many' does not exist in Existence, which is accepted by the siddhāntin as the locus of all but It does not exist in all (see *mayā hi sati sarvaḥ prapañcaḥ vartata itīṣyate na tu tat sarvatra vartata iti*, NRD, p. 101).

The pūrvapakṣin makes another proposal to drive home his point of view. He says that the absence of non-difference between existence, consciousness and bliss should be made the probandum just as the absence of non-difference other than the difference, etc. of the seer and the seen is accepted by the siddhāntin. The siddhāntin replies in the negative saying that that kind of absence of non-difference (*abhedābhāva*) is not recognised by the pūrvapakṣin and hence it cannot be made the sādhya. He further adds that when either of the two, that is, bheda and abheda, is denied, the other stands accepted since, according to the pūrvapakṣin, both existence and non-existence are realities. Therefore, the unestablished absence of non-difference (*abhedābhāva*) which is other than the difference, etc. of the seer and the seen cannot become the sādhya of the syllogistic proposition. Moreover, this also goes against the scriptures : Beginning with 'It was only existence...' Chāndogya Upaniṣad 6. 2. 1 and concluding with 'That thou art' Ch. Up. 6. 8. 7, the Upaniṣad conveys with a purpose that Brahman of the nature of existence is one with consciousness. Therefore, the contradiction of the scripture cannot be avoided if an attempt is made to infer the absence of non-difference of existence from consciousness. From this the siddhāntin concludes that neither difference from existence is inferable nor the absence of non-difference.

Even on accepting the non-difference of existence, consciousness and bliss (*saccidānandānāmabhede'pi cidātmanorbhedo'stīti śaṅkate*, VV, p.102), the opponent points out that the difference of knowledge from the soul is known by the mind since it (the soul) is known as the locus of the experience 'I know'. If the soul is accepted to be known by the mind, then it may be understood to be other than the soul like pleasure, etc. To him who does not believe this to be true, this syllogistic proposition should be put forward to prove that knowledge has a different locus and a different content : The knowledge of 'I' has a different locus and a different content because of the state of being knowledge like the knowledge of a pot (cf. *ahamiti jñānaṁ pakṣīkṛtyānumānamāracayati*, ibid., p. 102). In case an objection is raised that the reason in the syllogism has an upādhi consisting in the objecthood of that which is other than the soul, then it can be set aside by saying that in the knowledge of other's soul, the upādhi is not concomitant with the *sādhya* as, in the knowledge of other's soul, the soul itself is the object of knowledge, and not that which is other than the soul. So, the objecthood of that which is other than the soul is not an upādhi (*etenātmāviṣayatvopādhirapāstaḥ*, ibid., p. 103). If it is doubted that an upādhi exists since there is no contradiction against the soul being the object of the knowledge that has the soul as its locus (*ātmani svāśrayajñānaviṣayatve bādhakābhāvādupādhiśaṅketi cet*, ibid., 103), then that also can be set aside in the following way : If it is admitted that during deep sleep the soul does not become manifest by its own eternal light, then the soul, which is the subject of the experience 'I slept happily' would not be recollected. But such a recollection is an empirically verified phenomenon. So, the contingency of the absence of remembrance of the soul of deep sleep constitutes a contradictory argument against the soul's not being made manifest by its own eternal light and hence also against the possibility of the upādhi referred to above.

The siddhāntin does not subscribe to the view of the opponent saying that the soul cannot be known by the mind. Consequently, the difference having the soul as the pratiyogin cannot be known by the mind. He adduces śruti as evidence : Which is not known by the mind but by which the latter is known. He further consolidates his view saying that since the soul is self-luminous, it does not require any means of knowledge for its own knowledge. To explain why the difference of the self-luminous soul is not capable of being comprehended by a means of knowledge, it is desirable to gain familiarity with the well-known views on the nature of difference as to whether difference is the property of a thing or it is the very nature of the thing itself. The former view belongs to the Nyāya system of philosophy whereas the latter view is held by the Prābhākara Mīmāṁsaka. If we take into account the view of the Naiyāyika, then it may be said that a means of knowledge not comprehending the dharmin and the pratiyogin cannot reveal their difference. In case the existence of the dharmin itself is considered to be conducive to the cognition of difference to arise, then only bare difference would be known, and not as 'this is different from that' (*tathātve ca bheda ityavabhāseta. na tvidamasmāt bhinnamiti*, NRD, p. 103 and also cf. VV, p.103). The same fault would be applicable if the view of the Prābhākara Mīmāṁsaka is taken into consideration and the difference is construed as the nature of the thing itself (*svarūpabheda*) because it also does not require anything else for its cognition. To point out another defect, the siddhāntin takes recourse to an option of alternatives : Is the well-known difference, being the domain of a relative view (*sāpekṣa*), said to constitute the very nature of a thing or does it constitute something other than this? The first alternative is not logically justifiable since the identity of something which requires a reference (*sāpekṣa*, i.e. difference) and that which does not require it (*nirapekṣa*, i.e. a thing) is evidently not intelligible. When the second alternative that the unknown difference consists in the nature of a thing, is taken into consideration, it is only a difference of opinion about the nomenclature. For the opponent may designate the extramundane (*aprasiddha* or *alaukika*) assumed entity as difference whereas the siddhāntin does not intend to do so. So, it is a futile exercise. From this the siddhāntin concludes that difference does not consist in the form of a vastu nor does the knowledge of difference include the thing (vastu) its content.

Now the pūrvapakṣin makes another attempt to prove the tenability of difference. He says that a qualified cognition is preceded by the cognition of the qualifier but it does not make the qualifier its content. To drive home this point, he invokes the popular illustration of the qualified cognition 'the sandal wood is fragrant'. In this cognition, the fragrance of the sandal wood, which is a qualifier of the piece of sandal wood, does not become the object of the perceptual cognition at the time when the qualified cognition arises. According to this view, a qualified cognition does not include the cognition of the qualifier. On the basis of such a qualified cognition, the pūrvapakṣin holds the view that the cognition of difference of the self-luminous soul is not at all impossible. In other words the difference of the soul can be perceived without perceiving the soul as, being self-luminous, the soul first becomes manifest and then the qualified cognition 'the difference from the soul' can take place without the cognition of the soul at the time when the qualified cognition is taking place (in *ātmapratiyogika bheda*, the soul qualifies the difference). So, in consonance with this, the cognition of difference of the self-luminous soul is not incongruous. The siddhāntin does not accept that the qualifier does not become the object of the qualified cognition because this would give rise to the contingency of the visual perception of the difference of a word. To explain, first 'a form (*rūpa*)' is perceived by the eyes and 'a word' (*śabda*) by the ears. Then the qualified cognition 'a form is different from a word', which includes 'a word' in it, is liable to become visually perceptible (*śrotranetrābhyāṁ śabdarūpāvasāye rūpaṁ bhinnaṁ śabdāditi viśiṣṭajñānaṁ cākṣuṣam āpatet*, VV, p. 104). It is, therefore, held by the siddhāntin that in a qualified cognition the qualifier should also become an object of cognition. The siddhāntin further adds that, when an immediate cognition of something takes place in the absence of the causal apparatus, it takes place because of the eternal perception, that is, perception by the witness (*sākṣipratyakṣa*) just as the immediate perception of ākāśa in the cognition 'a bird flies in the sky' takes place. Here ākāśa is admitted by the siddhāntin to become an object of witness perception. On this view, the perception of the qualifier 'fragrance' in the qualified cognition 'the sandal wood is fragrant' can be explained in terms of the perception by witness consciousness unlike the Naiyāyika who holds that the frgarance is visually perceived by virtue of the extraordinary contact (*jñānalakṣaṇasannikarṣa*) which consists in the previous knowledge of fragrance. In this way, the siddhāntin concludes that, since the soul is self-evident, it does not require any means of cognition for its knowledge, nor for the difference from it.

आत्मनः स्वप्रकाशत्वे प्रमाणनिरूपणम्

नन्वात्मनः स्वयंप्रकाशत्वे किं मानम्। 'अत्रायं पुरुषः स्वयं ज्योतिरि'त्यागम इति चेन्न। 'वागेवास्य ज्योतिरि'तिवदात्मनो ज्योतिःकरणत्वाद् ज्योतिष्ट्वाभिधानाद्। अन्यथाहमिति वेद्यतानुभवविरोधः। एतेनानुमानमप्यपास्तम्। अपि च स्वयंज्योतिष्ट्वमन्यत्र प्रसिद्धमप्रसिद्धं वा। आद्ये असाधारणमात्मत्वादिसाधनं सपक्षाप्रवेशाद्। न च साधनान्तरमत्रान्वयि सम्भवेद्। आत्मानात्मनोः साधारणधर्मानङ्गीकाराद्। द्वितीये चाप्रसिद्धविशेषणः पक्षः। आत्मा स्वव्यवहारकारणप्रकाशः आत्मत्वात् कुम्भवदिति व्यतिरेकिप्रयोगे नायं दोष इति चेन्न। आत्मनः सर्वव्यवहारागोचरत्वाभ्युपगमात्। तद्गोचरत्वे चात्मनः किमपराद्धं ज्ञानगोचरत्वेन। किञ्च अहमिति प्रसिद्धस्य धर्मित्वे उक्तोऽनुभवविरोधः, तदितरस्य धर्मित्वे च परस्याश्रयासिद्धिः। अपि चात्मनो वेद्यत्वे न किञ्चिद् बाधकमस्ति। एतेनार्थापत्तिरपि निरस्ता। अनुपपत्तेरभावाद्। आत्मनो वेद्यत्वे प्रमातृत्वं न स्यादिति चेन्न। वेद्यानां नयनादीनां प्रमाणकरणत्ववदात्मनः प्रमाणोपादानत्वोपपत्तेः। तथापि कथमात्मनः स्वयंज्ञतेति चेद् गुरुत्ववद् ज्ञानस्य स्वाश्रयातिशयहेतुत्वे विरोधानुपलब्धेरिति ब्रूमः। एतेन स्वात्मनि वृत्तिविरोधो व्याख्यातः। नन्वात्मनः परप्रकाश्यत्वेऽहमनहं वेति कदाचित्संशयः स्याद्। न। दुःखादिवदात्मन्यपि संशयाभावोपपत्तेः।

स्यान्मतम्। ममेदनुकूलमित्यादिविशिष्टप्रत्ययो विशेषणप्रत्ययाधीनसद्भावः। तस्य च विशेषणस्यात्मनोऽनन्यथासिद्धिरुक्ता मकरन्दादिषु। अतः सिद्धा आत्मनः स्वयंप्रकाशतेति। न। अनुकूलाद्यन्वयिनोऽहंप्रत्ययिनः स्वप्रकाशताया वेदान्तिनोऽप्यनिष्टत्वात्। तदन्यस्य चाशनायाद्यतीतस्यासङ्गस्य नानुकूलाद्यर्थान्वयः सम्भवी। न चेयमनुमानादिमानोक्तिः सम्भवति। साध्याप्रसिद्ध्यादिग्रस्तत्वाद्। अतो यत्किंचिदेतद्। एवमात्मनः स्वयंज्योतिष्ट्वासिद्धेः प्रसिद्धत्वाच्च दृश्यत्वम् इत्यास्थेयम्।

Proof for soul's self-luminosity

Trans. : What is the evidence for the self-luminosity of the soul? If it is said that the scriptural statement 'In this state the person becomes self-luminous' is a proof for this, then this is not so. Being an instrument of light the soul is described as light like the statement 'Speech is his light'. Otherwise, the experience of knowability in 'It is I' would be contradicted. By this the (vyatirekī) syllogistic proposition (to prove the self-luminosity of the soul) is set aside (see VV, p. 105). And also, is self-luminosity elsewhere well-known or not? If the first alternative is admitted, then the reason, the state of being a soul, would suffer from the fallacy known as *asādhāraṇa anaikāntika* as sapakṣa has no place in this syllogism (*sapakṣāpraveśāt*: as there cannot be any illustration of positive concomitance (*anvayī*) in the kevalavyatirekī syllogism). And another reason, having the positive concomitance (*anvayī hetu*) is not possible here as there is no property which is accepted to be common to both the soul and other than it. If the second alternative is accepted, then the *pakṣa* would be having an unknown sādhya. This fault would not be there in the following vyatirekī syllogism : Being a soul, it is the causal light of its own usage (un)like a pot. This is not so since the soul has been accepted as not being the object of any usage. In case the soul is accepted as an object of all usages, then what is the harm in its having the state of being an object of knowledge? Moreover, if what is well known as 'I' (*ahaṅkāra*) is the dharmin, then (the contingency of) the contradiction of the experience (of knowability) has already been pointed out. If other than 'I', i.e. the witness consciousness is accepted as the dharmin, then the fault of *āśrayāsiddhi* is incurred (as the pūrvapakṣin does not accept witness consciousness). And also, there is no contradiction if the soul is accepted as knowable. By this, the arthāpatti evidence stands discarded since there is no unintelligibility (in respect of the knowability of the soul). If it is said that, on accepting the soul as knowable, the soul's state of being knower would not be available, then this is not so because the soul's instrumentality of a valid cognition can be possible like the instrumentality of the eyes, etc. which are knowable. Even then, how can it be proved that the soul is self-luminous? This can be explained by the illustration of gravitation. We say that there is no contradiction of the causality of knowledge to produce excellence in its locus (consisting in its being knowable) just as the quality of gravitation inhering in a pot, etc. produces excellence in them to facilitate their fall. By this the opposition to the view that an activity cannot be produced in the self by itself (*karmakartṛvirodha*) gets explained. The objection that if the soul is accepted as being illuminated by other than itself, then sometimes there could be a doubt about one's own self 'whether I am or I am not'. No, this is not so. (This can be explained by the illustration of pain.) The absence of any doubt about the existence of the soul is possible just as one does not have any doubt about one's own pain, etc.

The (following) view could also be possible. The qualified cognition 'it is favourable to me', etc. is dependent on the knowledge of the qualifier. The unconditional establishment of the qualifier soul is described in Nyāyamakaranda, etc. Therefore, the self-luminosity of soul is taken as established. No, it is not desirable even for the Vedāntin to hold that self-luminosity belongs to him who, having the idea of ego, has the cognition 'this is favourable to me', etc. And there cannot be any relation of the cognition 'this is favourable to me', etc. with the other which is unattached, beyond hunger, etc. Also the statement about the syllogistic proposition, etc. (that self-luminosity would be available by the process of elimination) is not possible because of being vitiated by the faults such as the unestablished sādhya and the like. Therefore, (being an infructuous syllogism) this does not deserve any consideration. Thus, the self-luminosity of the soul remaining unestablished, the soul's state of being perceivable, being well-known, should be adhered to.

Ann. : This section discusses the problem of self-luminosity of the soul. The siddhāntin quotes the scripture *atrāyaṁ puruṣaḥ svayaṁjyotirbhavati*, Bṛhadāraṇyaka Upaniṣad, 4. 3. 9 'In this (dream) state the person turns self-luminous' to prove the self-luminous nature of the soul. The pūrvapakṣin does not accept this and says that the word *jyotis* here has been used metaphorically in the sense of an instrument of light as it has been used in *vāgevāsya jyotirbhavati*, Bṛh. Up. 4. 3. 5. If this is not accepted then the knowability of the self in the experience 'I am' would be contradicted. This dismisses the following kevalavyatirekī syllogism to prove the self-luminosity of the soul : The soul is self-luminous because of the state of being a soul (un)like a pot. The pot is not a soul. Hence it does not possess self-luminosity. Self-luminosity in an entity other than the subject of the syllogism, i.e. the soul, could be construed as either familiar or unfamiliar. If it is accepted as familiar, then the reason 'the state of being a soul' would be rendered fallacious as there would be no illustration where 'the state of being a soul' can be shown since the soul is the subject (cf. *sati sapakṣe pakṣamātravṛttitvāt*, VV, p. 105). Another reason (*hetu*) which could be common to both the soul and that which is other than the soul is not possible. The reason is that such a property as could be common to both is not known. In case the second alternative is accepted, then the sādhya would be rendered unestablished (*aprasiddha*) and the subjecet (*pakṣa*) would become *aprasiddhaviśeṣaṇa*. Regarding the second fault, the pūrvapakṣin says that this fault does not exist in the following kevalavyatirekī syllogistic proposition : Being a soul, the soul is the causal light of its own usage (un)like a pot. It means that which does not have the state of being a soul does not become the causal light of its own usage. A pot does not have the property of soulhood and as such it does not have a causal light of its own to manifest itself The contention of the pūrvapakṣin that this syllogism does not suffer from the defect of *aprasiddhaviśeṣaṇapakṣa* is not acceptable as the soul is not accepted as an object of any usage. As this is not an established fact that the soul is not an object of any kind of usage, let it be conceded that it could be an object of some usage. In case the soul is accepted to be an object of some kind of usage, then it can also be accepted as an object of a cognition.

If the ego is admitted to be the subject (*pakṣa*), then the experience of knowability is contradicted as the ego is the agent of the act of cognising. So, how can it become the object of cognition (see NRD, p. 105). In case, the other, that is the witness, is accepted as the pakṣa, then the fault known as *āśrayāsiddhi* becomes applicable as the witness of the ego (witness consciousness) is not accepted by the pūrvapakṣin. Moreover, there is no contradictory argument against the view that the soul is knowable. That the soul is not inanimate confers knowership on the self and this is not possible if the soul is not admitted to be self-luminous. This kind of argument does not favour the view of the knowability of the soul. Also the knowability of the soul does not favour the view that it is the knower. But this can be taken care of in the following way : Even though the eyes, etc. are knowable, still they are considered to be instrumental in generating a valid cognition. In the same manner, the soul can be accepted to be instrumental in producing a valid cognition even though it is accepted to have the property of being knowable. However, the acceptance of this view raises another problem. The sense organs, eyes, etc. are instrumental in generating knowledge but they themselves do not become an object of the cognition generated by them. Similarly the soul also would not become an object of the cognition generated by it. It would all the more become difficult to explain the soul's cognition when we take into account the view that the agent of the act of cognition cannot become its own object because of the contradiction known as *karmakartṛvirodha.* In this situation, it is quite an exercise to explain how the soul comes to know itself. The upholder of the view of the knowability of the soul says that the soul's knowing itself can be explained by taking the illustration of gravitation. A cognition or knowledge generated by the soul would bring about excellence in it and that excellence could be construed as 'the state of being knowable by itself' just as the gravitation residing in a pot, etc. does good to them by facilitating their fall. This explains the contradiction known as *karmakartṛvirodha*. To endorse his position, the upholder of the view explained above says that if the soul is accepted as illuminable by an entity other than itself, then it would give rise to a doubt about oneself. This objection is answered by invoking the illustration of pain, etc. As one is never in doubt about the pain one feels so the subject would never be in doubt about himself.

In the context of the self-evident nature of the soul, the author also discusses the qualified cognition. He says that it is preceded by the cognition of a qualifier in the manner in which the cognition of a person with a stick follows the cognition of the stick. Similarly the qualified cognition 'it is favourable to me' is consequent upon the cognition of the self which is a qualifier in the present cognition. It has been discussed in detail in the works, Nyāyamakaranda, etc. that the self cannot be proved and established by any other means. Consequently, it is concluded that the self is established unconditionally, i.e. it does not need anything else to prove itself; it is self-evident. The pūrvapakṣin does not accept this saying that even the Advaitin would hesitate to subscribe to the view that this kind of self-luminosity belongs to the self which has the cognition 'this is favourable to me' (*anukūlādyanvayino'hampratyayinaḥ svaprakāśatāyā vedāntinopyaniṣṭatvāt*, see NRD, p.107). This qualified cognition also cannot belong to the soul which is unattached, beyond hunger and so on.

After rejecting the syllogistic propositions put forward to prove self-luminosity by pointing out the faults, namely, the unestablished sādhya, āśrayāsiddhi, etc. and the assumption evidence as there is no unintelligibility in accepting the property of knowership in the soul even without subscribing to the view of self-luminosity, the pūrvapakṣin concludes that the soul is knowable.

आत्मनो दृश्यत्वे दोषकथनम्

प्रयोगस्तु — आत्मा दृश्यः, न्यायविषयत्वाद् धर्मवद् । न तावदस्य न्यायविषयत्वमसिद्धम् । शारीरकानारम्भप्रसङ्गाद् । अयमेव च विपक्षे बाधकस्तर्कः । नापि विरुद्धतादिदोषः शङ्क्यः । सपक्षवृत्त्यादेः स्फुटत्वादिति । अत्रोच्यते — न तावद् 'अत्रायं पुरुषः स्वयंज्योतिरि'तित्यागमस्याहमिति वेद्यतानुभवविरोधः । अहंकारद्रष्टुरेव स्वयंज्योतिष्ट्वबोधकत्वाद् । अहमनुभवामीत्यहंकार एव द्रष्टा प्रत्यक्षसिद्ध इति चेन्न । देहस्येव अहंकारस्याप्यनात्मन आत्मसंभेदादेव द्रष्टृत्वप्रतीत्युपपत्तेः । अनात्मत्वं चाहंकारस्य छन्दोगोपनिषद्यात्माहंकारादेशयोः पृथक्पाठात् सिद्धम् । तत्र हि 'अथात आत्मादेशः' इत्यात्मादेशात् पृथग् अहंकारादेशः पठ्यते 'अथातोऽहंकारादेशः' इति । स्मृतौ च 'अहंकार इतीयमि'त्यहंकारमुक्त्वा पृथगात्मोच्यते 'अपरेयमितस्त्वन्यामि'ति । तदेवं स्वयंज्योतिष्ट्वश्रुतेर्न विरोधगन्धोऽपि । विरोधाभावादेव च न वागादिवद् भाक्तमात्मनो ज्योतिष्ट्वम् । एतेनानुमानेऽपि विरोधोऽपास्तः । प्रयोगस्तु — आत्मा आत्मव्यवहारकारणप्रकाशः द्रष्टृत्वात् कुम्भवदिति व्यतिरेकी । न तावदाश्रयासिद्धिः । उभयसिद्धस्यैवाहंकारद्रष्टुराश्रयत्वाद् । न च प्रमाणसिद्ध एव धर्मी । प्रतिबिम्बादेरपि धर्मित्वाद् । वक्ष्यते चैतन्मिथ्यात्वानुमाने ।

Shortcomings of the view that soul is perceivable

Trans. : The syllogistic proposition (to prove that the soul is perceivable) is as follows : The soul is perceivable or knowable since it is the subject of reasoning (*nyāyaviṣaya*) like dharma. It is not that its being the subject of reasoning is not established. Otherwise, why would Śaṅkara undertake to write a commentary on the Brahmasūtras (Śārīrakabhāṣya)? And this itself constitutes a contradictory argument against the contrary view.

Also there should not be any apprehension about the faults known as *viruddhatā*, etc. since the residence (of the reason) in the illustration (*sapakṣa*), etc. is evident.

Now the siddhānta view is going to be presented : The Upaniṣadic statement 'In this state the Self turns self-luminous' does not contradict the experience of knowability of 'I' since it makes known the self-luminosity of the seer of 'I'. In case it is said that it is established by the perceptual evidence that the 'I' in 'I experience' is the seer, then this is not true. The cognition of the 'I' being the seer, which is other than the soul, can be possible on account of its (superimposed) identity with the soul like that of the body (which is so obviously other than the soul). That the 'I' is different from the soul is established from the separate instructions about the soul and the 'I' in the Chāndogya Upaniṣad; for in that Upaniṣad the instruction of 'I (*ahaṅkāra*)' in 'Now the instruction about the 'I'' Ch. Up. 7. 25. 1 has been given separately from that of the self in 'Next, the instruction about the self' Ch. Up. 7. 25. 2. The smṛti, i.e. the Bhagavadgītā, having first stated the 'I' in 'and also 'I = ahaṅkāra'' Bh. G. 7. 4, separately mentions the self in 'The Prakṛti of Mine which is different from this' Bh. G. 7. 5. In this way there is not even an iota of conradiction of the śruti which describes the self-luminosity of the soul. And on account of the absence of contradiction (of the self-luminosity) there is no metaphoric use of soul's self-luminosity like that in respect of speech, etc. By this, the fault of contradiction in the syllogism (that follows) also stands dismissed. The vyatirekī syllogistic proposition reads : The soul is the causal light of its own usage (cognition, etc.) because of being the seer (un)like a pot. No defect known as *āśrayāsiddhi* is applicable since only the seer of 'I', which is recognised by both the sides, is the pakṣa. However, it is not necessary that that which is established by a means of valid cognition should be the dharmin. Even the reflection (*pratibimba*, see VV, p. 110) can become the subject (*pakṣa*) and this will be mentioned in the syllogism to prove the indeterminability (*mithyātva* = *anirvacanīyatā*) of the phenomenon (see ibid., pp. 227-28).

Ann. : This section dwells upon the problem regarding the perceivable nature of the soul. The pūrvapakṣin holds the view that the soul is perceivable and adduces the following syllogism as evidence : The soul is perceivable since it is a subject of deliberation like dharma. The reason exists in the illustration as dharma can also become a subject of logical discussion. In the same manner the soul also becomes a subject to be discussed for its various aspects. The pūrvapakṣin says that if the soul had not been the subject of reasoning, Śaṅkara would not have undertaken to write the famous commentary on the Brahmasūtras, which is also known as Śārīrakabhāṣya. This proves the authenticity of the reason used in the syllogism. This also constitutes a contradictory argument against the contrary view : If it had not been knowable, it would not have been the subject of logical reasoning and the Śārīrakabhāṣya would not have been initiated at all. The syllogism does not suffer from the defects of contrariness, etc. as the reason is obviously present in the illustration dharma, which is obviously a subject matter for deliberatioin. After the pūrvapakṣin has successfully demonstrated the perceivable nature of the soul, the siddhāntin undertakes to analyse his arguments. At the outset he brings to notice the point that in the scriptural statement about the self-luminosity of soul, that is, 'In the dream state the person turns self-luminous' does not run counter to the knowability of the self as expressed in the reflection 'I experience' since the scripture says that it is the seer of 'I' that is actually self-luminous. The siddhāntin further explains that although the 'I' appears to be the subject of a perceptual experience, it appears to be so on account of its identification with the soul just as the body, which is obviously different from the soul, appears to be the 'I'. Moreover, the soul and the 'I' are separately mentioned in clear terms in the Chāndogya Upaniṣad and the Bhagavadgītā. The Chāndogya Upaniṣad, 7. 25.1 'Now the instruction in terms of the 'I'' mentions the 'I' separately from the self which is mentioned in the same Upaniṣad, 7. 25. 2 'Next, the instruction in terms of the self'. The Bhagavadgītā also separately mentions both the self and the 'I' in the fourth and fifth verses of chapter seven. First, the 'I' is mentioned in 'and also 'I'' in Bh. G. 7. 4 and it makes a mention of the self in 'The Prakṛti of Mine which is different from this' Bh. G. 7. 5. In this way there is not even an iota of conradiction of the śruti describing the self-luminosity of the soul. Had there been some sort of contradiction of the self-luminosity of the soul, then there would have been some justification for the metaphoric use of luminosity in the sense of instrumentality in respect of the soul. Now since there is no contradiction of the self-luminosity of the soul, there is also no justification for the use of metaphor in this context as in respect of speech, etc.

The vyatirekī syllogistic proposition does not suffer from fallacies of any sort and is capable of proving the self-luminosity of the soul. The fallacy known as *āśrayāsiddhi* as pointed out by the pūrvapakṣin does not hold ground as the witness (seer) of the 'I' is the subject of the syllogism since this is an established fact according to both the sides. Nonetheless, it is not necessary that an entity which has been established by a means of valid cognition should be accepted as the subject of the syllogism. Even a reflection (*pratibimba*) can be accepted as the dharmin (see NRD, pp. 227-28). This will be discussed by the author in the second chapter of the present work in the context of the syllogism regarding the indeterminability (*mithyātva* = *anirvacanīyatā*) of the phenomenon.

अहंकारस्यानात्मत्वनिरूपणम्

नन्वात्मनि ते व्यवहार एव नास्ति। अतस्तत्कारणप्रकाशता अप्रसिद्धा। अस्त्यात्मनि वैदिकशब्दव्यवहार इति चेन्न। अपौरुषेयस्य प्रकाशकारणतासम्भवाद्। अतो भवत्पक्ष एवाप्रसिद्धविशेषणः पक्ष इति उच्यते — लोकेऽपि लक्षणयात्मनि शब्दप्रवृत्तिर्दृश्यते। 'गाढमहमद्य सुप्त' इति। तथापीत्थं परस्यात्मनि शब्दप्रयोगोऽप्रसिद्ध इति चेद्। नायं दोषः। विवक्षितस्यात्मनि शब्दप्रयोगमात्रस्योभयसिद्धत्वात्। तदेवं नाप्रसिद्धविशेषणः पक्षः। द्रष्टृत्वमप्यात्मनो 'नान्योऽतोऽस्ति द्रष्टे'त्याद्यया श्रुत्यैवानुमोदितम्। आत्मनो दृश्यत्वे किं बाधकमिति चेत् 'सुखमहमस्वाप्समि'ति परामर्शासम्भवप्रसङ्ग इति ब्रूमः। न हि सुषुप्तस्यात्मनि अनुभवः प्रमाणाभावात्। सुषुप्तिव्याहतिप्रसङ्गात्। न चासंविन्नो जडः परामृष्टुं शक्यः। सुषुप्तोत्थितः स्वापकालीनमात्मनि दुःखाभावमनुमिमीते 'सुखमहमस्वाप्समि'ति चेन्न। व्याप्त्याद्यनुसन्धानाभावाद्। न चाभ्यासपाटवात्तदभाव इति कल्प्यम्। अन्यथाप्युपपत्तेः, कल्पनाबीजाभावात्, स्वापकालीनधर्म्याद्यसिद्धेश्च नानुमानम्। अहं स्वप्नजागरान्तराले, न दुःखभाग् नियमेनास्मर्यमाणतदातनदुःखत्वात् कुम्भवदित्यनुमेति चेद्। न अन्तरालकालासिद्धेः साध्यहेत्वोरप्रसिद्धत्वात्। प्रकृतपरामर्शकालः पूर्वकालादपरः परामर्शकालत्वात्, संप्रतिपन्नवद् इति तत्सिद्धिरिति चेन्न। अन्योऽन्याश्रयत्वाद्। अनुमानतः परामर्शसिद्धौ हि तत्कालात्पूर्वकालसिद्धिः तत्सिद्धौ चानुमानतः परामर्शसिद्धिरिति। तस्मात्ते न सम्भवी स्वापपरामर्शः। अपि चात्मनः स्ववेद्यत्वे स्वात्मनि वृत्तिविरोधो दुर्वारः।

न च गुरुत्ववद् ज्ञानस्य स्वाश्रयातिशयहेतुत्वादविरोधः । कर्मकारकरहितस्य ज्ञानस्यासम्भवाद् । ज्ञानस्याश्रय एव तज्जन्यातिशयवत्त्वात् कर्मकारकमिति चेन्न । कर्मताव्यापकरहितत्वात् । परसमवेतक्रियाफलशालित्वं हि कर्मत्वव्यापकम् । तद्विरहश्च प्रकृते प्रसिद्धः ।

Trans. : (The pūrvapakṣin says :) According to you, there is no usage at all in respect of the soul. Hence it is not established (*aprasiddha*) that the soul is the causal light of its usage. (Should the siddhāntin say that) there is a Vedic usage in respect of the soul, the pūrvapakṣin does not accept this as it is not possible for the Vedic word of non-human origin to become the cause of the manifestation of (the eternally established) soul. So, the defect of the subject not having an established sādhya is incurred only in your case. The siddhāntin says that, in common parlance, a word is also used to indicate the soul as in the experience 'Today I slept well' ('I' by lakṣaṇā indicates the soul here). (The pūrvapakṣin says :) Nevertheless, such a usage (*lākṣaṇika*) in respect of the soul is not accepted by the opponent. The siddhāntin says that this does not constitute any defect as the bare verbal usage is intended in respect of the soul, which is acceptable to both the sides. So in this way, the subject (*pakṣa*) ceases to have the unestablished sādhya in it. Also the seership of the soul is endorsed by the śruti alone : 'There is no seer other than it', etc. (The pūrvapakṣin asks :) What is the argument that contradicts the view of the perceivable nature of the soul? The siddhāntin replies that the impossibility of the act of remembering the experience 'I slept happily' would constitute the contradiction of the view of the perceivable nature of the soul. The pūrvapakṣin denies that a person in deep sleep has any experience since there is no evidence to this effect. In case this is admitted, then the very existence of the state of deep sleep would be contradicted. (The siddhāntin replies that) an unconscious senseless person cannot recall anything. (The pūrvapakṣin replies :) When awakened from deep sleep, he infers the painlessness of deep sleep in the soul when he says 'I slept happily'. The siddhāntin replies in the negative (that is, there is no inference) as there is no remembrance of the concomitance, etc. And it should not be assumed that the absence of the recollection of concomitance, etc. is due to the force of habit (*abhyāsapāṭavāt*). (The siddhāntin says that) there is no justification for inference : 1. because the remembrance can be explained otherwise also (that is, by virute of the self-luminosity of the soul), 2. because there is no ground for such an assumption and 3. because there is no knowledge of the dharmin (*pakṣa*), etc. during the state of deep sleep. (But, the pūrvapakṣin puts forward the following syllogism for the establishment of the dharmin, etc. :) During the interval between the dream and waking states I experience no pain as the pain of that state is invariably not remembered by me like a pot. The siddhāntin does not accept this syllogistic proposition as the probandum and the reason remain unestablished on account of the unestablished status of the interval between the two states (see *ato'ntarālaviśiṣṭasādhyahetvorasiddhernānumānamiti siddhāntī svābhiprāyaṁ prakaṭayati*, VV, p. 113). (However,) the interval (between the dream and waking states) can be established by the following syllogism (insists the pūrvapakṣin) : The time of remembrance, which is under consideration, is other than the earlier time since it has the state of being the time to remember like the known time. But this cannot be proved as it suffers from the defect of mutual dependence : After the remembrance (*parāmarśa*) has been established by inference, the time earlier than the time of remembrance gets established and when the time earlier than the remembrance has been arrived at, the remembrance is also established by the inference. So, in your case the remembrance of deep sleep is not possible. And also if the soul is admitted to be capable of being known by itself, then the contradiction of one's own activity in oneself cannot be avoided.

The contradiction (*svavṛttivirodha*) regarding the cognition of the soul cannot be resolved by invoking the illustration of gravitation which brings about an excellence in the locus where it inheres since a cognition which does not have an object (*karma*) is not possible. Let then the locus of a cognition be the object (*karma*) because some excellence has been added to it by the cognition itself. No, (the locus of a cognition cannot be an object) since it does not have the pervader of the state of being an object, which consists in having the result of an activity which inheres in the other but the absence of that is well-known in the locus, i.e. the soul, which is under consideration (*ātmani noktaṁ karmatvamasti tasya jñānajanyaphalaśālitve'pi jñānāśraya-tvāditi vyāpakarāhityam*, VV, p. 114).

Ann. : The pūrvapakṣin refers to the syllogism put forward above : The soul is the causal light of its own usage (cognition, etc.) because of being the seer (un)like a pot. He points out that there is no usage in respect of the soul. As such, the sādhya 'the soul is the causal light of its own usage' in the syllogism remains unestablished. The siddhāntin replies saying that, even in the absence of popular usage with regard to the soul, the Vedic usage does exist in respect of the soul. However, the pūrvapakṣin observes that the existence of the sādhya cannot be established as the Vedic word, being of non-human origin, is not invested with any denotative faculty and consequently, it cannot be construed as the cause of the manifestation of the eternally established soul. So, the defect of *aprasiddhaviśeṣaṇapakṣa* still exists so far as the siddhāntin's view is concerned. The siddhāntin takes recourse to the indicative faculty and says that, in our day-to-day practice, we use the word 'I' (*ahaṅkāra*) when we mean 'the soul'. The word *ahaṅkāra* conveys the sense of soul by the indicative faculty as is clear from the usage 'Today I had a sound sleep'. Nevertheless, such a verbal usage with reference to the soul is not accepted by the pūrvapakṣin. But the siddhāntin is of the view that the bare verbal usage is intended here to convey the sense of the soul and it is acceptable to both the sides. Therefore, the defect of an unestablished sādhya in the subject ceases to exist.

To prove that the soul is not an object of knowledge (*dṛśya*), the siddhāntin quotes the śruti 'There is no seer other than him', Bṛhadāraṇyaka Upaniṣad, 3. 7. 23 to make the pūrvapakṣin understand the fact that the soul is the seer, and not the seen. Otherwise, the remembrance of the experience 'I slept happily' would not be possible. The pūrvapakṣin controverts this saying that there is no experience during the state of deep sleep since there is no proof to this effect. If the incidence of experience was accepted, then the very status of deep sleep (*suṣupti*) would be compromised. If it is said that an unconscious and senseless person is not able to recall anything, then the pūrvapakṣin makes the following observation : When a person awakens from deep sleep, he infers the absence of pain during that state and says 'I slept happily'. The siddhāntin raises an objection saying that the inference of painlessness is not possible as there is no remembrance of the concomitance, etc. The pūrvapakṣin's reply that the absence of the remembrance of concomitance, etc. may be due to the state of having been habitually accustomed, is not convincing because there is no ground to assume the absence of pain during deep sleep and because the experience of pleasure can be explained by the self-luminosity of the soul. Besides, because of the non-establishment of the dharmin, etc. during deep sleep, there is no scope for inference. Still the pūrvapakṣin does not give up his attempt to convince the siddhāntin by putting forward another syllogistic proposition to prove that the absence of pain during deep sleep is inferred : During the interval between dream and waking states I experience no pain as the pain of that state is invariably not remembered by me like a pot. A pot does not remember, pain etc. In the same manner a person like me does not remember the pain, etc. of deep sleep. The siddhāntin does not accept this syllogism as the probandum and the reason are not established because of the unsettled status of the interval between the dream and waking states. The pūrvapakṣin presents another syllogism to do away with the defect of non-establishment of both the probandum and the reason and to prove the settled status of the interval which becomes an object of remembrance. The following is the inference to prove the time of deep sleep (the interval between dream and waking states) : The time of remembrance which is under consideration follows the earlier time since it has the state of being the time to remember as the known time (*sampratipannavat*). The veracity of the act of remembrance depends on that of the interval between the dream and waking states. After the remembrance has been proved by the inference, the time earlier than the time of remembrance gets proved and when the earlier time has been proved, the remembrance is inferred on the basis of the earlier time. Thus the syllogism put forward to prove the veracity of the interval between the states of dream and waking is rendered infructuous because of the defect of mutual dependence. As such, it is not possible to establish the reality of the interval (*antarāla*). Moreover, if the soul is admitted to be knowable by itself, then the contradiction of one's activity in oneself (*svavṛttivirodha*) becomes unavoidable. The pūrvapakṣin makes another attempt to resolve the contradiction pointed out by the siddhāntin. He says that gravitation brings about excellence in the locus where it inheres and there is no contradiction involved in it. Likewise a cognition can bring about excellence in the locus where it resides. Thus the contradiction of one's activity in oneself can be resolved in a satisfactory manner. The siddhāntin says that a cognition which does not have an object is not possible. The pūrvapakṣin replies that the very locus of cognition can be construed as an object. The siddhāntin rejects the contention of the pūrvapakṣin saying that the locus of a cognition does not fulfil the criterion of being an object. The pervader of the state of being an object consists in having the result of an activity that inheres in the other. But such is not the case in the present context. Hence in the absence of the state of being an object, the incidence of cognition of the soul is not possible. In case it is insisted upon, then the defect consisting in the contradiction of one's activity in oneself remains applicable.

नन्वात्मनो वेद्यतास्वप्रकाशत्वोभयमप्यात्मनो मास्त्विति प्राभाकरस्य पूर्वपक्षः

नन्वात्मनो वेद्यतास्वप्रकाशत्वोभयोरभावे किमनुपपन्नम् अपरोक्षतेति चेद् । न । अनुभवाश्रयतया तदुपपत्तेः ।

यत्तु मानं संवेदिता न संविदधीनप्रकाशः संवित्कर्मतामन्तरेणापरोक्षत्वात् संविद्वदिति । तत्र यदि संविदधीनत्वं प्रकाशस्य संविज्जन्यत्वं तदा तन्निषेधे सिद्धसाधनम् । कुम्भादिसंविद्रूपत्वनिषेधे साध्यविकलता दृष्टान्तस्य । अथात्मा न संविदाश्रयतयाऽपरोक्षः अपरोक्षत्वात् कुम्भवदित्यनुमानम् । न । विपक्षे बाधाभावाद् अद्रष्टृत्वोपाधिकत्वाच्च । तस्मात्संविदाश्रयतया आत्माऽपरोक्ष इति ।

Prābhākara's view that the soul is neither knowable nor self-luminous

Trans. : The pūrvapakṣin asks 'What will be unintelligible if the soul is not held to be knowable and self-luminous?' If it is said that the immediate experience (of the soul would be unintelligible), (then the Prābhākara will say) 'no' (and reply that) this (immediate knowledge of the soul) can be intelligible by virtue of its having the state of being the locus of knowledge (experience).

The following syllogism is being restated (see VV, p. 114) in support of the self-luminosity of the soul : The knower, for its manifestation, does not depend on a cognition since it is immediately given (in experience) without being an object of cognition like a cognition. In this syllogistic proposition, if dependence on cognition is construed as having the state of being a product of cognition, then its denial leads to the defect of proving that which is already proved. If the cognition of a pot is denied having the property of a cognition, then the illustration would cease to have the sādhya in it. Then let the following be the syllogism (to prove the immediate cognition of the soul) : The soul is not immediately known by being the locus of a cognition because of its being immediatelty known (un)like a pot. No, since there is no stultifying argument against the contrary view and because it has an upādhi in the form of 'not having the state of being a seer'. Therefore, the soul is immediately known because of its being the locus of knowledge (thus concludes the Prābhākara).

Ann. : In order to situate the issue of the immediate knowledge of the soul, the Prābhākara raises a query : What would be unintelligibile should the soul be admitted to be neither knowable nor self-luminous? The siddhāntin replies that the immediate cognition of the soul would be rendered unintelligible in that case. The Prābhākara does not accept this and holds the view that the immediate knowledge of the soul can become intelligible because of its being the locus of knowledge. But immediate knowledge of the soul by being the locus of a cognition goes against the syllogism that proves the self-luminosity, which the Prābhākara restates (cf. *ātmanaḥ saṁvidāśrayatvenāparokṣatvamanumānaviruddham ityāśaṅkya svaprakāśatvānumānamanuvadati,* ibid., p. 114). In the syllogism which is restated by the Prābhākara, it is sought to be proved that the knower is not dependent on the cognition for its manifestation as it is immediately cognised without itself becoming the object of a cognition. The manifestation of the soul is likened to the manifestation of a cognition. In other words, the syllogism seeks to prove that the soul is self-manifest like the cognition. The syllogism reads as follows : The knower, for its manifestation, does not depend on a cognition since it is immediately given (in experience) without being an object of cognition like a cognition. The siddhāntin points out saying that if the manifestation dependent on cognition is construed as the product of a cognition, then its denial would incur the defect of proving that which is already proven. Secondly, if the cognition of a pot is not accepted as having the nature of a cognition, then the sādhya would be absent in the illustration. In this way, the syllogism is rendered ineffective to prove the intended self-luminosity. The Prābhākara apprehends another syllogism which goes against his accepted position. The syllogism reads as follows : The soul is not immediately known on account of its being the locus of a cognition since it is an object of immediate knowledge (un)like a pot. The Prābhākara rejects the syllogistic propostion on two counts : 1. There is no stultifying argument against the contrary view that the soul is known immediately by being the locus of a cognition. 2. The reason 'the state of being immediately cognised' is vitiated by the presence of an upādhi consisting in 'the state of not being a seer'. 'The state of not being a seer' is concomitant with the sādhya, that is, 'not being immediately cognised by being the locus of a cognition'. There is no concomitance of 'the state of not being a seer' with the reason consisting in 'the state of being immediately cognised'. This can be demonstrated as follows :

yatra saṁvidāśrayatayā aparokṣatvābhāvaḥ tatra adraṣṭṛtvaṁ yathā kumbhe.

yatra aparokṣatvaṁ tatra adraṣṭṛtvaṁ na yathātmani.

Thus after rejecting the syllogistic proposition of the siddhāntin, the Prābhākara concludes saying that the soul is immediately known on account of its being the locus of knowledge.

प्राभाकरशङ्कासमाधानम्

न। उक्तविधयात्मनोऽपरोक्षत्वे मानाभावाद्। अथ 'कुम्भमहमनुभवामी'त्यध्यक्षं मानम्। न। कुम्भवदात्मानुभवयोरपि प्रत्यक्षविषयताप्रसङ्गाद्। न चोक्तविधयाऽपरोक्षत्वं स्वप्रकाशत्वेन वानुभवाश्रयत्वेन वापरोक्षत्वम्। अननुभवत्वादनात्मत्वाच्च। अतोऽनुभवाश्रयतयात्मनोऽपरोक्षत्वं प्रत्यक्षविषयतयाऽऽस्थेयम्। तथा चात्मानुभवयोरपि प्रत्यक्षविषयत्वप्रसङ्गो दुर्वारः।

प्रयोगस्त्वत्र दृष्टान्ताभावादपास्तः। केवलव्यतिरेकी तु प्रयोगो भवता नाद्रियते। तदादरणे चाप्रसिद्धविशेषणता। न चाहमिति संविदनुपपत्तिरमुमर्थं गमयेद्।

मतान्तरानुसारेणापि तदुपपत्तेः। तदेवमात्मनोऽस्वयंप्रकाशत्वे बाधकसद्भावाद् नाप्रयोजकत्वशङ्कापि। यदपि न्यायविषयत्वादित्यात्मनो दृश्यत्वे मानम्। तदपि 'अविज्ञातं विजानतामि'त्यागमबाधितम्।

किं च किं वास्तवं दृश्यत्वं साध्यं, किं वा अवास्तवम्, आहोस्विद् दृश्यत्व-मात्रम्। आद्ये साध्यशून्यो दृष्टान्तः। इतरयोस्तु सिद्धसाधनता। अस्मत्साध्यं तु व्यवहारहेतुत्वोपलक्षितं प्रकाशात्मत्वम्। तच्च प्रकाशभेदाभावोपलक्षितं स्वरूपं सत्यं च। उपलक्षितमपि क्वचित्साध्यम्। यथा नाशोपलक्षितसत्तायोगि-त्वमनित्यत्वमिति निरवद्यम्।

The resolution of the Prābhākara's doubt

Trans. : No, (this cannot be accepted) because there is no evidence of the immediate cognition of the soul in the manner discussed above. Let then the perception 'I cognise a pot' be the evidence. No, for this would make both the soul and its knowledge the content of perceptual cognition like a pot. Also the state of being immediately cognised is not in the said manner : Neither because of the state of being self-luminous nor because of the state of being the locus of a cognition. And also because the soul and a pot do not enjoy the state of being a cognition nor do a pot and its cognition share the nature of the soul (cf. VV, p. 115). Therefore, it should be held that the immediate knowledge of the soul by being the locus of a cognition is in the manner of being the content of a perceptual cognition. And if that is accepted, then the contingency of the soul and its cognition becoming a content of the perceptual cognition cannot avoided..

The syllogistic proposition has been discarded because of the absence of an illustration and you show no concern for the kevalavyatirekī syllogism. In case you show a concern for the kevalavyatirekī syllogism, then the defect of the sādhya not being well-known (*aprasiddhaviśeṣaṇatā*) would be incurred. Also it is not that the unintelligibility of the cognition 'I am' would imply this meaning (i.e. the immediate cognition of the soul by being the locus of a cognition), for this can be made intelligible by taking recourse to another stand-point. Since in this way there is a contradictory argument against the view of the absence of self-luminosity of the soul, there is no apprehension of the absence of a favourable argument (in favour of the self-luminosity of the soul). The evidence that the soul has the state of being perceivable because of its being a subject of deliberation has been stultified by the scriptural statement 'It is unknown to them who proclaim that they know it'.

Moreover, does the real or unreal state of being perceivable or barely the state of being perceivable constitute the sādhya? If it is the first, then the illustration will cease to have the sādhya in it. On accepting the second and third alternatives, the defect of proving that which is already proved becomes applicable. Our sādhya is of the nature of being luminous indicated by the state of being a cause of the usage (regarding itself) and that luminosity is of the true nature indicated by the absence of difference of luminosity. The indicated (state of being luminous) could at some place constitute a sādhya just as 'the non-eternity consisting in having a relation with the sattā universal indicated by destruction' may be construed as an inferable without incurring any fault (see VV, p. 117).

Ann. : According to Prabhākara, knowledge is self-luminous. Its object is revealed since it has the state of being its content, whereas the agent is revealed because of its being the locus of knowledge. Thus not only the objects but even the knower and the knowledge are revealed in perception. This is what is called tripuṭī-saṁvit. In accordance with the view of tripuṭīsaṁvit, the Prābhākara explains the immediate cognition of the soul by its being the locus of knowledge. The siddhāntin does not accept the view of the Prābhākara that the soul becomes manifest because of its being the locus of knowledge. The reason is lack of evidence in this regard. In case the perceptual experience 'I know a pot' is given as an evidence, then the analysis of the three components of this perceptual experience, to wit, a pot, its cognition and the soul would give rise to three defects according to the interpretation of Ānandajñāna in Vedāntaviveka. The options with regard to these three components are : 1. Do all these components constitute the content of the perception, or 2. are they the loci of the perceptual cognition, or 3. are they self-luminous. If the first alternative that all the three components are the content of the perceptual cognition is accepted, then the knowledge and the self would be on a par with the pot and, as such, would become the content of the perceptual cognition. In case the second alternative is accepted, then the contingency of both the knowledge and its object, the pot sharing the nature of the soul would be incurred. If the third alternative is admitted, then both the self and the pot would be on a par with knowledge and hence they would have to be accepted as self-luminous, which is obviously not tenable. (see, *atra hi pratyakṣe kumbhānubhavātmānaḥ tadviṣayā vā tadāśrayā vā svaprakāśā vā iti vikalpyādyaṁ dūṣayati – na kumbhavaditi. na dvitīyaḥ, ghaṭasaṁvidorapyātmatvāpatteḥ. tasyaiva saṁvidāśrayatvaniyamāt. na tṛtīyaḥ ghaṭātmanorapi saṁvittvaprasaṅgāt*, VV, p. 115). The second and third alternatives are apparently not worth considering. However, the first alternative that the soul is immediately known by being the locus of a cognition deserves some consideration. But, according to this view, both the soul and knowledge would assume the state of being an object of knowledge itself like a pot, and consequently the soul would be known immediately as an object of the perceptual knowledge. As such, the contingency of both the soul and the knowledge becoming the object of perceptual knowledge cannot be escaped (cf. *tathā cātmānubhavayorapi pratyakṣaviṣayatvaprasaṅgo durvāraḥ*, NRD, p.115).

However, Ānandajñāna draws our attention to the possible syllogisms as regards the third alternative view. He says that the anvayavyatirekī syllogism cannot serve the purpose for lack of an illustration since there is nothing other than the soul, which, by being the locus of a cognition, becomes immediately known (*ātmātiriktasya saṁvidāśrayatayā'parokṣasyāniṣṭatvādityarthaḥ*, ibid., 115). The pūrvapakṣin does not feel inclined to use the kevalavyatirekī syllogism as it is not free from defects. The following is the kevalavyatirekī syllogism : The soul, by being the locus of a cognition, is immediately cognised since it has seership unlike a pot. In case, there is something other than the soul, which is immediately given in experience by being the locus of a cognition, then the fallacy known as *asādhāraṇa anaikāntika* becomes applicable since the state of being a seer cannot exist in that entity which is other than the soul. If it is said that seership exists in that, then the syllogism ceases to be kevalavyatirekī. If the state of being immediately cognised by virtue of being a locus of knowledge is not well-known anywhere else, then the defect known as *aprasiddhaviśeṣaṇatā* applies (see *saṁvidāśrayatvenāparokṣatvaṁ anyatra siddhaṁ cettatra hetvavṛttāvasādhāraṇatā tadvṛttau vyatirekitvāyogaḥ. tasyānyatrāsiddhau aprasiddhaviśeṣaṇatā*, VV, p. 115). Thus, the syllogisms suffer from fallacies. So, they are not effective to prove their sādhya. The assumption evidence is being discarded as the immediate knowledge of the soul, which is the substratum of 'I' could also be explained by virtue of the self-luminosity of the soul (*ahaṅkārādhiṣṭhānātmakacaitanyasya svaprabhavatve'pi ahamityaparokṣānubhavasambhavāditi hetum āha matāntareti*, ibid., pp. 115-16). However, the cognition 'I am' may be accepted as an evidence of the immediate knowledge of the soul since if it were not accepted, then the I-consciousness would not be cogently explained. Also there is an argument that stultifies the view of the non-luminosity of the soul. The doubtlessness about one's own existence is enough to show that the soul is self-luminous. The evidence that the soul is the object of a cognition (*dṛśya*) because it becomes the subject of reasoning can be set aside by the Upaniṣadic statement 'The soul remains unknown to them who proclaim to know it', Kena Up., 2. 3.

Now the author discusses the soul's state of being perceivable (*dṛśyatva*), which is sought to be proved because of its being the subject of reasoning (see NRD, p. 108). Is this state of being perceivable real or unreal or neither (that is, barely perceivable)? If the first alternative is accepted, then the illustration (*dharma*) obviously does not have it as dharma is not deemed to be perceivable. On accepting the other two alternatives, the defect of proving that which is already proved would be incurred as such a sādhya is already well-established according to the Advaita view.

The siddhāntin says that the sādhya, according to him, is the self-luminosity which is indicated by the cause of the verbal usage regarding it. In other words, the real nature of the self-luminosity of the soul indicated by the absence of difference of luminosity constitutes the sādhya. There is nothing unintelligible in this as that which is indicated also can be accepted as the sādhya just as the concept of non-eternity defined in terms of 'indicated by' (*upalakṣita*) has been accepted : Non-eternity consists in the state of its being related to the sattā universal indicated by destruction (*nāśopalakṣitasattāyogitvamanityatvam*, NRD, p. 117 which means 'The co-locatedness of destruction with existence (*sattā*) like that of a pot indicates non-eternity'). The case of the soul is exactly opposite since the soul has relation with sattā but there is no destructibility in it. Thus, the siddhāntin concludes his view about the nature of the sādhya (self-luminosity) which he seeks to establish by the syllogism. Now he enters into the logical niceties regarding the syllogism in the following section so that his view of the self-luminosity of the soul may get further strengthened.

अनात्मत्वं चास्माकमुपाधिः, पक्षेतरत्वस्योपाधित्वे प्रसिद्धानुमानभङ्गः स्यादितिचेन्न। तत्रोपाधेरसम्भवात्। साधनाव्यापकः साध्यसमव्याप्तिर्ह्युपाधिः। तथा च कथय कथमग्निमत्त्वाद्यसमव्याप्ति पक्षेतरत्वमुपाधिः स्याद्। अतः क्वचित् पक्षेतरत्वमपि साध्यसमव्याप्तित्वादुपाधिः स्यात्। को दोषः? वक्ष्यते च सम-व्याप्तेरेवोपाधित्वम्। अतो नात्मनो वेद्यत्वमनुमेयम्। अदृश्यत्वे चात्मनस्तद्याथा-त्म्याकारन्तःकरणवृत्तिद्वारा संसारनिदानाज्ञाननिवृत्त्यर्था वेदान्ताः। ब्रह्ममीमांसापि तत्रैवोपकारजननीति न बाधः कश्चित्। किञ्च संविद्रूप एवात्मा 'विज्ञानघन' इत्यादिश्रुतेः। संविच्च न संविदो विषयः, समत्वात्। समयोर्हि न विषयविषयिभावो दृश्यते युज्यते वा दीपयोरिव। करयोरविशेषयोरपि ग्राह्यग्राहकता दृश्यत इति चेन्न। तयोर्विशेषवत्त्वात्। प्रयत्नावष्टब्धो हि करो ग्राहकः। स्वरूपेण चेतरो ग्राह्य इति न समत्वं तयोः। तस्मात् संविदगोचर एव संवित् स्वतः प्रकाशते।

प्रयोगस्तु — विवादपदं स्वव्यवहारहेतुप्रकाशः, संवित्त्वात् कुम्भवदिति व्यतिरेकी। न तावदप्रसिद्धविशेषणता। संविद्व्यवहारहेतुप्रकाशो हि प्रसिद्धः। अतस्तत्स्वरूपत्वं साध्यं नाप्रसिद्धम्। संवित्प्रकाशभागे सिद्धसाधनमिति चेन्न। तस्याधर्मिभागत्वात्। संवित्प्रकाशो ह्यसंप्रतिपन्नो न प्रकृतविवादपदम्। अतो न धर्मीति न भागे सिद्धसाधनता। हन्तैवं विवादपदमिति विशेषणं व्यर्थम्। न। पराभिमतसिद्धसाधनतापरिहारार्थत्वात्।

ननु संवित् स्वव्यवहारस्य विषयतया हेतुः प्रकाशश्चेति कथं न सिद्धसाधनता? न। शब्दाभिलापव्यवहारस्य विषयाजन्यत्वाद्। अन्यथा कथमतीतादौ तत्सम्भवः। व्यवहारान्तरस्य चात्रानभिमतत्वात्।

Trans. : We hold that 'the state of being other than the soul' is an upādhi. Construing this upādhi as 'the state of being other than the pakṣa', the pūrvapakṣin raises an objection that if 'the state of being other than the pakṣa' is accepted as an upādhi, this will demolish the well-known instance of syllogism. The objection is not viable since the occurrence of the pakṣetaratva upādhi is not possible there. (To establish that the upādhi is not possible in the well-known instance, its definition is being given :) An upādhi is that which is not concomitant with the sādhana but which is co-extensively concomitant with the sādhya. (The siddhantin asks :) Then tell how in that manner 'the state of being other than the pakṣa' can be an upādhi when it is not co-extensively concomitant with the fire, etc.? Therefore on account of being co-extensively concomitant with the sādhya, 'the state of being other than the pakṣa' could possibly be accepted as an upādhi in some instance. There is no harm in it. And it will be explained that that which is co-extensively concomitant with the sādhya is an upādhi. Hence the knowability of the soul is not inferable and in spite of the soul being unknowable, the Upaniṣads are purported to remove ajñāna, the cause of saṁsāra, by virtue of the mental mode of the form of the true nature of the soul. The Brahma-mīmāṁsā also is an aid only in the removal of ajñāna (by removing the obstacles in the form doubt, etc.) and there is no stultification of the unknowability of the soul. Moreover, knowledge itself is the soul as the śruti (Bṛhadāraṇyaka Upaniṣad, 2. 1. 8 & 4. 3. 7) says '(Puruṣa that) consists of consciousness', etc. The cognition is not the object of another cognition because of their being mutually equal. The cognition-and-its-content-relation (*viṣaya-viṣayibhāvasambandha*) is not seen between two equals nor does it look appropriate just as there is no such relation between two lamps. If it is said that there is the seizer-seized (*grāhya-grāhakatā*) relation between two similar hands, then this is not so since they have some distinction (in the context of such a relationship). The hand to which effort has been applied is 'the seizer' whereas the other by itself remains 'the seized'. Thus there is no equal status of the two. Therefore, only cognition which is not an object of (another) cognition shines by itself, that is, it is self-luminous.

The kevalavyatirekī syllogism, too, is as follows : A pot-cognition (the subject of dispute) is the manifesting cause of its own verbal usage because it is a cognition unlike a pot. The defect of the sādhya not being well-known does not apply here as a cognition as the manifesting cause of a verbal usage about itself is well-known. Therefore the sādhya consisting in the nature of a cognition is not unknown. If it is said (from the Nyāya point of view) that it suffers from the defect of proving that which is already proved in the context of the inner perception (*saṁvitprakāśa = anuvyavasāya*), then also this is not so as it (*anuvyavasāya*) does not form a part of the subject (*dharmin*); for the inner perception, which as such is not agreed upon, is not 'the subject of dispute' (*prakṛtavivādapadam*). Thus it is not the dharmin and, as such, there is no defect of siddhasādhanatā. Oh! thus the qualifying expression 'the term under dispute' would be of no use. This is not so since this expression is used to avoid the fault of siddhasādhanatā from the point of view of the other (the Naiyāyika).

The pūrvapakṣin replies that a cognition is the cause of its own manifestation by being its own content (*viṣayatayā*). Then how does the defect of proving that which is already proved not become applicable? The siddhāntin says that the defect of siddhasādhanatā would not be applicable, since the verbal usage is not generated by the content (i.e. the cognition in this case). Otherwise, how can the verbal usage have any relation with (a thing) the past? No usage (*vyavahāra*) other than the verbal one is intended in the present context.

Ann. : The siddhāntin further analyses the syllogism put forward by the pūrvapakṣin to prove the knowability of the soul (see NRD, p. 108 for the syllogistic proposition under consideration). He says there is an upādhi consisting in 'the state of being other than the soul' which in other words may be construed as 'the state of being other than the subject (*pakṣa*)' because the soul is the pakṣa. The state of being knowable or perceivable is the sādhya. The reason is 'that it is the subject of deliberation'. The pūrvapakṣin points out saying that the invocation of the upādhi in this case would lead to the abandonment of the well-known instance of inference : The hill has fire because it has smoke. The siddhāntin replies that there is little possibility of the presence of the upādhi consisting in 'the state of being other than the subject' in the well-known syllogism. The siddhantin, by implication, makes a distinction between 'the state of being other than the soul' and 'the state of being other than the subject'. He further lays down the criterion of an upādhi in this context. That which, not being concomitant with the reason, is co-extensively concomitant with the sādhya is an upādhi. Taking this criterion into consideration, the upādhi consisting in 'the state of being other than the subject' does not exist in the popular instance 'the hill has fire becasue it has smoke' as there is no co-extensive concomitance of 'the state of being other than the pakṣa' with 'the fire'. The siddhāntin furnishes an instance where the upādhi of the form of 'the state of being other than the pakṣa' is present. The presence of 'the state of being other than the subject' can be seen where the absence of the sādhya has been verified by some other definite means of cognition. In the syllogism 'the fire is cold since it is a substance', the absence of the state of being cold is verified by the tactile perceptual cognition. So, the sādhya is stultified and the criterion of the co-extensive concomitance of 'the state of being other than the subject' with 'the sādhya' is fulfilled in the following way : where 'the state of being cold' is, there is 'the state of being other than the fire (*pakṣa*)' and where 'the state of being other than the fire (*pakṣa*)' is, there is 'the state of being cold'. Likewise 'the state of being other than the soul' is co-extensive with the sādhya 'knowability' (*dṛśyatva*) in the syllogistic proposition 'the soul is knowable because it is the subject of deliberation like dharma'. This can also be demonstrated as follows : where 'the state of being other than the soul' is, there is 'knowability' and conversely, 'where 'knowability' is, there is 'the state of being other than the soul'. Thus having the co-extensive concomitance with the probandum, 'the state of being other than the soul' is an upādhi and, as such, the syllogism put forward by the pūrvapakṣin cannot prove the knowability of the soul. The siddhāntin concludes saying that the upādhi is very much present in the syllogism put forward by the pūrvapakṣin to prove the perceivable nature of the soul. As such, the state of being perceivable (knowable) of the soul remains unsubstantiated.

After rejecting the syllogism to prove the knowability of the soul, the siddhāntin states that the purpose of the Upaniṣads is to inculcate conviction about the true nature of the Ultimate Reality and help him attain the state of deep meditation in which he succeeds in having his intellect modalised into the form of the self-luminous soul, which terminates his ignorance, the cause of saṁsāra. The deliberation on Brahman is definitely beneficial for the seeker to attain such a state. And it has been mentioned in the scriptures in clear terms that the soul consists of consciousness or intelligence.

It is the nature of the cognition that it does not become an object of another cognition since both of them are equal and there is no cognition-content relation (*viṣayaviṣayibhāvasambandha*) between two cognitions. The illustration given by the siddhāntin in this context is that of two lamps. Neither can be said to manifest the other. They manifest themselves by themselves. The illustration given by the pūrvapakṣin to prove the contrary is also taken care of by the siddhāntin. The pūrvapakṣin says that the seizer-and-the-seized (*grāhyagrāhaka*) relation is seen between two hands, which are equal. The siddhāntin makes an observation saying that the two hands between which the seizer-and-the-seized relation exists are not equal. The hand which is made to grasp or seize the other hand is 'the seizer' whereas the hand to which no effort has been applied becomes 'the seized'. So there is no equality between the two as claimed by the pūrvapakṣin. In this way, the siddhāntin concludes saying that a cognition which does not become a content of another cognition shines by itself. In other words it is self-luminous and the soul which is of the nature of cognition, consciousness or intelligence is also self-luminous. The siddhāntin makes use of the following kevalavyatirekī syllogism to prove his stand-point : The cognition of a pot (the subject of dispute) is the cause of its own verbal usage since it is a cognition unlike a pot. The verbal usage in respect of a pot depends on its cognition whereas a verbal usage regarding a cognition depends upon the cognition itself. Hence it is self-luminous unlike a pot. The function of the cognition, which is well-known, in this regard does away with the defect known as *aprasiddhaviśeṣaṇatā*. But the Naiyāyika says that there is a defect of proving that which is already proved as the cognition is made known by the inner perception (*anuvyavasāyaḥ = saṁvidaḥ prakāśaḥ*). The siddhāntin points out saying that the concept of anuvyavasāya is not recognised by him and hence it is not 'under dispute' and as such it does not form the subject of the syllogistic propositon. Consequently, there is no partial siddhasādhanatā as the Naiyāyika has pointed out. The qualification 'the term under dispute' is also not without any purpose as it is purported to avoid this very fault of siddhasādhanatā pointed out by the Naiyāyika.

The pūrvapakṣin says that the defect of siddhasādhanatā is still applicable as the cognition is the cause of its own usage by being its own content. The siddhāntin holds that the verbal usage of the cognition is not generated by its content as is clear from the fact that a verbal usage also can refer to a thing of the past. Had the verbal usage been generated by the content, then it would not have had any reference to a thing of the past. As such, the defect of siddhasādhanatā does not apply here as the usage or vyavahāra in this context is intended to signify a verbal usage. Ānandajñāna makes an observation that, although the perceptual cognition of the objects is the cause of the verbal usage in respect of the objects, the cognition does not depend on another cognition for its manifestation. (cf. *pratyakṣā saṁvidyadyapi viṣayeṣu laukikābhivadanahetuḥ tathāpi tasyāḥ na saṁvidantaranibandhanatvam. na hi saṁvedane'bhivadanātiriktavyavahārāntaraṁ saṁvedanākhyaṁ samasti anavasthāprasaṅgāt*, VV, p. 120). Since the verbal usage of a cognition is not dependent on another cognition, the defect known as siddhasādhanatā is not applicable (*saṁvidabhivadanasya saṁvidantaranibandhanatvābhāvānna siddhasādhyatetyabhisandhiḥ*, ibid., p. 120).

ननु संवित्त्वं न ते जातिः। एकव्यक्तेजातिरसम्भवाद्। नाप्यौपाधिकम्। उपाधेरनिरूपणाद्। अतः संवित्त्वं ते न सिद्धम्, न। घटाकाशवदौपाधिकत्वाद्। अन्तःकरणपरिणामश्च घटवदुपाधिः। परस्येत्थं संवित्त्वमसिद्धमिति चेन्न। संवित्त्वमात्रस्यैव हेतोरुभयसिद्धत्वाद्। न चाप्रयोजकत्वम्। उपाधेरसम्भवात्। संवित्प्रकाशत्वमुपाधिरिति चेन्न। साध्याव्यापकत्वात्। प्रकाशरूपत्वं हि साध्यम्। तच्च स्वस्याव्यापकम्। अथ मतं विशेषणभेदाद्विशिष्टसाध्योपाधिभेदः। व्यवहारहेतुत्वं हि साध्यविशेषणम्। संविद्विषयत्वं चोपाधेः। अतो न साध्याव्याप्तिरिति। न। अत्र विशिष्टद्वयाभावाद्। विशेष्यस्याभिन्नत्वाद्। न च ते विशिष्टं विशेष्यादिभ्यस्तत्त्वान्तरम्, तत्त्वान्तरत्वे तु विशिष्टद्वयाश्रययोस्साध्योपाध्योरव्याप्तिः। अस्माकं तु विशेषणारोपितं विशिष्टं न तत्त्वान्तरम्। अतो न धूमवत्त्वादेरव्याप्तिः। संविद्दृश्यताप्रयोगस्त्वात्मदृश्यताप्रयोगवदपास्यः। तर्हि संवित्पदमात्मपदं च स्वविषयगोचरज्ञानजन्यं लौकिकपदत्वात् पदत्वाद्वा कुम्भपदवदित्यनुमीयताम्। न। दृष्टान्ते स्वशब्दार्थस्यानुगमाभावात्। तस्य साध्यविकलत्वाद्। विषयशब्देन अविवक्षितविशेषं विषयमात्रमिष्यते, किं वाच्योऽर्थः अथवा लक्ष्यः, तत्र न तावत् प्रथमद्वितीयौ सिद्धसाधनतापत्तेः। अभ्युपेयते हि संविदात्मपदस्य वाच्यस्य ज्ञानगोचरता। तृतीये तु मुख्यार्थोविवक्षया प्रयुक्तगङ्गापदेन व्यभिचारः। यदि किञ्चिदात्मनः संविदो वा प्रकाशभेदसाधनमुत्प्रेक्ष्येत तदपि सत्यत्वादिना साध्यं विकल्प्यापास्यम्। अथाग्निमत्त्वादिवल्लौकिको भेदः साध्यः, तदा सिद्धसाधनता।

ननु संविदो वेद्यत्वे को दोषः स्यात्। असंवित्त्वप्रसङ्ग इति ब्रूमः। ननु सर्वत्रैवं स्वप्रकाशत्वं साधयितुं शक्यम्। न। कुम्भादिभावेऽपि ते तत्प्रकाशाभावाद्। ननु ते प्रकाशो नित्यः, सत्यम् तथापि प्रकाशे सति कुम्भादेरभावान्न तदात्मनोपलम्भसम्भवः। मायामयस्यैव च वेद्यत्वाद्वेद्यत्वेऽसंवित्त्वं नियतमा-

पद्येत । न हि माययानध्यस्तस्य संवित्सम्बन्धस्सम्भवी । संयोगादेरत्रासम्भवाद् । न चान्तरेण संवित्सम्बन्धं संवेद्यत्वं स्याद् । अनियमापत्तेः । विषयविषयिभावोऽपि सम्बन्धापेक्षः । अन्यथातिप्रसङ्गात् । प्रपञ्चितं चैतदिष्टसिद्धिविवरणे । यदप्यत्र मिश्रेण प्रलपितम् 'अनुभूतेरननुभाव्यत्वे शशविषाणवदननुभूतित्वप्रसङ्ग' इति तत्र व्याप्त्यभावात् प्रशिथिलमूलता । न हि पण्डितम्मन्यस्य शशविषाणेऽसिद्धे व्याप्तिः सिद्ध्येद् । अननुभाव्यत्वं चाप्रसिद्धम् ।

ननु तवैवेयं व्याप्तिरस्तु । शशविषाणासिद्धेरननुभाव्यत्वसिद्धेरात्मनि निश्चयाभ्युपगमात् । तर्हि शशविषाणेऽननुभाव्यत्वाभावाद्व्याप्त्यसिद्धिः । विपर्ययप्रमाणाभावाच्चायमप्रसङ्गः । प्रपञ्चितश्च संविद्वेद्यत्वे प्रमाणाभावः । तस्मात्तत्त्वदर्शनाज्ञानजद्वेषान्मिश्रेण प्रलपितमित्युपेक्षणीयम् । एवं निरवद्यं संवित्स्वप्रकाशत्वम् । सति चैवं संविद्रूपात्मनि स्वप्रकाशत्वं सिद्धम् ।

Trans. : (The pūrvapakṣin tells the siddhāntin that) 'the state of being a cognition' in your (siddhāntin's) case does not constitute a universal since a universal cannot inhere in an individual. Nor is it an upādhi since it has no description as an upādhi (just as the upādhi *ākāśatva* has the description : *śabdāśrayatva*). Therefore, the status of 'the state of being a cognition' (*saṁvittva*) remains unestablished in your case. The siddhāntin replies in the negative and adds that it is adjunctival like the pot-space. And (here) the intellectual modification is an upādhi like a pot. If it is said that 'the state of being a cognition' in this way is not subscribed to by the opponent, then this is not so because both the sides accept 'only the bare state of being a cognition' as the reason (*hetu*). And the reason is not ineffective because of the absence of an upādhi. Let 'the state of being the manifestor of a cognition' be an upādhi. The siddhāntin replies in the negative since it is not concomitant with the sādhya. The state of being luminous (*prakāśarūpatva*) is the sādhya and it cannot be concomitant with itself. The pūrvapakṣin holds that the qualified sādhya and the qualified upādhi are different because of difference in the qualifiers. To explain, 'the state of being the cause of a verbal usage' is the qualifier of the sādhya and 'the state of being a content of the cognition' is that of the upādhi. So, the concomitance of the sādhya is not absent. No, this is not so because the two qualified (entities) do not exist because the substantive is the same. And, according to you, the qualified is not essentially different from the substantive, etc. In case they are (accepted to be) essentially distinct, then there can be no concomitance between the two qualified substrata : the sādhya and the upādhi. As per our view, the substantive qualified by a qualifier does not become different in essence. Therefore, the concomitance of that having the smoke, etc. is not absent (that is, 'a hill qualified by the fire' is inferred from 'that qualified by the smoke'). The syllogism to prove the knowabiltiy of a cognition should be discarded like the one used to prove the perceivable nature of the soul. Then let it be inferred that the terms *saṁvit* and *ātman* are produced by the cognitions having the denotata of these terms as their domain (*viṣaya*) because of 'the state of being a common word (*laukika pada*)' or because of 'the state of being a word (*pada*)' like the term 'pot'. This is not so because the meaning of the word *sva* is not comprehended in the illustration (*kumbhapada*) since the sādhya does not exist in it. Is the bare content, without any specifications, intended to be conveyed by the term *viṣaya*, or a denoted meaning or an indicated one? The first and the second alternatives are not feasible as this would give rise to the fault of proving that which has already been proved (*siddhasādhanatā*) since it is an accepted fact that the denotative meanings of the terms *saṁvid* and *ātman* do become the content of a cognition. So far as the third alternative is concerned, there is deviation in respect of the term *gaṅgā* spoken with the intention to convey the primary meaning 'the stream of gaṅgā'. If any syllogism to prove the difference of luminosity from the soul or the cognition was assumed, it should also be discarded by juxtaposing the sādhya with the options of the state of being real, etc. In case a popular instance of difference like the fiery (hill), etc. is to become the sādhya, then that would amount to proving that which has already been proved (*siddhasādhanatā*).

The pūrvapakṣin raises a query : What would be the harm if the knowability of a cognition was going to be proved? The siddhāntin replies that then the cognition would lose its nature as a cognition. The pūrvapakṣin expresses his apprehension that in this way the self-luminosity could be proved everywhere. The siddhāntin replies in the negative and says that even when a pot, etc. are present, they are not manifest (unless they come into contact with the sense organs).

Again the pūrvapakṣin asks 'Do you subscribe to the view that the luminosity is eternal?' The siddhāntin admits that it is true. Even then a pot, etc. are not perceived as such when they are not present even if the light (luminosity) is present. It is only the creation of māyā, which is knowable and, as such, if the cognition was knowable, then it would invariably be rendered devoid of the property of being a cognition. There is no possibility of a cognition having any relation with that which is not superimposed by māyā since relations such as conjunction, etc. are not possible in it (cognition) and without any relation of a cognition, knowability (in it) just does not exist. In case this is not accepted, then disorder would result (e.g., a piece of cloth would become knowable by virtue of the cognition of a pot). The state of being the cognition-and-its-content (*viṣayaviṣayibhāvà*) also requires a relation otherwise over-extension would result. We have elaborately discussed this in Iṣṭasiddhivivaraṇa. The irresponsible statement made by Śivāditya Miśra in this context is that knowledge (*anubhūti*), if not knowable, would be treated as not being knowledge like the hare's horn (*śaśaviṣāṇavat*). Because of the absence of the concomitance there, the syllogism has a weak foundation (*praśithilamūla*). In the event of the hare's horn being unreal, the concomitance with it cannot be proved by him who masquerades as an arrogant scholar. Also the state of being unknowable is not well-known.

(The pūrvapakṣin proposes :) Let this be the concomitance only in your case because you are definite about the presence of the sādhya (the state of being unknowable) in the soul (= *anubhūti*) and also about the hare's horn (according to the Māyāvāda). Then the absence of the state of being unknowable ceases to exist in the hare's horn and consequently, the concomitance (used by Miśra) would remain unestablished. Also there would be no undesirable contingency as there is no evidence to the contrary. That there is no proof for the knowability of a cognition has already been discussed. Consequently, what is spoken irresponsibly by Śivāditya Miśra out of the animosity born of ignorance about the intuition of the Truth should be overlooked. In this way, the self-luminosity of a cognition remains without any blemish. And such being the case, the self-luminosity of the soul, which is of the nature of a cognition, gets established.

Ann. : Now the pūrvapakṣin questions the very status of the reason (*hetu*) 'the state of being a cognition (*saṁvittva*)'. He says that it can be neither a universal nor an adjunctival property. It cannot be the former since a universal does not exist in a single individual. Nor can it be an adjunctival property because there is no description of an upādhi as regards this just as the upādhi *ākāśatva* has been described as *śabdāśrayatva*. It is, therefore, clear that the status of 'the state of being a cognition' still remains unestablished in the siddhāntin's view, avers the pūrvapakṣin. The siddhāntin rejects the standpoint of the pūrvapakṣin and clarifies saying that it is an upādhi like a pot in the pot-space and in this case the intellectual modification would be taken as an upādhi like a pot. But this kind of the being of a cognition is not accepted by the pūrvapakṣin. The siddhāntin drives home his point of view stating that 'barely the state of being a cognition' is intended here and that is acceptable to both the sides.

The syllogistic proposition put forward by the siddhāntin is kevalavyatirekī : A pot-cognition is the manifesting cause of its own verbal usage because it is a cognition unlike a pot. He says that there is no upādhi here. In the absence of an upādhi there is no such argument as would go against the reason used in the syllogism by the siddhāntin. Still the pūrvapakṣin finds fault with the syllogism of the siddhāntin and comes up with an upādhi in the form of *saṁvitprakāśatvam*. It is a genitive tatpuruṣa compound (*saṁvidaḥ prakāśaḥ, tasya bhāvaḥ*) and consequently the term means the manifestation (*prakāśa*) of a cognition (*saṁvit*). That virtually comes to mean 'the state of being *anuvyavasāya*' (inner perception) which manifests the vyavasāya cognition). Evidently the objection comes from the Naiyāyika's side. The sādhya is 'the state of being the manifestor of the verbal usage of a cognition' (*svavyavahārahetu-*

prakāśatvam), whereas the *saṁvidprakāśatvam* constitutes the upādhi which has been interpreted as the state of being a cognition which is the content of another cognition (*saṁvidviṣayaprakāśatvam*). Having the nature of being luminous, both are one and the same. Neither can pervade the other as both share the same nature. By treating them as different on account of the difference in their qualifications, there can be concomitance between the two in the inner perception as follows : Where 'the state of being a manifestor of the verbal usage of a cognition' (*saṁvidvyavahārahetuprakāśatvam*) is, there is the state of being a cognition which is the content of another cognition' (*saṁvidviṣayaprakāśatvam*). But this concomitance is not tenable as that which is qualified is only one, and not two (*atra viśiṣṭadvayābhāvāt*, VV, p. 122). The substantive remains the same. In case the qualified ones are treated as essentially different, they would cease to be mutually concomitant (*tattvāntare tu viśiṣṭadvyāśrayayossādhyopādhyoravyāptiḥ*, ibid., p. 122). According to the siddhāntin, the qualified substantives are not different from the bare ones. That is why it is said that they infer the hill qualified by the fire from the hill qualified by the smoke (cf. *asmākaṁ tu viśeṣaṇāropitaṁ viśiṣṭaṁ na tattvāntaram, ato na dhūmavattvāderavyāptiḥ*, NRD, p. 122). This comes to mean that the reason of the siddhāntin's syllogistic proposition is not vitiated by any upādhi. He further adds that the syllogism to prove the knowability of a cognition should be discarded like the one used to prove the perceivable nature of the soul.

The other syllogism put forward by the pūrvapakṣin to prove the knowbility of a cognition or the soul is : the terms *saṁvit* and *ātman* are produced by the cognition of the content (*viṣaya*) of these terms since they have either 'the state of being a common word (*laukikapada*)' or 'the state of being a word (*pada*)' like the term 'pot'. The siddhāntin says that this syllogism is not tenable as the meaning of the word *sva* (*saṁvit*) is not comprehended in the illustration (*kumbhapada*). As such, the sādhya ceases to exist in the illustration. Then the three alternative interpretations of the word *viṣaya* are taken up for consideration : Is the bare content without any specifications intended to be conveyed by the term *viṣaya*, or a denoted meaning or an indicated one? The first and second alternatives are not feasible as this would incur the defect of proving that which has already been proved (*siddhasādhanatā*) because it is accepted that the denotative meanings of the terms *saṁvid* and *ātman* do become the content of a cognition. So far as the third alternative is concerned, there is deviation in respect of the term *gaṅgā* spoken with the intention to convey the primary meaning 'the stream of gaṅgā' since the word *gaṅgā* in this case does not have the sādhya consisting in 'the state of being generated by the cognition of the word *gaṅgā* invested with the faculty of indication' although it has the reason consisting in 'the state of being a pada'. Thus the syllogism put forward by the pūrvapakṣin is not worth considering according to the siddhāntin. He continues to corroborate his view of the unknowability of either a cognition or the soul by proposing that the possibility of the difference of light or a cognition or the soul should be rejected by juxtaposing the difference with the optional alternatives of 'the state of being real' etc. If the empirical difference is to be proved, then the defect of siddhasādhanatā is incurred. However, the siddhāntin points out that if a cognition is held to be knowable, then it would lose its status as a cognition. The cognition as light is eternal and it has no relation with that which is not superimposed by māyā, clarifies the siddhāntin. And without having any relation with a cognition, nothing comes to have the state of being knowable. If this is not accepted, then disorder would reign supreme and a cognition of a piece of cloth would arise even from that of a pot. Thus knowability is the characteristic of that which is superimposed on the Ultimate Reality.

The author of NRD also refers to the view of Śivāditya Miśra who holds the view that if a cognition is not admitted to be knowable then it would cease to be a cognition because then it will be on a par with the hare's horn. The concomitance between the state of being unknowable (*ananubhāvyatva*) and the state being of not knowledge (*ananubhūtitva*) is not possible since the illustration, the hare's horn is absolutely unreal (alīka). The pūrvapakṣin says that the existence of the hare's horn can be possible in the philosophy of Māyāvāda. The siddhāntin retorts saying that, even then, the concomitance would not be possible as in that case the hare's horn would cease to be unknowable (*ananubhāvya*). Moreover, the siddhāntin says that the absence of an evidence for the contrary instance has already been discussed. Therefore what is spoken by Miśra is out of ignorance about the intuition of the Truth and hence does not deserve any consideration. In this way the self-luminous nature of a cognition remains without any fault and the self-luminosity of the soul, which is of the nature of cognition, gets established without any hurdle.

नन्वेवं विज्ञानवादप्रवेशप्रसङ्गः। बौद्धोऽपि विज्ञानमात्रं तत्त्वमभ्युपगच्छति। इच्छति च भवानपि तावन्मात्रं तत्त्वमिति। न च नित्यत्वेन विशेषः। अत्यन्ताद्वैतवादिनो नित्यत्वधर्मस्याभावात्। स्वरूपत्वे च स एव विज्ञानवादप्रवेशप्रसङ्गः। धर्मसंभवे च द्वैताद्वैतमतप्रसङ्ग इति। न। वेदान्तवादिभिश्चैकस्यैकता न स्याद्। मनोभेदोत्पत्तिविनाशानां मायामयत्वाश्रयणाद्। बौद्धास्तु विज्ञानानि स्वरसभङ्गुराण्यविरतोदयानि निजभेदभिन्नानि स्वविषयाण्यभ्युपगच्छन्तीति कथं तथागतमतावकाशो वेदान्तेषु। यदि किंचित्साम्यान्मतान्तरता, तदा सर्वमतसाङ्कर्यप्रसङ्गः। तस्मात्सिद्धं स्वतस्सिद्धस्याविषयत्वाद् भेदो न मानगम्य इति।

ननु सर्वज्ञानाविषयस्याविषयत्वसिद्धिरपि कथं स्यात्। सा चेत् कथंचिद्भवेद् भेदसिद्धिरपि तथैव भवेत्। स्यान्मतम् — अविषयस्य सिद्धावसिद्धौ चाविषयत्वसिद्धिर्न वारयितुं शक्येतेति। तर्हि भेदसिद्धिरपि तथैव शक्या न वारयितुम्। अस्माकं स्वप्रकाशतया विषयसिद्धेरविषयत्वं साधयितुं शक्यम्। भेदस्तु नैवं ते सिध्यति। तस्य विषयतासिद्धेः। तर्हि, तथैव ते भेदसिद्धिरप्युपपद्येत। किञ्च आत्मनः सतो भानेऽप्यविषयत्वज्ञानाविषयत्वान्न तस्याविषयत्वज्ञानं स्याद्। आत्मनः संविद्विषयता नेष्यते न तु वृत्तिज्ञानविषयतापीति चेत्, तथाप्यात्मनोऽविषयता न संविन्ना स्याद्। यदपि मतं स्वप्रकाशस्याप्यदृश्यत्वाद्यवच्छिन्नस्य स्यादेव दृश्यतेति, तत्सुहृदां कर्णेषु जप्तव्यम्। न तु सभ्यम्। इत्थंभावे मानाभावात्। तस्मान्नाविषयत्वं कस्यचिद्। अतो भेदसिद्धिर्नानुपपन्नेति।

उच्यते — आत्मनोऽदृश्यत्वेऽपि तदविषयत्वादिना भानं नानुपपन्नं। तथाहि— आत्मनि स्वप्रकाशतया प्रकाशमाने लोकसिद्धाविषयत्वव्यतिरेकव्याप्त्यादिबलादात्माविषयत्वाकारा मनोवृत्तिर्जायते। तस्यामभिव्यक्तो दृगात्मा। तस्मिन् स्वाध्यस्तस्याविषयत्वावच्छिन्नरूपत्वस्य सिद्धिः प्रमाणफलमिति गीयते।

नन्वेवमात्मभेदोऽपि मानतः सिध्येत्। सिध्येद्यदि स आत्मन्यविषयत्वादिवदध्यस्तः स्यात्। तदध्यासे च ते दर्शनहानिः।

नन्वविषयत्वादेरध्यस्तत्वे विषयत्वादि सत्यं स्याद्। न। स्वाप्नयोरिव उभयोरपि मिथ्यात्वोपपत्तेः। तथापि नैवं परार्थानुमानं सम्भवेत्। परो ह्यात्मानं तन्निर्देशाद् विषयतयैवावगच्छति। स कथमनुमानात्तमविषयत्वेनावगच्छेद्। विरोधाद्। उच्यते। धर्मिनिर्देशादात्माकारा बुद्धिवृत्तिरुत्पद्यते। अनुमानाच्चात्मनः संविद्विषयत्वं गम्यते। अतो न विरोधगन्धोऽपि।

ननु बुद्धिरेव संविद्। न। बुद्ध्यभावेऽपि सुषुप्तौ संविद्भावाद्। अन्यथा 'न किञ्चिदवेदिषमि'ति सुषुप्तिपरामर्शः कथं स्याद्। न चायं परामर्शोऽन्यथा सम्भवतीत्युक्तम्। अतो बुद्धेरन्या संविदवश्यमभ्युपेयेत्यनुमानमव्याहतम्। तस्मादात्मनो विषयत्वादिसिद्धिरवद्येति तस्य सच्चिदानन्दादेः भेदसिद्धिर्नानतस्समस्तीति सिद्धम्।

Trans. : Thus (i.e. if consciousness itself is the soul, then) the Doctrine of Momentary Consciousness (Vijñānavāda) is liable to become contingent. The Buddhist also subscribes to the view that only consciousness is the Reality and you also regard that much as Reality. And there is no distinction on account of its being eternal because the property of being eternal does not exist for the absolute non-dualist. In case eternity is the nature of consciousness, then the same Doctrine of Momentary Consciousness is liable to become contingent. If a property (both identical and different) is assumed to be possible, then the non-dualism-cum-dualism view becomes applicable (i.e. the view of absolute non-dualism would be in jeopardy, cf. *bhinnābhinnadharmasambhave cādvaitamatavyāhatiḥ*, VV, p. 125). No, since the Vedāntins do not hold that oneness is the property of the One since the difference, origination and destruction of the mind are held to be the product of māyā. On the other hand, the Buddhists view consciousnesses as fleeting by nature, incessantly arising, distinct by themselves (not due to any upādhi) and having themselves as the content. Then how can the Buddhist Doctrine have any scope in the Upaniṣads. If due to a little similarity a doctrine is considered to be another doctrine, then an amalgam of all views would be the result. Therefore, it is established that the difference of the self-proven Reality cannot be known by a means of knowledge since it does not become an object (of knowledge).

The pūrvapakṣin asks : How can that which is not an object of any cognition be proved that it is not an object? If somehow that is proved, then the difference can also be proved in the same way. This could also be assumed : The establishment of the state of not being an object cannot be avoided whether that which is not an object has been proved or not. Then the establishment of difference could also not be avoided in the same manner. (The siddhāntin holds the view that) the state of not being an object can be proved by us since the object (soul) is established on account of its being self-luminous. But the difference cannot be proved like this in your case since the state of its being an object is not established. Then the establishment of difference could be made intelligible in the same manner (by taking the soul as the *dharmin*). Moreover, even though the soul is comprehended as existent, the cognition of its having the state of not being an object cannot be had because of its not being an object of the cognition of the soul's state of not being an object. The soul's state of being an object of a cognition is not desirable but its being an object of a mental mode (*vṛttijñāna*) is not denied. Even then the soul's not being an object (of knowledge) is not known (asserts the pūrvapakṣin). Also the view that the self-luminous delimited by the state of being unperceivable could however assume the state of being perceivable should be told to friends in private, and not in public since there is no proof of this kind of view. Therefore there is nothing which does not have the state of being an object. Hence the establishment of the difference is not unintelligible (impossible).

(The siddhānta view) is being explained : Even though the soul is not perceivable, its comprehension as having the state of not being an object, etc. is not unintelligible. To explain, when the soul shines by being self-luminous, the mental mode of the form of soul's non-objectivity arises by the force of the empirically verified non-objectivity, negative concomitance (*vyatirekavyāpti*), etc. The seer soul becomes manifest in that (mental mode). The establishment of the state of being a form qualified by the state of not being an object superimposed on the soul is described to be the result of the vṛtti (*pramāṇa*).

The pūrvapakṣin says that in this way the difference of the soul can also be established by a means of cognition. The siddhāntin observes that if the difference is proved then that would be construed as superimposed on the soul like the state of not being an object, etc. If the superimposition of difference is accepted, then your view would be rendered untenable.

The pūrvapakṣin states that if the state of not being an object, etc. is accepted to be superimposed, then the state of being an object would have to be real. The siddhāntin replies in the negative since the unreality of both (*viṣayatva* and *aviṣayatva*) can be justified like those of a dream. Nonetheless, in this way the syllogism meant for the other person would not be possible since the other comprehends the soul only as an object when it is pointed out (as being the dharmin in the syllogism). (Then) how can he know from the syllogism that the soul is not an object when there is a contradiction between the states of being an object (*viṣayatva*) and not being an object (*aviṣayatva*)? It is explained (by the siddhāntin) : When the dharmin (soul) is indicated, the mental mode of the form of the soul (perception) takes place and its having the state of not being an object of cognition is known from the inference. Consequently, there is not even an iota of contradiction.

(The pūrvapakṣin does not accept the above view of the siddhāntin because) the mind itself is the cognition. The siddhāntin replies in the negative as there is no mind in dreamless sleep although the cognition (*saṁvid*) exists. Otherwise, how could the recollection of dreamless sleep take place in the form 'I did not know anything'? It has already been mentioned that this recollection is not possible in any other way (than that explained just now). So, it has to be admitted necessarily that the cognition is different from the mind (*buddhi*). And, as such, the syllogism (of the siddhāntin) remains uncontradicted. Therefore, the view of the soul's having the state of being an object, etc. is faulty and consequently, it is established that its difference from Existence, Consciosness and Bliss cannot be proved by a means of cognition.

Ann. : The siddhāntin has established the state of being self-luminous of the soul which is consciousness but the pūrvapakṣin points out saying that, if only consciousnes is held to be the Reality, then the Yogācāra doctrine (Vijñānavāda) viewing consciousness alone as reality would render Advaitavāda redundant (*ātmaiva tvanmate tattvam. sa yadi saṁvid eva tarhi saṁvinmātraṁ tattvamiti yogācāramatānumatiṁ śaṅkate*, VV, 125). The siddhāntin states that, if such a view is held on account of some kind of similarity, then an amalgam of all doctrines would result. If, to avoid this kind of confusion, it is said that there is a distinction between the two : The Yogācāra school holds consciousness to be momentary, whereas, according to the Advaitin, it is eternal (*nityatvaṁ saṁvido* *vedāntibhiriṣyate yogācāreṇa tvanityatvam,* ibid., p. 125), then there is no confusion between the two and the Advaita doctrine would hold on its own. Upon this the opponent points out saying that the state of being eternal can be either the nature or an attribute of consciousness but neither is possible. The state of being eternal cannot be held to be the nature of consciousness as this would make the Advaita view confused with the Yogācāra doctrine (*svarūpatve ca sa eva vijñānavādapraveśaprasaṅgaḥ,* VV, p. 125) as pointed out just now. Concerning the view that it is an attribute, Ānandajñāna suggests three alternative interpretations : The state of being eternal as an attribute is either 1. different or 2. identical or 3. identical-cum-different. Taking into consideration the first alternative interpretation that it is different, he says that there is no scope for any such assumption as per the theory of absolute non-dualism as it would compromise it (*atyantādvaitavādino nitya-tvadharmasyābhāvāt,* NRD, p. 125). If the attribute is understood as identical-cum-different according to the third interpretation, then also the Advaita doctrine stands compromised (*bhinnābhinna-dharmasambhave cātyantādvaitamatavyāhatiḥ,* VV, p. 125). In case it is taken as identical with consciousness or as its nature, then this would again usher in the Buddhist doctrine of consciousness, to wit, Vijñānavāda (*svarūpatve ca sa eva vijñānavādapraveśaprasaṅgaḥ,* NRD, p. 125 and also cf. *svarūpapakṣeṇa sahābhedapakṣaṁ prati-kṣipati,* VV, p. 125).

According to Vijñānavāda, cognitions arise incessantly. They are fleeting by nature and have themselves as objects since nothing external to consciousness exists according to this doctrine. They are different because of their being unique. In other words, they are not different due to some external factor (upādhi). They are just different by themselves. Given this, how can Vijñānavāda have any scope in the context of the Upaniṣads which conceive an eternal self-luminous Reality which admits of no change. A little similarity is not a sufficient ground to put the two absolutely different views on a par. So, the consciousness (which in Advaita is identical with the soul) being established as a self-luminous entity, does not become an object of any means of cognition. So, it does not have the state of being an object. Accordingly, the reality of difference concerning the self-luminous consciousness cannot be proved through a means of knowledge.

The siddhāntin has dismissed the possibility of the reality of difference with reference to the soul as it does not have the state of being the object of a cognition. But the pūrvapakṣin does not see eye to eye with the siddhāntin on the view that the soul does not become an object. He asks how the soul which does not become an object can be known to have the state of not being an object. He further remarks that whatever way the siddhāntin adopts to prove the non-objectivity of the soul, the reality of difference can be proved the same way. The siddhāntin replies that the state of not being an object can be comprehended vis-a-vis the state of being an object because the soul is self-luminous (*asmākaṁ svaprakāśatayā viṣayasiddheraviṣayatvaṁ sādhayituṁ śakyam*, NRD, p. 126). But such a possibility does not obtain on the view of the pūrvapakṣin as difference does not enjoy the status of being an object because the counter-positive is beyond the means of knowledge (*bhedastu naivaṁ te sidhyati. tasya viṣayatāsiddheḥ*, ibid., p. 126. *tatra hetumāha – tasyeti. ātmano viṣayatvābhāvāt tadbhedo mānato na sidhyatīty-arthaḥ*, VV, p. 126). However, the pūrvapakṣin makes a proposal that the difference of the soul can be proved just as the soul's having the state of not being an object has been proved on the basis of self-luminosity (*aviṣayatvasiddhivat bhedasiddhirapi svapra-kāśatvenāviṣaye pratīci sambhavatītyāha*, ibid., p. 126). The pūrva-pakṣin continues to lay stress on his standpoint by remarking that although we become aware of the soul, how can its state of not being an object be comprehended when it does not become the object of that cognition which has as its content the state of not being an object. He further adds that the Advaitins hold the view that the soul being pervaded by the mental mode, is not pervaded by the phala, the reflection of the self in the mind. Even then the soul's state of not being an object is not recognised, asserts the pūrvapakṣin. If it is held that the self-luminous self can become perceivable by being qualified by the state of not being perceivable, etc. then this, advises the opponent, may be treated as a personal view and not philosophical as there is no evidence in support of such a stand-point. This is why the pūrvapakṣin concludes that there is nothing which does not have the state of being an object. As such, the reality of difference is not impossible.

The pūrvapakṣa view is criticised by the siddhāntin as follows: Although we do admit the unperceivable nature of the soul, still the awareness of the soul's having the state of not being an object, etc. is not unintelligible. The soul shining by itself, the mental mode of the non-objectivity of the soul takes place on the force the state of not being an object, vyatireka concomitance, etc. which are empirically verified. The soul which is the seer becomes manifest in that mental mode. The result of the means of knowledge, that is vṛtti, is the awareness of the state of not being an object which is superimposed on the soul, reflected in the mental mode. The pūrvapakṣin says that the difference of the soul could likewise be proved by a means of knowledge. The siddhāntin replies saying that if this is accepted, then the difference would be taken as superimposed on the soul like *aviṣayatva*. By this, the pūrvapakṣin would be compelled to abandon his philosophical position.

Again the pūrvapakṣin raises an objection saying that if the state of not being an object, etc. is held to be superimposed, then the state of being an object would have to be real. The siddhāntin does not accept this saying that the unreality of the state of being or not being an object can be explained cogently on the analogy of dream objects. The pūrvapakṣin says that if the siddhāntin's view is accepted, then the syllogism used for the sake of the other would not be possible as the other would know the soul in the form of an object when it is conveyed to him by describing the soul as a dharmin (subject) in the syllogism for the other. Then how can he know it as not having the state of not being an object from the syllogism when *viṣayatva* and *aviṣayatva* are mutually contradictory. The siddhāntin, however, resolves this contradiction by stating that, when the dharmin is indicated, the mental mode of the form of the soul takes place and in that mental mode (perception) the soul becomes manifest and from the syllogism it comes to be known that the soul is not the object of cognition. Thus there is no contradiction between the two modes of knowing. However, the pūrvapakṣin says that the mind itself is the cognition (*saṁvid*). But the siddhāntin does not accept this saying that the cognition exists in the dreamless sleep when the mind is not present as it is submerged in ajñāna. Otherwise, how can the recollection of deep sleep as 'I did not know anything' take place? It should, therefore, be admitted that the cognition is different from the mind. In this way, the evidence of the soul's having the state of being an object is faulty. Hence, it is conclusively established that the difference of Existence, Consciousness and Bliss, which constitute the Ultimate Reality, cannot be proved with the help of a means of cognition.

आनन्दरूपश्चायमात्मा स्वापेऽवभासते । 'सुखमहमस्वाप्समि'तिपरामर्श-दर्शनाद् । 'एषोऽस्य परम आनन्द' इति भेदश्रुतेर्नैवमिति चेन्न । तदा भेदासम्भ-

वात्। 'न तु तद्द्वितीयमस्ती'ति तदा भेदो निषिध्यते। तस्मा'देषोऽस्य'ति भाक्तो निर्देशः। यथा 'आनन्दं ब्रह्मणो विद्वानि'ति [तत्रापि] भेदनिर्देशाद् ब्रह्मणो गुण इति चेन्न बह्वागमविरोधात्। तथा हि — 'आनन्दाद्ध्येव खल्विमानि भूतानि जायन्ते' 'आनन्दो ब्रह्मेति व्यजानाद्' 'विज्ञानमानन्दं ब्रह्मे'त्यादिबह्वागमविरोधो ब्रह्मानन्दभेदनिर्देशे स्याद्। आनन्दशब्द एव भाक्तो दुःखाभावं ब्रूयादिति चेन्न। मुख्ये सम्भवत्यमुख्यस्यान्याय्यत्वात्।

स्यान्मतम् — दुःखाभाव एवानन्दशब्दस्य मुख्यार्थः। ज्वरभारभयादिदुःखनिवृत्तौ 'अहो सुखमि'त्युपलम्भाद्। न हि तत्र सुखस्य क्लृप्तौ हेतुरस्ति। यत्तु ज्वरादिनिवृत्तिविषयवत् सुखस्य व्यञ्जिकेति मतं तत् प्रक्रियामात्रम्। अभावस्य सुखव्यञ्जकत्वे मानाभावाद्। यदपि मानम् — सुखं न दुःखाभावः तदनिरूप्यत्वात् कुम्भवदिति, तदपि वार्तम्। विपक्षे बाधाभावात्। प्रलयेन व्यभिचाराच्च। प्रलयो हि सर्वकार्याभावत्वाद् दुःखाभावोऽपि। न चासौ दुःखनिरूप्य इति कथं न व्यभिचारः। प्रलयस्य सर्वाभावतया सर्वनिरूप्यत्वाद् दुःखनिरूप्यत्वमिति चेत्, तर्हि सुखस्यापि दुःखाभावतया दुःखनिरूप्यत्वात्तदनिरूप्यत्वं ममासिद्धम्। अतो दुःखाभाव एवानन्द इति।

न। आनन्दस्य भावत्वानुभवविरोधाद्। ब्रह्मरूपताश्रुतिविरोधाच्च। दर्शितानि हि तद्विषयाणि श्रुतिवाक्यानि। अतो लौकिकमपि सुखं न दुःखाभावः नित्यमेवात्मसुखं विषययोगजान्तःकरणवृत्तिव्यङ्ग्यं सद् विषयसुखमिति गीयते। ज्वराद्यभावोऽपि विषयवदात्मसुखस्य व्यञ्जको भवेद्। अभावस्य व्यञ्जकता च नादृष्टचरी। मूर्तद्रव्याभावस्याकाशव्यञ्जकतादर्शनाद्। अत आत्मैव सुखं स्वापेऽपरोक्षं भातीति परामर्शाद् गम्यते।

ननु स्वप्नान्तेऽनुभूतं सुखं सामीप्यात् स्वापकालीनत्वेन भ्रान्त्या परामृश्यते। यथा 'दुःखमहमस्वाप्समि'ति परामृश्यते। न। युक्तं हि दुःखं भ्रान्त्या तथा परामृश्यत इति। सुषुप्तौ दुःखस्याभावात्। सुखपरामर्शे तु बाधाभावान्न तस्य भ्रान्तित्वं युक्तम्। तस्मात्स्वापे सुखरूपेणात्मनः स्फुरणं नापलपनीयम्। एवमनुभवसिद्धं तावदात्मनः सुखरूपत्वम्। तदनुभवे च विप्रतिपन्नस्य परामर्शानुपपत्तिरुक्ता। तथाऽऽगमतोऽपि सुखरूपतात्मनः सिध्यति। तथा हि — 'सत्यं ज्ञानमनन्तं ब्रह्म। यो न वेद निहितं गुहायामि'ति ब्रह्मप्रत्यगात्मनोरैक्यमुक्त्वा 'आनन्दाद्ध्येव खल्विमानि भूतानि जायन्ते। आनन्देन जातानि जीवन्ति। आनन्दं प्रयन्त्यभिसंविशन्ती'ति। आनन्दो ब्रह्मेति सतात्पर्यं ब्रह्मात्मन आनन्दरूपतोच्यते। एवमनुमानतोऽप्यात्मनः सुखरूपता ज्ञायते। तदयं प्रयोगः — आत्मा सुखमनन्यार्थत्वे सति प्रियत्वाद् दुःखवदिति व्यतिरेकी। न च वाच्यं सुखस्यात्मार्थत्वादनन्यार्थत्वविशिष्टो हेतु सपक्षाप्रवेशादनध्यवसित इति। आत्मनः सुखतादात्म्यस्य साध्यत्वात् सपक्षासिद्धेः। तर्हि कालात्ययापदेश इति चेन्न। सुखादात्मनो भेदे प्रमाणस्यासंप्रतिपत्तेः।

न च 'अहं सुखी'ति प्रत्ययबाधः। अहमोऽनात्मताया उक्तत्वाद्। दर्शितं ह्यहंकारात्मनोर्भेदे मानम्।

ननु प्रीतिः सुखं, तत्साधनं च प्रियम् अतो हेतुप्रतिज्ञयोर्व्याघात इति। न। प्रियस्येच्छाविशेषविषयस्य प्रसिद्धत्वात्। कथमन्यथा सुखं प्रियमिति प्रसिद्धिः साध्वी स्याद्। 'भक्तिमान् मे प्रियो नरः' इति प्रयोगदर्शनाच्च। न हि भक्तेनेश्वरे सुखं जन्यते। यदि च प्रियपदेन सुखसाधनमेवोच्यते, तदा आत्मनस्तु सर्वं प्रियम्भवतीति वक्तव्यं स्याद् न पुनः 'आत्मनस्तु कामाय सर्वं प्रियं भवती'ति। आत्मनः सुखसाधनमिति युज्यतेऽन्वयो न त्वात्मनः कामाय सुखसाधनमिति। अतः स्नेहविषय एव सर्वत्र प्रियपदेनोच्यते। अनानन्दोऽप्यात्मा प्रीतिविषयः स्यात्, को बाध इति चेत्, प्रीतिविषयत्वभङ्ग इति ब्रूमः। यतो दुःखतत्साधनेभ्य उद्विजते लोकः, तृणादिषु चोदास्ते। सुखसाधने च न निरुपाधिप्रेमोपपद्यते। अतोऽत्र तादृशप्रेमविषयत्वान्यथानुपपत्तिप्रसूतार्थापत्तिरपि शक्यते प्रमाणयितुम्। सुखलक्षणलक्षितत्वादिति व्यतिरेकिप्रयोगादपि सुखस्वरूप आत्मा। सुखलक्षणं च यदर्थमन्यदुपादीयते। यच्च नान्यार्थमिति। तथारूपश्चात्मा।

ननु सुखमात्मार्थम्। न। अकिंचित्करत्वात्। सुखं स्वज्ञानं जनयतीति चेद् न, तज्ज्ञानस्याजन्यत्वात्। तज्जन्यं चेत् सुषुप्तौ न स्याद्। दर्शितं च सुषुप्तौ तज्ज्ञानम्। विपक्षे चात्मन उक्तरूपता न स्यादिति बाधः। सुखमात्मैव चेत्तज्जन्यं कथं स्यात्? न कथञ्चिद्। या त्वन्तःकरणवृत्तिरात्मसुखव्यञ्जिका सुखसम्भेदात् सुखाकारा सैव जायते नश्यति। भिन्ना आत्मार्था वेद्या चेत्येवमादिदशामाविशतीति न विरोधगन्धोऽपि। सुखमेव चेज्जन्यं तत् स्वापे न स्यात्। साधितं च स्वापेऽपि सुखम्।

नन्वात्मनः सुखत्वे कथं तद्भाने सुखाभानम्। कामोपप्लुतान्तःकरणावच्छिन्नत्वादिति ब्रूमः। अत एव कामोपशमे विदुषां सुप्तानां च सुखाभिव्यक्तिरुपपद्यते। कामाभावाच्चानन्दस्य शतगुणोत्कर्षः श्रूयते। 'ते ये शतं मानुषा आनन्दास्स एक' इत्यादौ 'श्रोत्रियस्य चाकामहतस्य'ति श्रवणाद्। यथा ह्यवच्छेदकदोषात् क्वचित्प्रतिबिम्बिते रूपे भात्यपि तदभिन्ना शुद्धिर्न भाति। एवमात्मस्वरूपमपि सुखं तद्भानेऽपि न भातीति किमनुपपन्नम्?

Trans. : And the soul having bliss as its nature shines in deep sleep since the experience that 'I slept happily' is recollected. (The pūrvapakṣin says :) Not like this since there is a scriptural statement of difference, 'this is its supreme bliss'. (But the siddhāntin replies :) There is no possibility of any difference in that state because the existence of difference then is denied (by the śruti) 'and there is none second to it'. Therefore, the difference seen in the scriptural statement 'This is its supreme bliss' is figurative, as in 'One who knows the bliss of Brahman'. There also, could bliss not be considered to be a property of Brahman because of the indication of difference? (The siddhāntin says :) No, because this stand would contradict many scriptures. To explain, 'All these creatures are indeed born out of Bliss only', 'He knew that Bliss was Brahman', 'Consciousness and Bliss are Brahman', many such scriptural statements would be contradicted if difference is indicated between Brahman and Bliss. Let then the word *ānanda* figuratively mean 'absence of pain'. No, when the primary denotation is possible, to take resort to the secondary meaning is not justified.

The pūrvapakṣin makes a proposal 'Let 'the absence of pain' itself be the primary meaning of the word *ānanda* since the experience of happiness, 'How happy I am' is seen after the cessation of pain from fever, burden, fear, etc. because there is no ground for the assumption of happiness in that context. The view that 'freedom from fever, etc. manifests happiness as the sense objects do' is merely a way of description because there is no evidence (to support the view) that absence can manifest happiness. The syllogism 'Pleasure is not the absence of pain since it is not described by it (pain) like a pot' does not merit any consideration since there is no contradictory argument against the contrary view and there is also deviation in respect of the dissolution. Being the absence of all effects, the dissolution is also constituted by the absence of pain. And that (dissolution) is not describable by the pain. So, why should not there be any deviation? Let then the dissolution be construed as describable by pain since, being the absence of all, the dissolution is describable by all. Then happiness also being the absence of pain is describable by pain. So, I do not accept that it is not describable by pain. Therefore, only absence of pain constitutes bliss (avers the pūrvapakṣin).

(Siddhāntapakṣa) : No, since it is contradictory to the experience of bliss as being positive and also to the scriptural statements which describe Brahman as bliss. The scriptural statements depicting the blissful nature of Brahman have already been cited. Therefore, the worldly pleasure also is not the absence of pain. Only eternal bliss of the soul which is manifested by the mental mode produced by the contact of sense objects is described as sense pleasure. Let the absence of fever, etc. manifest the bliss of the soul as the sense objects do. The manifesting aspect of absence is not uncommon. It is seen that the absence of embodied objects manifests ākāśa (e.g. in a well, etc.) Therefore, it is known by the recollection that the soul itself being bliss immediately shines in deep sleep.

The pūrvapakṣin suggests that the pleasure experienced at the end of a dream is illusorily recollected as belonging to the state of deep sleep because of its proximity just as the experience 'I slept unhappily' is recollected. The siddhāntin says 'no' as it is proper to say that the pain is remembered illusorily in that way (i.e. that it belongs to the state of deep sleep) since there is an absence of pain in the dreamless sleep. It is not proper to construe the recollection of happiness as illusory as there is no contradiction of the remembrance of happiness. Consequently, the experience of the soul as bliss in deep sleep should not be denied. Thus the blissful nature of the soul is indeed established by experience. The impossibility of the recollection is explained to him who is opposed to the experience of bliss (in deep sleep). Likewise the blissful nature of the soul is established also on the basis of the scriptures. To explain, 'Brahman is Truth, Knowledge and Infinity. He who knows him hidden in the cave of the heart (obtains all his desires)', Taittirīya Upaniṣad, 2. 1. 1. Thus after describing the oneness of Brahman with the individual soul, it has been said 'All these creatures are born out of Bliss only, they live by bliss and return to bliss at the time of death'. Brahman has been described of the form of bliss with a purpose. In this way the blissful nature of the soul is also known from the syllogism. This is the vyatirekī syllogism : The soul is bliss since it is dear though not meant for anything other than itself unlike pain. And it should not be objected that bliss being for the sake of the soul, the qualification 'not being for anything other than itself' of the reason remains indefinite because of its not residing in the sapakṣa, which remains unestablished as the identity of the soul and bliss is the probandum (*sādhya*). Then it is sublation (since in the absence of the identity between the soul and bliss, the state of being blissful does not remain in the soul). No, since there is no acknowledged evidence of the difference of bliss from the soul. And it (the identity of the soul and bliss) is not contradicted by the experience 'I am happy' as it has already been explained that the 'I' is not the soul; for the evidence of the difference between the 'I' and the soul has been demonstrated (see NRD, p. 109).

(The pūrvapakṣin says :) Let happiness be pleasure and that which is a means to it be dear. Therefore, there is a contradiction between the reason (*hetu*) and the proposition (*pratijñā*). The siddhāntin replies in the negative since it is well-known that the object of a specific desire is dear. Otherwise how could the well-known fact that pleasure is dear be true? And also because there is a usage 'The man who has devotion is dear to me'. It is definite that pleasure is not produced in God by a devotee. If the word *priya* denotes 'a means to happiness' only, then it should be said that everything is dear to the soul instead of 'but for the love of the soul (*ātman*) all is loved', Bṛhadāraṇyaka Upaniṣad, 4. 5. 6. The syntactic relation consisting in 'the soul's means to pleasure' would then be proper and not 'a means to pleasure for the love of the soul'. Therefore, everywhere the object of affection alone is called by the term *priya*. (The pūrvapakṣin asks :) What would stop us from saying that the soul bereft of bliss could be an object of love? The siddhāntin says that then the soul would cease to be the object of love because man avoids pain and that which causes pain, and remains indifferent to chaff, etc. And there is no unconditional love for that which is a means to pleasure. In this context, therefore, the assumption (*arthāpatti*) that otherwise the unconditional love (for the soul) would be unintelligible can be adduced as an evidence (*pramāṇa*). It is also known from the vyatirekī syllogism that the soul has blissful nature : The soul is bliss since it is defined in terms of 'the nature of bliss' unlike pain (see VV, p. 134 for the vyatirekī syllogism). Happiness is that for the sake of which something else is acquired and which is not for the sake of anything else. The soul has such nature.

(The pūrvapakṣin makes another proposal :) Let beatitude be for the sake of the soul. The siddhāntin replies in the negative because it cannot induce any excellence in the soul. Bliss produces its own knowledge. No, (the siddhāntin remarks saying that) its knowledge cannot be generated. Had it been a product, it would not have been there during deep sleep and it has been shown that the cognition (experience) of bliss does take place in deep sleep. That the soul would otherwise be devoid of bliss constitutes a contradictory argument against the contrary view. If it is admitted that bliss itself is the soul, then how can it be a product? Not in any way. The mental mode which manifests self's bliss is of the form of bliss because of being suffused with it. It is the mental mode that takes birth and perishes. And it assumes the states as 'it is different', 'it is for the sake of the soul', 'it is knowable', etc. and, as such, there is not an iota of contradiction. If bliss was a product, it would not be there in deep sleep and it has been proved that bliss exists also in deep sleep.

The pūrvapakṣin asks why bliss is not known during the cognition of the soul if it is itself bliss. The siddhāntin replies: (that bliss is not experienced) because the soul is delimited by the mind which is overwhelmed by desires. Therefore, it is plausible that bliss becomes manifest when desire does not exist and also in them who are fast asleep. It is heard that bliss is experienced a hundred times more because of the absence of desires, for it is given in the scriptures 'A hundred such human blisses are one', etc. 'of the one who is proficient in the Vedas and not overwhelmed by desire', Tai. Up. 2. 8. 1-2. There is nothing unintelligible if bliss, though identical with the soul, is not experienced even when the soul is being cognised, just as purity (*śuddhi*) identical with a form (*rūpa*) is not perceived because of the defect of a delimitor (e.g. a mirror) even when the form is reflected (in it).

Ann. : In the present section the problem of bliss as the nature of the soul has been analysed. The siddhāntin invokes the experience of deep sleep as an evidence of the blissful nature of the soul. He says that the recollection of everybody that he slept happily is a proof that the soul is essentially blissful or bliss itself. There are two kinds of statements in the scriptures. One kind of statements indicate difference between bliss and Brahman. The other kind of statements which are in abundance show that there is identity between bliss and Brahman. The scriptural statement from which it appears that bliss is different from Brahman is 'This is its Supreme Bliss', Bṛhadāraṇyaka Upaniṣad, 4. 3. 32. But on the basis of the following statement from the same Upaniṣad 'There is no second (for him to see)', Bṛh. Up. 4. 3. 23 , the siddhāntin urges that the indication of difference should be construed as metaphoric. The statement 'Knows the bliss of Brahman', Tai. Up. 2. 9. 1 must not be interpreted as showing bliss as a property of Brahman since this would contradict many scriptural statements. For example, the famous statement of the Taittirīya Upaniṣad 'He came to know that bliss is Brahman as verily from bliss are born these beings and when born they live by bliss and return into bliss at the time of death' and the following one 'Consciousness is Brahman and bliss is (also Brahman)' Bṛh. Up. 3. 9. 28, which show identity between bliss and Brahman, would be contradicted. The pūrvapakṣin makes a suggestion that the word bliss may be interpreted in a metaphoric way and as such it may mean 'absence of pain'. The siddhāntin disagrees and says that, when the primary meaning is possible, there is no point in hunting for the secondary meaning. Nevertheless, the pūrvapakṣin continues to buttress his position by saying that, when a man is relieved of pain and other ailments, he expresses his joy interjectionally, which fact shows that the absence of plain may legitimately be taken as bliss. In other words, the absence of pain may be construed as manifesting happiness just as in Advaita a sense object is understood as a manifestor of pleasure. To this the siddhāntin replies that to feel happy from the recovery from fever, etc. is only a method of describing happiness or pleasure but, in reality, the absence of pain cannot be accepted as the cause of the manifestation of bliss since there is no evidence to this effect. To buttress his view that the absence of pain cannot be accepted as bliss, the siddhāntin puts forward a syllogistic propostion : Pleasure is not absence of pain since it is not described by pain like a pot. It means that if absence of pain is construed as pleasure even when it is not described by pain, then even a pot would assume the state of being pleasure since the absence of pain can be put on a par with a pot. The pūrvapakṣin does not consider the syllogism to be worth considering as there is no contradictory argument against the contrary view that the absence of pain is pleasure. Moreover, this syllogism suffers from deviation in respect of the state of dissolution. The dissolution may be taken as the absence of pain as it is constituted by the absence of all effects. But it is not described by pain. So, there is deviation. According to the pūrvapakṣin, the dissolution can be understood as described by pain since it is constituted by the absence of all effects and as such it can be construed as described by all including pain. The pūrvapakṣin further says that he does not subscribe to the view that pleasure is not described by pain as being absence of pain it can be construed as describable by pain. From this he concludes that the absence of pain is bliss.

The siddhāntin does not accept the view of the pūrvapakṣin that it is the absence of pain that constitutes bliss as the argument given by him is not convincing since bliss is experienced as something positive. If the absence of pain is accepted as bliss, then the positive aspect of bliss would be contradicted. It is all the more not acceptable as it contradicts many scriptural statements which describe Brahman as bliss. The statements to this effect have already been mentioned. Hence pleasure at the empirical plane also cannot be described in terms of absence of pain as the eternal bliss which becomes manifest by the mental mode induced by the contact of sense objects is often described as pleasure. He futher clarifies saying that the absence of fever, etc. may also be understood as a manifesting factor of the bliss of soul. It is not uncommon that absence can also be construed as a manifestor. Even the absence of embodied products becomes the cause of the manifestation of space (*ākāśa*) in a well, etc. (*na ca mūrtābhāvasyāpi vyañjakatvamasampratipannamiti sāmpratam. tasya kūpādāvākāśavyañjakatāyāḥ sarvapratipannatvāditi bhāvaḥ*, VV, p. 131). It is therefore cogent to hold the view that the soul is identical with bliss and that this bliss is immediately experienced in deep sleep is known from the recollection 'I slept happily'.

The pūrvapakṣin again makes an observation that the bliss that is experienced at the end of a dream could be recollected as illusorily belonging to the dreamless sleep just as the experience 'I slept unhappily' is illusorily recollected as belonging to the dreamless sleep. However, the siddhāntin does not accept the observation of the pūrvapakṣin and clarifies saying that it is possible that pain could be recollected as illusorily belonging to the state of dreamless sleep since there is absence of pain in that state. Since there is no sublation of the experience of bliss, it would not be logically tenable to construe the recollection of bliss as illusory. Therefore it should not denied that the soul is bliss. It is all the more so when the bliss aspect of the soul is proved by the experience itself. If someone does not feel reconciled to such a fact then he should be confronted with the assumptive means of cognition (*arthāpatti*). This can be explained as follows : Had the soul not been essentially blissful, then the recollection of the experience of bliss in deep sleep would not have been possible. Since this kind of experience is widely recognised, there should be no misgiving about the nature of the soul as bliss. The scriptures also abundantly demonstrate this fact: After establishing the unity of Brahman and the innermost soul in 'Brahman is truth, knowledge and infinity. He who knows him hidden in the heart obtains all his desires', Taittirīya Upaniṣad, 2. 1. 1, it has been said in the same Upaniṣad that 'All these creatures are born out of Bliss alone and they live by bliss and return to bliss at the time of death'. Thus Brahman has been described of the nature of bliss with a purpose in the scriptural statement 'Bliss is Brahman',Tai. Up. 3. 6 (cf. *āgamagamyamapi brahmātmanaḥ sukhatvamādityāderyūpatvādivadavivakṣitam ityāśaṅkyāha satātparyamiti*, VV, p.132). The scriptural statements in abundance demonstrate that Brahman is Bliss and so is the individual soul which is not different from Brahman. The siddhāntin presents a syllogistic proposition to endorse this standpoint : The individual soul is bliss since it is not meant for anything other than itself yet it is dear unlike pain. That which is not dear is not bliss, for example, pain. But the individual soul is not such. Hence it is bliss. And there is no evidence to the effect that the individual soul is different from bliss. The experience 'I am happy' cannot contradict the individual soul's identity with bliss since it has been already explained that the 'I' (*ahaṅkāra*) is different from the soul (see NRD, p. 109).

Now the pūrvapakṣin considers the problem of pleasure from another angle. He proposes, let happiness (*prīti*) be pleasure (*sukha*) and the means to achieve it be dear. But as a consequence there would not be any compatibility between the proposition (*pratijñā*) and the reason (*hetu*) in the syllogistic proposition : The soul is bliss since it is a means to it. It is simply not possible to comprehend how pleasure and its means can be the same. The qualifying expression 'not meant for anything else than itself' is also not feasible as a means to pleasure is obviously for the sake of pleasure, which means that it is manifestly for the sake of other than itself. If the term *priya* is construed as meaning something other than a means to pleasure, then there would be no incompatibility between the proposition and the reason. The siddhāntin clarifies this stance explaining that that which is dear is an object of a specific desire. Otherwise, the fact that pleasure is dear would not be true. The statement of the Bhagavadgītā, 12. 17 'He who is filled with devotion is dear to me' also endorses this as pleasure or happiness is not generated in God by the devotee. So, the term *priya* does not signify 'a means to pleasure'. Moreover, if the term *priya* had meant 'a means to pleasure', then the famous expression 'but for the love of ātman all is loved' of Bṛhadāraṇyaka Upaniṣad, 4. 5. 6. should instead have been 'everything is dear to the soul'. So, by the term *priya* is meant an object of affection or love. Besides it may be said that there is no unconditional love for a means to pleasure. But there is unconditional love for the soul and hence the soul is nothing but bliss. The bliss should not be understood as a product. Had the bliss been a product, then it would not have been present in the dreamless sleep. Nonetheless it has already been shown on the basis of the recollection 'I slept happily' that bliss is invariably experienced in deep sleep. The appearance and disappearance of bliss can be attributed to the mental mode of the form of bliss. When such a mental mode comes into existence, it appears that happiness is generated and when it disappears, it looks as if it has been destroyed.

The pūrvapakṣin asks if the soul is bliss, then why is bliss not experienced when one is aware of the soul? The siddhāntin replies that, although the individual soul is identical with bliss, it is not experienced when the mind is overwhelmed by desires. It is these desires which obstruct the manifestation of the bliss. It is generally seen that a man who is free from desires and expectations of any kind experiences beatitude. In the dreamless sleep when all the sense organs stop working or when the mind itself submerges in its cause, that is ajñāna, the bliss of the soul manifests itself. That is why it is always bliss that is experienced in deep sleep. The bliss which is experienced by a desireless person is thousand times more than that of the one who is not free from desires and expectations. The siddhāntin explains by giving an illustration from our day-to-day life why bliss is not manifest when one is aware of the soul : The purity (*śuddhi*) which is identical with a form (*rūpa*) is not clearly perceived when the form is reflected in a mirror which is covered with dirt, etc. When the purity of form, which is not perceived even though the form is reflected in the mirror, it does not mean that purity is different from the form. In the same way bliss which is the nature of the soul is not experienced due to the condition of the mind which reflects it. The non-perception of the pure whiteness of the form has been compared to that of the blissful nature of the soul. According to the siddhāntin, the pure whiteness (*śuddhi*) of the form has been postulated to be identical with the form in the manner in which bliss has been conceived to be identical with Brahman or the individual soul. In the coming section, the discussion revolves around this pivotal point.

ननु केयं रूपस्य शुद्धिः, यदि मलविरहः यदि वा रूपसामान्यविशेषः । अथ वा वैशेषिकतन्त्रमनादृत्य रूपस्यापि गुणोऽस्तीत्युच्यते । सर्वथापि न रूपाभिन्ना शुद्धिरिति । उच्यते — न तावद्रूपशुद्धिर्मलविरहः । प्रक्षालितमलेऽपि मृतकलेवरादौ स्वाच्छ्यादर्शनाद् । न च रूपस्वरूपत्वमपि तस्यास्तद्रूपेण व्यभिचरतीति वाच्यम् । रूपविशेषस्य स्वच्छस्याभ्युपगमात् । नाप्यस्या द्वितीयपक्षे सम्भवः । प्रसिद्धगौरत्वसामान्येन स्वाच्छ्यस्य परापरभावाभावाद् । न हि गौरत्वं परम्, अगौरस्यापि स्वच्छस्य दर्शनाद् । नापीतरस्य परत्वम् । गौरस्यापि क्वचिदस्वच्छत्वाद् । अथैकव्यक्तिनिष्ठयोरप्यपरापरभावे न काचित् क्षतिरिति मतम् । तत्र न तावत्सामान्ययोस्तुल्यव्यक्तिता सम्भविनी । तथा क्वचिदप्यनुपलब्धेः । हस्तपाण्यादिशब्दानां च पर्यायत्वाभावप्रसङ्गाद् । हस्तत्वादिशब्दप्रवृत्तिनिमित्तभेदप्राप्तेः । एकव्यक्तिगतसामान्ययोः परस्परव्यभिचारे च शिंशपात्वादिना वृक्षत्वानुमानं न स्यात् । तत्रापि व्यभिचारशङ्कासंकोचासम्भवाद् । एकव्यक्तिगतसामान्ययोः परस्परव्यभिचारे च न क्वचिदपि प्रमाणमस्ति । निर्बीजा च कल्पनाऽतिप्रसङ्गिनी । सुवर्णघटप्रतीतिस्तु घटसमानाकारविषयतयाऽन्यथासिद्धा न घटत्वव्यभिचारे मानम् । ज्वालाप्रत्यभिज्ञेव, स्थायित्वे । विमतं पृथिवीत्वाव्याभिचारि, तन्न्यूनवृत्तित्वे सति जातित्वाद् गोत्ववदित्यनुमानविरोधाच्च ।

कथं चोकर्षादिमत् स्वाच्छ्यं सामान्यं स्याद् । न हि गोत्वादि क्वचिदुकर्षादिमद् । नन्वेवं रूपस्वरूपमपि नोत्कर्षादिमत् । सत्यम् । अत एव बहुधवलादिवद्रूपविशेषः स्वाच्छ्यमिष्यते । एतेन तृतीयपक्षोऽप्यपास्तः । न हि रूपस्य गुणोऽस्तीत्यस्ति प्रमाणम् । तथापि प्रतीतस्य तदैवाप्रतीतिरस्ति भेदे प्रमेति चेन्न । प्रतीयमानदूरस्थवस्त्वभिन्नस्य भेदप्रकर्षादेरप्रतीयमानत्वाद् । अतो यथा, रूपाभिन्नापि शुद्धिः तद्भानेऽपि न भात्युपाधिदोषाद् एवमात्मनि भात्यपि आनन्दो न भात्यभिन्नोऽपीति न किञ्चिदनुपपन्नम् । तस्मादात्मैवानन्द इति न्यायानुभवशरणैरादरणीयम् । तदेवं सच्चिदानन्दात्मैकरसं ब्रह्मागमगम्यमिति सिद्धम् ।

Trans. : What is this purity of form[1] (*rūpaśuddhi*)? Is it the absence of dirt or is it a particular universal of form (*rūpasāmānyaviśeṣa*) or can we say that this is a quality of the form disregarding the Vaiśeṣika system (according to which a quality does not reside in another quality)? Purity in any manner is not identical with the form. The siddhāntin says : The absence of dirt does not constitute the purity of form as we do not cognise any purity in a dead body, etc. even when they have been washed of dirt (by water, etc.). And it should not be stated that the very form constitutes purity as the latter deviates from the former (i.e. even without dirt, a dead body has the form but it is not considered to be pure). The reason is that a specific form has been admitted to be pure (i.e. a particular form having whiteness, etc. is understood to be pure; see *śvaityādivadrūpavyaktiviśeṣasya pariśuddhasya svīkārāt*, VV, p. 137). The second alternative form (of purity) is also not possible since purity does not have the state of being more or less extensive vis-a-vis the well-known universal whiteness (*gauratvasāmānya*); for whiteness (*gauratva*) is not more extensive (than purity) as purity is seen even in that which is not white; nor is the other (purity) more extensive as the white is also seen to be impure in some cases. If it is held that there is no harm in accepting the absence of being more or less extensive (*parāparatvābhāva* of purity and whiteness) in an individual, then in that case there is no possibility of two universals residing in an equal number of individuals because such an instance is not found anywhere. (If such an instance was accepted, then) it would lead to the absence of synonymity in the words *hasta, pāṇi*, etc. since in that case the difference in the reasons (*pravṛttinimittas* = *hastatva* and *pāṇitva*) for the use of the terms (*hasta* and *pāṇi*) would be available. If the universals inhering in an individual mutually deviate, then the state of being a tree (*vṛkṣatva*) would not be inferred from the reason (*hetu*) consisting in the state of being a *śiṁśapā* (tree) because there is no possibility of the apprehension of violation being restricted even there (cf. *vṛkṣa-*

---

1. The English equivalent 'colour' is generally used to signify the *rūpa* quality of the Vaiśeṣika system. I have instead used the word 'form' to denote it.

tvasya śiṁśapātvavyabhicāre'pi tasyetarāvyabhicārādanumānopapattiriti cet, VV, p. 138). (The siddhāntin now says :) There is no evidence anywhere that the universals residing in a single individual mutually deviate. And a postulate which is not based on any evidence would lead to over-application. (Upon this, the pūrvapakṣin now presents a perceptual evidence of the mutual violation of the universals residing in the same individual :) However (the siddhāntin retorts saying that) the perception of a golden pot, which stands otherwise established due to the form similar to that of a pot, does not qualify as an evidence for deviation in respect of the state of being a pot just as the recognition of the flame (*jvālāpratyabhijñā*) is not (considered to be) a proof for the stability (of the flame). Also (because) this would contradict the (following) syllogism : The state of being a pot (i.e. *ghaṭatva* which is the subject of dispute) does not deviate from 'the state of being earth' since, being a universal, it resides in a smaller number of individuals (than (*pṛthivītva*) the state of being earth) like cowness.

How can purity which has (gradation of) excellence be a universal? For cowness, etc. do not have such (gradation of) excellence at all. (The pūrvapakṣin says :) In this way the form itself also does not have (any gradation of) excellence, etc. The siddhāntin says : It is true. That is why a particular form having abundant whiteness, etc. is intended to be purity. By this the third alternative view (about purity) also stands discarded as there is no proof for a quality to exist in a form (which term has been used here in the sense of a quality). Even then the non-cognition of the form which has (already) been cognised constitutes a valid cognition of difference (between the form and its purity) according to the pūrvapakṣin. The siddhāntin does not accept this view since the difference, identified with a distant object (as per the view of those who hold difference to be the nature of the thing itself), is not pre-eminently perceived. Therefore, purity which is identical with the form is not comprehended because of the defects of the adjunct even when the form is comprehended. In the same manner, it is not unintelligible that the bliss, which is identical with the soul, does not become an object of experience even when there is an awareness of the soul. Consequently, that the soul itself is bliss should gracefully be accepted by those who have regard for logic and experience. Hence in this way, it is proved that Brahman having the nature of undivided oneness of Existence, Consciousness and Bliss can be known from the scriptures (alone).

Ann. : It has been established in the preceding section that bliss is the essential nature of the soul. The pūrvapakṣin asks if the soul is bliss, why is it that the bliss is not experienced when there is an awareness of the soul? To explain this, the siddhāntin gives an illustration of the purity of form (purity is identical with the form according to the siddhāntin). He says that the bliss is not experienced even when there is an awareness of the soul just as the purity is not visible in a mirror in which the form is reflected. He further adds that it is sometimes not cognised on account of some defect of the medium, that is a mirror in this instance. If the mirror is covered with dust, dirt, etc., then the purity of form is not clearly cognised even if the form is seen reflected in it. Likewise, if the mind is overwhelmed by desires, expectations, etc., the bliss is not experienced even if the soul is reflected in it, i.e. even if one is aware of the soul. It is in this context that the author discusses the nature of the purity of form (*rūpaśuddhi*). I have translated the term *rūpa* into 'form', though both 'shape' and 'colour' are also denoted by it, and *śuddhi*, into purity. The siddhāntin says that if the pūrvapakṣin does not subscribe to the view of the identity of purity with the form, then he can have at most the following three interpretations of the term *śuddhi* that occurs in the compound word *rūpaśuddhi* : Does it denote 1. the absence of dirt or, 2. a specific universal of form or, 3. a quality of the form which is itself a quality (which is in contravention of the Vaiśeṣika Sysem of Philosophy)?

The pūrvapakṣin says that the view of the siddhāntin that purity is the nature of the form is not acceptable. The reason is that this view suffers from the fault of deviation (*vyabhicāra*); for purity is not concomitant with the form as purity may be absent even when the form is present. This deviation is evident in a dead body as explained above. Hence, purity cannot be identical with the form.

The siddhāntin now discusses the alternative meanings one by one. According to the first alternative denotation, purity has been interpreted as the absence of dirt. As such, it cannot be conceived to be identical with the form as there can be no identity between existence and non-existence (*na tāvat prathame śuddhirūpayor-abhedasiddhiḥ bhāvābhāvayostadayogāt*, VV, p. 137). Here the form (*rūpa*) is evidently existent whereas the absence of dirt (*malābhāva =śuddhi*) is of the form of non-existence. Thus, to show the untenability of the first construal, the illustration of a dead body is given. Although a dead body is cleaned of its dirt, etc. by water, perfume, etc., still it is considered to be impure (*mṛtaśarīre śvapacādau ca malavigame'pi śuddhatvabuddhyabhāvānna malābhāvaśśuddhiḥ*, ibid., p. 137). For the form of the dead body exists, whereas purity does not. In this way, the first meaning of the term *śuddhi*, being not tenable, may be relinquished.

Secondly, if purity is construed as a particular universal, then also there can be no identity between the two (form and purity) as an individual and a universal are extremely opposite to each other (*na tayorabhedaḥ jātivyaktyoratyantabhinnatvāt*, ibid., p. 137). Moreover, if purity is to be understood as a particular universal, then the state of its being more or less extensive does not exist when we compare the well-known whiteness (*gauratva*) with purity existing in an individual. It is not acceptable that whiteness is more extensive than purity, since something which is not white is seen to be pure; nor can it be accepted that purity is more extensive than whiteness because a white thing is also seen to be impure. Since the state of being more or less extensive does not exist vis-a-vis purity and whiteness, purity cannot be a particular universal (*yadi śuddhatvaṁ sāmānyaviśeṣaḥ tadā tulyavyaktivṛttijātidvayasya parāparabhāvaniyamādasyāpi svasamānāśrayeṇa gauratvena parāparatvaṁ vaktavyam. na ca tadasti. ato na jātiviśeṣaḥ śuddhatvamityāha*, ibid., p. 137). The pūrvapakṣin's view that there is no harm in assuming the absence of the state of being more or less extensive of two universals existing in a single individual is not worth considering for the following reasons : 1. If the absence of being more or less extensive is accepted by saying that it is due to their existing in an equal number of individuals, then this does not happen anywhere. In case this is insisted upon, then the synonymity of the words would cease to exist because the reasons for the use of words (*pravṛttinimitta*) would in that case become liable to be different. To explain, the words *ghaṭa* and *kalaśa* are synonymous. If *ghaṭatva* and *kalaśatva* are construed as two separate universals, then the reasons for the use of words to convey their significations would be different. As such, they would cease to be synonymous, which fact renders the first alternative as untenable. 2. The second relates to the fault of deviation. In case two universals residing in an individual, for example, the state of being a tree and the state of being *śiṁśapā* are assumed to be mutually violative, then 'the state of being a tree' would not be inferred from the reason consisting in 'the state of being a *śiṁśapā* tree'. Although the tree-universal (*vṛkṣatva*) deviates from *śiṁśapātva*, still the latter does not deviate from the former. As such, there will be no problem in inferring the tree-universal from *śiṁśapātva* (cf. *vṛkṣatvasya śiṁśapātvavyabhicāre'pi tasyetarāvyabhicārādanumānopapattiriti*, VV, p. 138). The pūrvapakṣin insists that even in this illustration also, the apprehension of deviation cannot be restricted (i.e. cannot be avoided). But, the siddhāntin avers that it is a well-known fact that there is no proof of mutual violation of the two universals inhering in an individual. Despite this, if somebody presupposes something without basing it on an evidence, then this would lead to the defect of overextension. In order to meet the objection of the siddhāntin, the pūrvapakṣin presents a perceptual evidence of the mutual violation of two universals existing in the same individual. He says that this violation is seen in a golden pot. The state of being gold and the state of being a pot are different universals but they occur in a single individual, to wit, a golden pot. The former (*suvarṇatva*) is a sub-universal of the fire-universal and the latter (*ghaṭatva*) is a sub-universal of the earth-universal. Both deviate mutually. (*suvarṇatvaghaṭatvayoḥ rucakaghaṭayormitho vyabhicāre'pi suvarṇaghaṭe sahabhāvadṛṣṭerekavyaktigatajātyormitho vyabhicāre pratyakṣaṁ pramāṇamityāśaṅkya pariharati*, ibid., p. 138). But, the siddhāntin points out saying that the perception of the golden pot as such depends on the form which is similar to that of a pot and, hence this cannot be construed as an evidence for the deviation of potness from the state of being gold. He likens the untenability of this evidence to that of the recognition-evidence of a flame, which is not considered to be an evidence of the stable nature of the flame (see the relevant text of NRD, p.138). Now the siddhāntin gives an example to show that the two universals existing in an individual are not mutually violative. The universals *ghaṭatva* and *pṛthivītva* can exist in a pot. The universal *ghaṭatva* is not violative of *pṛthivītva* as there is an invariable concomitance in the following way : Where *ghaṭatva* is, there is *pṛthivītva*. The siddhāntin says that if the view of the pūrvapakṣin was accepted, then it would contradict the following syllogistic proposition also: The potness (the subject of dispute) is not violative of earthness since being a universal it exists in a smaller number of loci than earthness like the cow-universal (*gotva*). This is with regard to the nature of universals but purity cannot enjoy the status of a universal for the reasons discussed above.

The siddhāntin now uses another argument to demonstrate the identity of purity with the form. He asks the pūrvapakṣin how purity, which has no gradation of excellence, can be a universal. The cowness, for example, does not have any such gradation of excellence, etc. The pūrvapakṣin reminds the siddhāntin that the form itself also does not have any gradation of excellence, etc. The latter accepts what the pūrvapakṣin says and speaks his mind that it is precisely this reason why he intends to conceive that a particular form is purity. As such, purity is that which consists in a particular form which possesses whiteness, etc. in abundance. In this sense a specific form is assumed to be purity. By this the third alternative meaning of purity also stands discarded as there is no evidence that the form can have another quality in it.

Now if purity is conceived to be identical with the form according to the siddhāntin, then the question of its cognition arises. Why does purity which is not different from the form not become an object of perception when the form is seen reflected in a mirror? The siddhāntin explains saying that this is because of some defect in the adjunct or medium as, for example, the mirror covered with dust, etc. does not reflect purity of the form although the form is seen reflected in it. The siddhāntin sheds light on the purpose of this illustration (*dṛṣṭānta*) by stating that in the same way bliss is identical with the soul (*dārṣṭāntika*) but at certain moments it is not cognised. To explain, even though the soul can become an object of awareness at any given time, still the bliss can escape being experienced because of desires and other such obstructions, which overwhelm the mind in which the soul is reflected. However the non-cognition of bliss does not mean that it is different from the soul. Consequently, the siddhāntin concludes averring that it is known from the scriptures that the soul is bliss and this should be respected by those who have regard for scriptures, logic and experience.

महावाक्यानामखण्डार्थता

ननु सर्वत्र वाक्येषु पदान्तरस्पृष्ट एव पदान्तरार्थः प्रसिद्धः। अतः संसृष्टपदार्थो वाक्यार्थः। न त्वेकरसं वस्तु असंसृष्टम्। पदानि हि वाक्यम्। तेन संसृष्टपदार्थ एव वाक्यार्थो युक्तः। यद्यपि 'प्रकृष्टप्रकाशश्चन्द्र' इति वाक्यं चन्द्रस्वरूपमात्रप्रश्नोत्तरम्। तथापि न तस्याखण्डार्थता। प्रकर्षगुणवतः प्रकाशस्य चन्द्रत्वप्रबोधनात्। कथं गुणविशिष्टार्थं वाक्यं चन्द्रस्वरूपप्रश्नोत्तरं भवेद्। गुणस्य चन्द्राभेदादिति ब्रूमः। अभिन्नस्यापि गुणता विशेषणता चाविरुद्धा। [**] भेदस्यापि भावाद्। यच्च 'सोऽयं चैत्र' इति वाक्यं तच्चैत्रमात्रस्य बुभुत्सिततत्वात् चैत्रस्वरूपमात्रं बोधयति। तदेतद्देशविशिष्टयोः तादात्म्यायोगाच्च। अतः कालादिसम्बन्धत्यागेन चैत्रस्वरूपमात्रं बुभुत्सितं लक्ष्यते। यच्च मतम् — पदान्तरवाच्यं मेयं च लक्ष्यम्। अतो न ब्रह्म लक्ष्यमिति, तदसद् अनियमात्। तथा हि इक्षुक्षीरादिमाधुर्यविशेषः अवाच्योऽपि लक्ष्यते। नात्र लक्षणापीति चेद्। न। अत्रेत्यनुवादाभावप्रसङ्गाद्। एवं लक्ष्यस्य न मेयत्वनियमोऽपि। स्वापे ह्यमेयमेव सुखं लक्ष्यम्। न च तन्मेयमित्युक्तम्। नापि तद्वाच्यम् अजन्यस्य तस्यालौकिकत्वाद् व्युत्पत्त्यसम्भवात्। तर्हि — लक्ष्यमिति निर्देशः कथम्? इत्थम् उपाधिरहितं लक्ष्यमिति निर्देशे उपाधिराहित्योपलक्षितं लक्ष्यमिति श्रोतुर्निश्चयोपपत्तेः। लक्षणाविशेषोऽपि भागत्यागरूपस्तावदुच्यते। सभागत्वं च लौकिकानन्दस्योपपादकान्तःकरणवृत्त्यवच्छिन्नत्वेन सिद्धम्। अन्यथा कथं ब्रह्मस्वरूपानन्दस्य मात्राश्रुतिः 'एतस्यैवानन्दस्यान्यानि भूतानि मात्रामुपजीवन्ती'त्युपपद्येत। एवं लौकिकसच्चिदादेरपि सभागत्वमूहनीयम्।

न च भागत्यागलक्षणाऽप्रसिद्धा। सोऽयमित्यत्रास्यावश्याभ्युपेयत्वात्। तत्र गत्यन्तराभावस्योक्तत्वात्। तदेवं 'तत्त्वमस्या'दिवाक्यमप्यखण्डार्थं प्रसिद्धम्। प्रयोगस्तु — विवादपदम् अखण्डार्थम्। अकार्यकारणद्रव्यमात्रविषयत्वे सति समानाधिकरणत्वात्। सोऽयमिति वाक्यवदिति। मृत्कुम्भ इति संसर्गविषयं समानाधिकरणं वाक्यम्। क्वचिच्च नीलमुत्पलमिति प्रसिद्धम्। अतो न विशेषणद्वयं व्यर्थम्। ब्रह्मणो जगदुपादानत्वेन द्रव्यत्वोपपत्तेश्च न हेत्वसिद्धिः। विपक्षे चोक्तसामानाधिकरण्यभङ्गो बाधः। दूषणान्तरविरहस्त्वतिरोहित एव। तस्माच्छ्रुतिस्मृतिन्यायबलान्मायाशक्ति जगदुपादानं स्वरूपतः सच्चिदानन्दात्मैकरसं ब्रह्म वस्तु नान्यत्किञ्चिदिति सिद्धम्

इति श्रीमत्परमहंसपरिव्राजकाचार्यश्रीमन्नारायणज्योतिःपूज्यचरणशिष्यस्य भगवत आनन्दानुभवस्य कृतौ न्यायरत्नदीपावल्यां प्रथमोऽध्यायः समाप्तः।

[**] As per the editor a portion of the text is missing. This comes to be known from the comments of Ānandajñāna in his Vedāntaviveka. See VV, pp. 140-145.

The Impartite Meaning of Identity Propositions

Trans. : The pūrvapakṣin says that it is well-known that in all sentences the meaning of a word is obtained only when it is syntactically connected with another word and, as such, the meaning of a sentence is relational and not the non-relational undivided Reality. It is indeed words that constitute a sentence. Therefore it is proper to hold that the import of a sentence is only relational. Although the sentence 'the most resplendent is the moon' is a reply to the question which is only about the nature of the moon, still the import of this sentence is not non-relational as it makes the light of an excellent quality known as being the moon. How can a sentence denoting a qualified object be a reply to a question regarding the nature of the moon? We say so because the quality is not different from the moon. Also it is not inconsistent if that which is not different from the qualified assumes the state of being its quality or qualification because there exists difference, too (it amounts to saying that a quality or a qualification is in identity-cum-difference relation with the qualified). And the sentence 'This is that Caitra' makes only the identity of Caitra known as Caitra alone is intended to be known since the identity of the two, which are qualified by this and that place, is not tenable. Therefore, the identity of Caitra only, which is intended to be known, is indicated after the relation of time, etc. has been relinquished. And the view – that which is the denotatum of another word and knowable can be the indicated meaning (*lakṣya*) and, as such, Brahman cannot be the indicated meaning – is not true as there is no such rule. To explain, the specific sweetness of sugarcane, milk, etc. is indicated, although it is not a denotatum (of any word). (The pūrvapakṣin makes a proposal:) Let there be no indication (*lakṣaṇā*) here. (The siddhāntin replies) in the negative as there can be no restatement (of an unknown thing; the term *atra* indicates a restatement which is not possible without accepting that the sweetness of sugarcane, milk, etc. is an indicated meaning). Likewise there is no such rule that an indicated meaning should also be a knowable object. In deep sleep, only the unknowable bliss is indicated. And it has already been mentioned that it is not knowable. Neither is it a denoted meaning since that unborn (bliss), being extramundane, cannot be an object of conventional learning. Then, how can it be described that it is indicated? (Even when Brahman is neither knowable nor denotable, there is a possibility of Its being indicated since It is self-luminous). Thus when Brahman, bereft of adjuncts (*upādhi*), is described as the indicated one, it becomes possible for the hearer to ascertain that the indirect meaning is indicated by the absence of adjuncts. Then this specific indicative faculty also is known as *bhāgatyāgalakṣaṇā*. That the worldly bliss has parts or divisions is explained by its being delimited by the mental mode. Otherwise how would the scriptural statement 'Other creatures live on a fraction of this bliss only', Bṛh. Up. 4. 3. 32. describing the measure of bliss, which is the nature of Brahman, become intelligible? In the same manner, it should be understood that the worldly existence, consciousness, etc. have parts or divisions.

It is not that the *bhāgatyāgalakṣaṇā* is not well-known. It has to be accepted in the context of such sentences as 'This is that', etc. It has already been mentioned that in such instances there is no other way out. Hence it is well-known that the sentences like 'thou are that', etc. convey an impartite (non-relational) meaning. The following is the syllogism (to endorse this standpoint) : The great proposition (*mahāvākya*) has an impartite meaning since the terms constituting it are co-referential, at the same time having as its domain the substance which is neither an effect nor a cause like the sentence 'this is that'. The sentence 'clay is a pot' being co-referential conveys a relational meaning and somewhere 'a blue lotus' is well-known (in this sense). Therefore, the two qualifications of the reason in the syllogism are not without a purpose. Brahman, being the material cause (in association with māyā) of this universe can legitimately be called a substance and, as such, the reason does not suffer from the asiddhi fallacy. The absence of the co-referentiality mentioned above would constitute a contradictory argument against the contrary instance (that is, the great proposition does not convey an impartite or non-relational meaning). The absence of other faults, too, is evident. Consequently, it is established on the basis of scriptures (*śruti*), traditional code (*smṛti*) and logical principles (*nyāya*) that (Brahman in association with) the power of māyā is the material cause of the universe, whereas by itself Brahman being non-dual Existence, Consciousness and Bliss is the Reality and nothing else (is real).

Here ends the first chapter of the Nyāyaratnadīpāvali, the work of the illustrious Ānandānubhava, the disciple of the glorious and honourable ascetic of the highest order, Nārāyaṇajyotis.

Ann. : This section deals with the problem regarding the non-relational meaning of the identity propositions (*mahāvākyas*). The pūrvapakṣin says that the import of a sentence is relational since in all sentences the meaning of a word is obtained always in relation with another word. The subject (*uddeśya*) and the predicate (*vidheya*) which constitute a sentence are mutually related as the substantive and the adjective. Even when we say, 'A mountain exists', it is interpreted to mean that the mountain is characterised by 'existence'. Hence it may be said that a sentence conveys the substantive-adjective relation (*uddeśyavidheyasambandha*). Take, for exmaple, the well known sentence *prakṛṣṭaprakāśaścandraḥ* 'the most resplendent is the moon'. Although this sentence is a reply to a question asked about the identity of the moon (*kaścandraḥ*), the moon is the subject and it is described by the compound word *prakṛṣṭaprakāśaḥ* 'that which is the most resplendent'. It is a case of the subject-predicate relation according to the pūrvapakṣin. Hence the meaning obtained would be relational (see *prakṛṣṭaprakāśaścandra iti vākyaṁ candrasvarūpamātrapraśnottaram. tathāpi na tasyākhaṇḍārthatā. prakarṣaguṇavataḥ prakāśasya candratvaprabodhanāt*, NRD, p. 140). The pūrvapakṣin pertinently asks how a sentence, which conveys the qualified meaning, can be a reply only about the identity of the object (the moon in the present context). He holds that a sentence is constituted by words and the meaning of a word is related to that of another word. In conclusion, he says that the meaning of a sentence is always relational.

The siddhāntin does not subscribe to the view expressed by the pūrvapakṣin and maintains that a sentence also conveys a non-relational meaning. According to him, the subject (*uddeśya*) and the predicate (*vidheya*) are not always two different entities which require some relation but they can demonstratively point to an identical entity. Consider, for example, the well-known sentence 'This is that Devadatta'. It is intended to convey the bare identity of Devadatta which is non-relational, and not to convey any other relation between Devadatta belonging to this time and place and the one belonging to that time (past) and place. When the bare identity is intended to be conveyed, the relation of 'this' and 'that' with Devadatta is incongruous. Only Devadatta (leaving aside the qualifications, this and that) is intended to be conveyed. Hence it is non-relational (*akhaṇḍārtha*). In conclusion, it may be stated that it is the intention of the speaker, which determines whether the statement is a relational description or a non-relational identity. In relation to the sentence *prakṛṣṭaprakāśaścandraḥ* 'the most resplendent is the moon', it may be submitted that the sentence is spoken not to express any relation of the moon to anything else but to indicate which the moon is. At first sight it would seem that in this sentence an adjective 'the most resplendent' is attributed to a substantive 'the moon'. But really this is not so. A quality can be predicated of a substantive, only when the substantive is already known. But here the substantive itself is unknown. Besides, the enquirer does not want to know what the moon is but which the moon is. Thus the meaning of the sentence *prakṛṣṭaprakāśaścandraḥ* 'the most resplendent is the moon' is non-realtional.[1]

The great or identity propositions, *vijñānamānandaṁ brahma* 'Brahman is Consciousness and Bliss', Bṛh. Ūp. 3. 9. 28, *tat tvam asi* 'Thou art that', Chā. Ūp. 6. 8. 7, *satyaṁ jñānamanantaṁ brahma* 'Brahman is truth, knowledge and infinity', Tai. Up. 2. 1. 1 and the like are intended to convey the Ultimate Reality which is non-dual, impartite (*akhaṇḍa*) and beyond all relations. Even sentences like 'This is that Caitra', 'The most resplendent is the moon', etc. indicate the bare identities of Caitra and the moon. So far as the first sentence is concerned, there is incompatibility between the meanings of the words 'this' and 'that' with reference to Caitra. If these terms and their meanings are given up, then only the identity of Caitra remains to be indicated. Thus we have to resort to the faculty of indication in order to arrive at this non-relational meaning. The pūrvapakṣin holds the view that the faculty of indication can

1. The Six Ways of Knowing, Datta, D. M., Calcutta, 1972, p. 325

be invoked only in the case of such words which have their own denotative meanings since we cannot comprehend the indicated meanings without knowing the denotations. So, according to him, the faculty of indication can be used in our day-to-day expressions but not in the case of Brahman which does not have any denotative meaning (*padāntaravācyaṁ meyaṁ ca lakṣyam*, NRD, p. 146). The siddhāntin does not agree with the pūrvapakṣin and says that it is not necessary that the faculty of indication can only be invoked with regard to an entity denoted by another term. He gives the illustration of the sweetness of sugar-cane, milk, etc. This kind of specific sweetness is not denoted by any term. Nevertheless it is conveyed by the faculty of indication. If the pūrvapakṣin says that there is no indication in this context. The siddhāntin asks how he can restate the term 'here (no *lakṣaṇā*)' if he does not accept the use of the faculty of indication in conveying the sweetness of sugar-cane, milk, etc. It is only the known thing which can be restated. And it is also not necessary that the indicated meaning should be a perceptible entity. Bliss in deep sleep is only indicated. It is not the signification of the term bliss (*sukha*) as it is used in the familiar sense in our day-to-day life as the bliss which we experience when we are awake is not present in deep sleep. What we experience in deep sleep is not the denotation of the word bliss. Since that bliss is not a product, it does not become an object of learning by convention (cf. *sukhamasvāpsamiti sukhaśabdaḥ sauṣuptasukhe prayujyate. na ca tasya tena vācyatā suṣupte prasiddhasukhābhāvāt. ātmasvabhāva-sukhasya ca ṣaṣṭhyādyabhāvenāvācyatvāt. etena padāntaravācyatāpi tasya nirastā*, VV, p. 146). Although Brahman is neither perceptible nor denotative, still it is indicated by virtue of its being self-luminous. The faculty of indication, which is resorted to here, is known as *bhāgatyāgalakṣaṇā*. The impartite nature of Bliss or Brahman is understood as having parts on the empirical plane on account of its reflection in the mode of the mind. This explains the scriptural statement which speaks of a fraction of Bliss, e.g. in 'Other creatures live on a fraction of this bliss only', Bṛhadāraṇyaka Upaniṣad, 4. 3. 32 describing the measure of bliss, although it is the nature of Brahman?.

The *bhāgatyāgalakṣaṇā*, which is invoked to obtain the non-relational and impartite meaning of the great propositions, is not unfamiliar as it has to be accepted in such sentences as 'This is that Caitra', 'Thou art that', etc. The siddhāntin also presents a syllogistic proposition to prove the undivided non-dual nature of the Ultimate Reality : The great proposition has an impartite meaning since it has reference to the same entity, having at the same time only that substance as its meaning which is neither an effect nor a cause like the sentence 'This is that'. In this syllogistic proposition the terms *tat* and *tvam* in the sentence *'tat tvam asi'* indicate the non-dual Reality as they have the common case-ending since they have a bare substance as their subject which is neither a cause nor an effect. The illustration is 'This is that'. In the clay-pot (*mṛtkumbhaḥ,* NRD, p. 147) illustration, clay and pot have the same case-ending, yet they are not construed as indicating a non-relational meaning. That is why the co-referentiality is qualified by 'having at the same time only that substance as its meaning which is neither an effect nor a cause'. The justification for Brahman being a substance lies in the fact that Brahman has been accepted as the material cause when it is in association with the power of māyā. Therefore, the reason does not suffer from the defect of svarūpāsiddhi. The absence of other faults bādha, viruddha, etc. in the syllogism is evident. Moreover, the contingency of giving up the co-referentiality of the terms occurring in the great propositions *tat tvam asi,* etc. is a deterrent to the contrary instance that the great propositions do not convey a non-relational and impartite meaning. In this way, accompanied by the qualification 'having at the same time only that substance as its meaning which is neither an effect nor a cause' the co-referential terms indicate an entity which is undivided and non-relational. The siddhāntin concludes saying that, although Brahman in association with the power māyā is the material cause of the universe, by nature It is one undivided Existence, Consciousness and Bliss.

Select Bibliography

Bhattacharya, Gopinath, *Tarkasaṅgrahadīpikā on Tarkasaṅgraha* by Annambhaṭṭa, Progressive Publishers, Calcutta, 1983.

Datta, D. M., *The Six Ways of Knowing*, University of Calcutta, 1972.

Gambhīrānanda, Swami : *Bhagavadgītā with the annotation Gūḍhārthadīpikā* by Madhusūdana Sarasvatī, Advaita Ashrama, Calcutta, 2000.

Gambhīrānanda, Swami : *Brahmasūtrabhāṣya of Śrīśaṅkarācārya*, Advaita Ashrama, 1983.

Goswami, Mahaprabhulal : *Nyāyakusumāñjali of Udayanācārya*, Darbhanga, 1972.

Gupta, Som Raj : *The Word Speaks to the Faustian Man*, Volume IV, MLBD, Delhi, 2001.

Mahadevan, T. M. P. : *The Sambandhavārtika of Sureśvarācārya*, University of Madras, 1972.

Mishra, Godabarisha, *The Anubhūtiprakāśa of Vidyāraṇya*, University of Madras, 1992.

Pandurangi, K. T. : *Prakaraṇapañcikā of Śālikanātha*, ICPR, Delhi, 2004.

Potter, Karl, H. : *Encyclopedia of Indian Philosophies*, Vol. XI, Advaita Vedanta from 800-1200, MLBD, Delhi, 2006.

Sarma, V. A. : *Citsukha's Contribution to Advaita*, Mysore, 1974.

Sastri, Ananta Krishna, N. S. : *Advaitasiddhi of Madhusūdana Sarasvatī*, Parimal Publications, Delhi, 1982.

Śāstrī, Harirāma Śukla : *Nyāyasiddhāntamuktāvalī of Viśvanātha with Dinakarī and Rāmarudrī*, Varanasi, 1972.

Shastri, J. L. : *Brahmasūtraśāṅkarabhāṣyam with the commentaries : Bhāṣyaratnaprabhā, Bhāmatī and Nyāyanirṇaya*, MLBD, Delhi, 1988.

Sastri, Subrahmanya, A. : *Prakaraṇapañcikā of Śālikanātha Miśra*, Banaras Hindu University, 1961.

Shastri, Subrahmanya, S. : *Upaniṣadbhāṣyam*, Vol. I, Mahesh Research Institute, Varanasi, 1979.

— *Chāndogyopaniṣat, Upaniṣadbhāṣyam*, Vol. II

— *Bṛhadāraṇyakopaniṣat, Upaniṣadbhāṣyam*, Vol. III

Sastri, Suryanarayana, S. S. : *The Siddhāntaleśasaṅgraha of Appayadīkṣita*, Madras, Vol. I [1935] & Vol. II [1937].

— & Saileswar Sen : *The Vivaraṇaprameyasaṅgraha of Bhāratītīrtha*, Andhra University Series, 1941.

Veezhinathan, N. : *The Saṅkṣepaśārīraka of Sarvajñātman*, University of Madras, 1985.

Yogīndrānanda, Swami : *Tattvapradīpikā* (*Citsukhī*), Varanasi, 1974.

INDEX